A Dialogic Teachi

MW00340626

Building on Robin Alexander's landmark *Towards Dialogic Teaching*, this book shows how and why the dialogic approach has a positive impact on student engagement and learning. It sets out the evidence, examines the underpinning ideas and issues, and offers guidance and resources for the planning, implementation and review of effective dialogic teaching in a wide range of educational settings.

Dialogic teaching harnesses the power of talk to engage students' interest, stimulate their thinking, advance their understanding, expand their ideas and build and evaluate argument, empowering them for lifelong learning and for social and democratic engagement. Drawing on extensive published research as well as the high-profile, 5000-student trial and independent evaluation of Alexander's distinctive approach to dialogic teaching in action, this book:

- Presents the case for treating talk as not merely incidental to teaching and learning but as an essential tool of education whose exploitation and development require understanding and skill;
- Explores questions of definition and conceptualisation in the realms of dialogue, argumentation and dialogic teaching, revealing the similarities and differences between the main approaches;
- Discusses evidence that has enriched the debate about classroom talk in relation to oracy, argumentation, student voice and philosophy for children as well as dialogic teaching itself;
- Identifies what it is about dialogic teaching that makes a difference to students' thinking, learning and understanding;
- Presents the author's rationale and framework for dialogic teaching, now completely revised and much expanded;
- Proposes a professional development strategy for making dialogic teaching happen which, like the framework, has been successfully trialled in schools;
- Lists resources from others working in the field to support further study and development;
- Includes an extensive bibliography.

Robin Alexander's *A Dialogic Teaching Companion*, like its popular predecessor *Towards Dialogic Teaching*, aims to support the work of all those who are interested in the quality of teaching and learning, but especially trainee and serving teachers, teacher educators, school leaders and researchers.

Robin Alexander is Fellow of Wolfson College at the University of Cambridge, Professor of Education Emeritus at the University of Warwick, and Fellow of the British Academy. He has also held chairs in education at the universities of Leeds and York and visiting posts outside the UK. His *Culture and Pedagogy* (2001) won the Outstanding Book Award of the American Educational Research Association, while *Children, their World, their Education* (2010), and his work as director of the Cambridge Primary Review, won the SES Book Awards First Prize and the BERA/ Sage Public Impact and Engagement Award.

A Dialogic Teaching Companion

Robin Alexander

Routledge
Taylor & Francis Group

LONDON AND NEW YORK

First published 2020
by Routledge
2 Park Square, Milton Park, Abingdon, Oxon, OX14 4RN

and by Routledge
52 Vanderbilt Avenue, New York, NY 10017

Routledge is an imprint of the Taylor & Francis Group, an informa business

© 2020 Robin Alexander

The right of Robin Alexander to be identified as author of this work
has been asserted by him in accordance with sections 77 and 78 of the
Copyright, Designs and Patents Act 1988.

All rights reserved. No part of this book may be reprinted or reproduced
or utilised in any form or by any electronic, mechanical, or other
means, now known or hereafter invented, including photocopying and
recording, or in any information storage or retrieval system, without
permission in writing from the publishers.

Trademark notice: Product or corporate names may be trademarks
or registered trademarks, and are used only for identification and
explanation without intent to infringe.

British Library Cataloguing-in-Publication Data
A catalogue record for this book is available from the British Library

Library of Congress Cataloging-in-Publication Data
A catalog record for this book has been requested

ISBN: 978-1-138-57034-4 (hbk)
ISBN: 978-1-138-57035-1 (pbk)
ISBN: 978-1-351-04014-3 (ebk)

Typeset in Sabon
by Apex CoVantage, LLC

For my grandchildren and those who teach them.

Contents

Acknowledgements

Formal acknowledgements are due to the agencies that funded projects to which this book refers: Economic and Social Research Council (ESRC) (Curriculum-Associated Discourse and Pedagogy in the Primary School, 1991–93); Leverhulme Trust, the British Council and the University of Warwick (Culture and Pedagogy, 1994–98 and 2002–3); the councils of North Yorkshire (Talk for Learning Project, 2002–8), the London Borough of Barking and Dagenham (Teaching Through Dialogue Initiative, 2003–6) and Bolton (Tapestry of Talk, 2008–11); Esmée Fairbairn Foundation (Cambridge Primary Review, 2006–12); Pearson Education (Cambridge Primary Review Trust, 2013–17); Education Endowment Foundation (Cambridge Primary Review Trust/University of York Dialogic Teaching Project, 2014–17).

'Goals for Productive Discussions and Nine Talk Moves', from *Talk Science Primer*, by Sarah Michaels and Cathy O'Connor, p. 11, is adapted with permission from the authors on behalf of TERC. 'Overview of Four ART Criteria and Eleven Practices', from *The Most Reasonable Answer: helping students build better arguments together*, by Alina Reznitskaya and Ian A.G. Wilkinson, p. 196, is adapted with permission from Harvard Education Press and the authors.

During those of the listed projects that were devoted exclusively to dialogic teaching, I learned much from working with Roger Luxton, David Reedy and David Rosenthal in Barking and Dagenham, Edna Sutton, Kathy Fiddes and their colleagues in North Yorkshire, Tony Birch and Nick Pounds in Bolton, and Kevan Collins at the Education Endowment Foundation. In the latter project, I greatly valued the three-year collaboration with my co-director Frank Hardman and project colleagues Jan Hardman, Mark Longmore, Taha Rajab and – again – David Reedy. In every case we depended upon, and were unstintingly given, the goodwill of schools, teachers and students.

In 2011, I was grateful to be asked to participate in an AERA-sponsored research conference on academic talk and dialogue at the University of Pittsburgh, organised by Lauren Resnick with Christa Asterhan and Sherice Clarke. This event and its resulting research compendium marked a critical moment in the development of dialogic pedagogy. Building on this, Neil Mercer and Jim Rose joined me in trying to persuade the UK government of the proposition that for children and students, talk really matters. In Tampere (2017), I enjoyed pooling ideas with EARLI symposium colleagues Alina Reznitskaya, Alexander Gröschner, Jonathan Osborne and Ian Wilkinson; and in Jerusalem (2018), an EARLI keynote allowed me to take dialogic teaching into the monologic worlds of political populism, evidence-denial and 'alternative facts'. In turning these contributions into publications, I was supported by editors Debbie Myhill, Ana Marjanovic-Shane and Eugene Matusov.

In the practical matter of writing this book, I am particularly grateful to Sarah Michaels, Cathy O'Connor, Alina Reznitskaya and Ian Wilkinson for their generosity in sharing papers, unpublished as well as published, and for allowing me to incorporate their hard-won ideas into two of the dialogic teaching repertoires in Chapter 7. I also thank Simon Jacobs, Claudia Austin and Marie Andrews of Routledge for tolerating deadline slippage and for their support throughout.

Over the years I have enjoyed discussions and email correspondence about pedagogy, classroom talk and dialogic teaching with more people, and in more countries, than I can remember. I thank all of them, but perhaps particularly Courtney Cazden, Maurice Galton, Frank Hardman, David Hogan, Kay Kinder, Adam Lefstein, Sarah Michaels, Martin Nystrand, Cathy O'Connor, Lauren Resnick, Alina Reznitskaya, Jim Rose and Ian Wilkinson; and, sadly no longer with us, Michael Armstrong, Jerome Bruner, Donald McIntyre and Brian Simon.

But especially, and as always, Karen.

1 Prologue

Dialogic teaching is good for students. It harnesses the power of talk to engage their interest, stimulate thinking, advance understanding, expand ideas and build and evaluate arguments, empowering them for lifelong learning and democratic engagement. Being collaborative and supportive, it confers social and emotional benefits too.

Dialogic teaching helps teachers. By encouraging students to share their thinking, it enables teachers to diagnose needs, devise learning tasks, enhance understanding, assess progress and assist students through the challenges they encounter.

Dialogic teaching is both talk and more than talk, for it enacts a dialogic stance on knowledge, learning, social relations and education itself.

If students need talk in order to learn about the world, teachers need talk in order to learn about students. The first condition is more generally understood than the second. Talk matters, and dialogic teaching positions it firmly and unreservedly at the heart of the student's learning and the teacher's practice. For all parties, it makes the process in which they are jointly engaged more visible and explicit, valuing evidence and mutuality above supposition and gamesmanship. John Hattie puts this well:

> What is most important is that teaching is visible to the student, and that the learning is visible to the teacher. The more the student becomes the teacher and the more the teacher becomes the learner, then the more successful are the outcomes.[1]

In its pursuit of the metalinguistic alongside the communicative, dialogic teaching is more than just 'classroom talk'. It is as distinct from the question-answer and listen-repeat routines which most of us experienced at school as it is from everyday conversation, aiming to be more consistently searching and reciprocal than both. Yet if that sounds a trifle too earnest, dialogic teaching also celebrates talk for talk's sake, relishing language in all its forms and rejoicing in expression, articulation, communication, discussion and argumentation. And, in so doing, dialogue takes us beyond classroom transactions into the realm of ideas and values, for dialogue is as much a stance or outlook – on human relationships, knowledge, education, culture and society – as it is a pedagogical technique.

And yet . . .

Notwithstanding these claims and the evidence we shall adduce to support them, talk other than that which emanates from the teacher has in many countries been accorded ambivalent, marginal or even negative educational status, and in England conspicuously so. There the residue of nineteenth century schooling and its attendant attitudes remains stubbornly detectable. To an extent, even research dedicated to illuminating classroom interaction may have been complicit, because until recently observation protocols attended more closely to the talk of the teacher than to that of the student. Some still do.[2]

So it was not wholly surprising when in 2012 a UK government education minister declined to ask schools to raise the profile of children's talk for fear of encouraging what he called 'idle chatter in class'. For good measure, he added that fostering oracy might imperil literacy, and this was a risk he was not prepared to take.[3]

Though, as we shall see, the minister's views may have been historically and politically understandable, they nevertheless offended both education and evidence, not least the evidence that marks the relationship between talking, reading and writing as symbiotic rather than mutually exclusive.[4] By May 2019, such attitudes appeared to be in at least partial retreat when an All-Party Parliamentary Group (APPG) launched a public enquiry into oracy under the banner 'Speaking for Change'. Its report was scheduled for May 2020,[5] though on past form its impact may turn out to be limited.

But let us not dwell overmuch on England's local difficulty. Dialogic teaching is embedded in a community of research and practice that from its roots mainly in the UK and US has now become vibrantly international. And since the community's members come from various disciplines as well as cultures, we shall need to devote some time to exploring their more significant differences in definition, perspective and preoccupation in matters relating to talk in general and dialogue in particular.

However, we give immediate notice that rather than follow those who believe that there is 'one right way' to handle classroom talk (that is, their way), this book emphasises the idea of *repertoire* and characterises dialogic teaching as an approach that encourages teachers to acquire and refine a broad array of interactive skills, strategies and moves, but to exercise their own judgement about how these are most effectively applied to the particular contexts in which they are working, using dialogic principles as reference points rather than obediently applying the nostrums of 'best practice'.

For dialogic teaching is about the agency of teachers as well as students, and with agency comes responsibility. So the character of the teacher's talk matters no less than that of the student, because although the student's talk manifests and drives his/her thinking and understanding and is therefore our ultimate concern, it is through the teacher's talk that the student's talk is mainly prompted, accelerated and enriched – or not, as the case may be. Hence 'dialogic *teaching*', where 'dialogic' qualifies both the classroom practice and the professional discourse, generating dialogues about dialogue and the education it seeks to advance.

This book

Some of the previous sentiments will be familiar to those who know *Towards Dialogic Teaching: rethinking classroom talk*, the short book which first appeared in 2004 and by 2019 had run to five editions and 22 printings. This book is its sequel and replacement. The first edition, much shorter than the final one (2017), which in turn was much shorter than this book, was drafted as part of an intended professional development pack for the Qualifications and Curriculum Authority (QCA), the statutory body which from 1997 to 2008 was responsible for England's national curriculum, tests, examinations and vocational qualifications. The pack fell foul of rivalry between QCA and the UK government's National Literacy Strategy (NLS), but the text was rescued, completed and published independently as *Towards Dialogic Teaching*.

Despite or perhaps because of its modest format – the final edition[6] was still a mere 60 pages stapled into no-nonsense soft covers, cheap enough to be scribbled on, small enough to be tucked into a pocket – *Towards Dialogic Teaching* proved extraordinarily popular, especially among serving and trainee teachers. This meant that the author's desire to replace it was repeatedly frustrated by the publisher's need to have stock at hand to meet customer demand, often in the form of bulk orders from schools and university bookshops, some of which re-ordered annually.

Although demand has not diminished, I have decided finally to call a halt to the cycles of tweaking and reprinting and instead offer something new. There are three reasons for this decision. First, the field of dialogic teaching as a whole has vastly expanded and diversified, attracting many additional members, accumulating fresh evidence and opening new lines of enquiry. Second, my own stance on dialogic pedagogy, too, has evolved. Third, although the particular approach I have developed over the years was, at a fairly early stage, evaluated in use,[7] in 2014–17 it was subjected to the greater rigours of a large-scale independent randomised control trial.[8] This validated not only the account of dialogic teaching set out in these pages but also a professional development strategy for bringing it to life. Since the strategy was also endorsed by the teachers who participated in the trial, I gained added confidence in its wider application and believed it should be adapted for inclusion here. For all these reasons, further updating of *Towards Dialogic Teaching* ceased to be an option.

Yet some things do not change. In 2004, the 'towards' in *Towards Dialogic Teaching* signalled work in progress, an unfinished journey of exploration into the riches and possibilities of classroom talk. The journey continues. Indeed to presume that we have reached our destination and can hang up our pedagogical boots would be contrary to the very spirit of dialogue. For if, as Mikhail Bakhtin believed, there is 'neither a first nor a last word' about anything, and dialogue is therefore as unending as he believed it to be ubiquitous,[9] then his maxim applies even more forcefully when the subject of dialogue is dialogue itself.

That sense of a journey is retained in the present book's title. The journey is companionable, not to say dialogic, inviting conversation with and about the book's ideas as the reader progresses, as well as providing sustenance along the way for those who need it. Echoing Chaucer's most celebrated of conversational journeys, this first chapter is even headed 'Prologue', though alert readers will point to a contradiction between Bakhtin's 'neither a first nor a last word' and the image of a journey with fixed points of departure and destination bracketed by prologue and epilogue. Teetering on the edge of being too clever about all this, we might however argue that the book as artefact is necessarily finite, but its journey of ideas is not.

The procession of projects

Here I should say something about my own journey thus far.[10] During the 1980s and early 1990s, working on projects as diverse as teachers' professional thinking and the pedagogical impact of large-scale systemic reform, John Willcocks, Kay Kinder, Nick Nelson and I made extensive use of classroom observation, lesson videography and transcript analysis, backed by interviews so as to access teachers' intentions and reactions.[11] This work confirmed not only the near-ubiquity of recitation – that familiar exchange structure of closed 'test' teacher question, recall student answer and minimal though usually judgemental teacher feedback – but also problems in the patterns of teaching which at the time were being advanced as recitation's antidote: protracted and unstructured reading and writing activities associated with low levels of pupil time on task and relatively superficial monitoring by the teacher; and an ostensibly gentler and more open kind of talk characterised by teacher-controlled pseudo-enquiry rather than genuine discussion, by hyperbolic but uninformative praise ('Brilliant!' 'Fantastic!' 'Well done!' . . .) rather than useful feedback, and by a low level of cognitive demand.

It was time to broaden perspectives on these matters, and in 1992, with the support of the Leverhulme Trust and British Council, the project *Primary Education in Five Cultures* was born. Between 1994 and 1998, accompanied by my wife Karen Lennox, I travelled in England, France, India, Russia and the United States to interview educational policy makers, administrators, school heads, teachers, parents and children, and to study what was going on in primary schools and classrooms, collecting observational fieldnotes, video recordings, lesson transcripts, photographs and interviews as our primary data and supplementing these with policy documents, teachers' lesson plans, teaching resources and samples of students' work.

Classroom talk was a prominent focus throughout, though never exclusively so. For it was pedagogy more broadly that I sought to understand and map (by pedagogy I mean not only the practice of teaching but also the intentions, ideas, theories, evidence and values that shape it). I was also keen to open up the possibility of alternatives to what I and others had reported over the years from British classrooms, where debate seemed doomed to be stuck forever in a sterile standoff between 'formal' and 'informal', 'traditional' and 'progressive', 'teacher-centred' (or 'subject-centred') and 'child-centred' – dichotomies that suited politicians and the media (and, sadly, some teachers) but misrepresented the conceptual complexity of teaching, let alone what was actually happening in classrooms.[12]

So across our five systems and cultures – a number, incidentally, that made such binary thinking impossible – we explored the relationship between talk and other aspects of teaching: classroom time, space and organisation; curriculum structure and content; relationships, rules and routines; learning tasks and activities; student diagnosis and assessment. We also extended the analysis to connect pedagogy with policy, history and culture. Language, self-evidently, is central to this pedagogic nexus, for it mediates culture as well as teaching and learning. That is why the project culminated in comparative analysis of classroom talk from our five countries, and culture did indeed shine through every exchange. And it is why it was this talk, whose immediacy was captured in video (130 hours of it) and transcript, that most excited those with whom it was shared at a seminar convened by QCA[13] in 2001, for it pointed the way towards possibilities for classroom interaction which at that time were rarely witnessed in British classrooms.

After the publication of the resulting book, *Culture and Pedagogy*,[14] I maintained the international focus on pedagogy broadly conceived while also delving more deeply into classroom talk. One strand of subsequent enquiry aimed to elevate pedagogy and classroom study within comparative educational research, where until then they had been somewhat neglected in favour of comparison of systems and policies.[15] A second strand critiqued the somewhat reckless inferences about 'effective' teaching that governments were by then busy drawing from international testing regimes such as PISA and TIMSS, and indeed the general naivety of policy-directed international comparison at a time of mounting PISA panic.[16] A third strand exposed the similarly simplistic treatment of pedagogy in the global monitoring reports tracking the progress of the UN Millennium Development Goals Education for All campaign, a campaign in which during two decades I worked on the ground with governments, NGOs and schools in India.[17]

But there was a fourth strand: translating into viable classroom strategies the insights we had gained from all this activity, first through preliminary materials[18] to help teachers explore alternatives to the defaults of actual or disguised recitation or IRF/IRE – the archetypal three-part classroom exchange consisting of (teacher) *I*nitiation, student *R*esponse and teacher *F*eedback or *E*valuation – and then by creating something more elaborate: a conceptual and practical framework for dialogic teaching, with interlocking repertoires of student and teacher talk validated by evidence and guided by principles of procedure.

During the next 15 years or so, this framework was applied, refined and evaluated with teachers in various parts of the UK, notably North Yorkshire, Bolton and the London Borough of Barking and Dagenham,[19] using successive editions of *Towards Dialogic Teaching* as the core text. We also expanded from primary into secondary and occasionally even higher education, and from the UK to other countries, notably Australia, Chile, Norway, Denmark, Sweden, Germany, Hong Kong/China, Singapore, the Netherlands, Israel and the United States.

Then, from 2014–17, in a project led by Frank Hardman and myself and funded by the Education Endowment Foundation (EEF), a further iteration of the dialogic teaching framework was subjected to randomised control trial (RCT) with 5000 students and 208 teachers in three English cities as one of EEF's 'what works' initiatives for tackling educational disadvantage.[20] The project was the largest of its kind yet to take place in the UK.[21]

The RCT, which was wholly independent, reported that after a dialogic teaching programme of only 20 weeks, preceded by training for the teachers involved, students in the intervention group were up to two months ahead of their control group peers in standardised tests of English, mathematics and science.[22] This encouraging result chimed with the findings of what was by then a large and growing body of research from several other countries, much of which had been reviewed in 2011 at an international seminar in Pittsburgh, USA and turned into a major book.[23] In 2020, this was supplemented by a research compendium from this book's publisher.[24] The case for the particular approach advanced in the present book could now be justified by evidence which was international rather than local, replicated rather than one-off, and which – in our case, at least – met what governments tend to regard, contentiously, as the 'gold standard' of educational research, the randomised control trial.

Meanwhile, a dialogic stance had informed two important strands in the Cambridge Primary Review: its discussion of pedagogy and its consideration of what education is for.[25] The Review, which I led from its inception in 2006 to its final report in 2010 and dissemination (2010–12), and then on into its successor the Cambridge Primary Review Trust (2012–17), was and remains the UK's biggest and most comprehensive research-based public enquiry into primary education.[26] There, as well as advocating dialogue in classroom interaction, we argued that education is itself a dialogue – of people, obviously, but also of ideas, arguments, values, cultures and ways of knowing.[27] This expansion of the idea of dialogue, from pedagogic practice to educational stance, was prefigured in 2006 in a companion booklet to

Towards Dialogic Teaching entitled *Education as Dialogue*,[28] which was published simultaneously in the UK and Hong Kong.

A collision of discourses

The journey towards dialogic teaching as educational ideal and infinitely perfectible practice is not only unending; it also takes unexpected turns. Recently, alongside the refinement and trial of the dialogic teaching framework, I have been increasingly exercised by what I see as a widening gulf between the ways of talking and reasoning that we try to cultivate inside the school and those that students encounter outside it.

Let me elaborate. For some students, the norms of pedagogical, curricular and wider cultural discourse may be more or less in harmony. Others experience those dissonances of class, race and gender that are well-researched yet still pressing; and they discover how academic and everyday registers diverge – inevitably so, for opening up new ways of knowing and understanding, and hence of naming, expressing and communicating, is the essence of schooling.

But from time to time – for these episodes are cyclic – and latterly during the decade punctuated by the Brexit debacle, the election of Donald Trump to the presidency of the United States and the rise of populist leaders with nationalist-authoritarian instincts in many of the world's so-called democracies (including, conspicuously, the UK), this divergence has become a strident confrontation. On the one hand we have the sedimented habits and values embodied in school curriculum domains and the more or less rational and courteous ways of accessing, interrogating and verifying the knowledge that such domains embody. But on the other hand we witness the sometimes raucous free-for-all of social media, the ascendancy of ephemeral and anonymous online content over the verifiable and attributable knowledge of book, studio and laboratory, the mischievous anarchy of fake news, the reduction of judgemental nuance to the binary 'like'/'dislike', the trolling and abuse that for many people have replaced discussion and debate, and the sense not so much that truth claims are open to question, as of course they always should be, as that for many in the public and political spheres truth is no longer a standard to which they feel morally obliged to aspire.

In a conference keynote in Jerusalem in 2018, I argued that taking dialogic teaching to scale makes educational as opposed to technical sense only if it also confronts this collision of discourses and values and in doing so re-asserts and explores four educational fundamentals that are currently caught in the cross-fire: truth, obviously, but also argument, voice and – that on which all of these depend – language.[29]

Hearteningly, students themselves have been at the forefront of resistance to some of the trends noted above, and here it is pertinent to note how the trajectory of this book's predecessor (2004–17) coincided with the growth of social media. Its first edition followed the launch of Myspace (2003). Its second coincided with that of Facebook (2004) and YouTube (2005); its third with Twitter

(2006); its fourth with Instagram (2010) and Snapchat (2011) – to name just a few of the many services, platforms and sites used by today's children and students for communication and information.

Social media allowed the leader of the world's most powerful nation to tweet to millions his airy dismissal of what the world's leading scientists have unreservedly accepted – evidence of potentially catastrophic climate change and biodiversity loss requiring urgent action if the onward rush to an irreversible tipping point is to be halted. But social media also enabled students to launch their counter-attack, abandoning their classes for the Friday climate strikes initiated in Sweden by Greta Thunberg (whose absence from school was surely a testament to education rather than a rejection of it), drawing attention to the crisis with a passion, directness, evidential mastery and fluency of articulation that shamed the equivocations of politicians and the self-interest of their media apologists and corporate backers.

Earlier, we saw and heard something similar in the United States, when in the wake of yet another mass school shooting students rose up and challenged the gun lobby while politicians who were either in its pocket or for other reasons didn't dare to speak out simply sat on their hands and mumbled about the Second Amendment of the US Constitution.[30] Once again, it was through their command of the dialogic essentials of language, argument and evidence that these students told and sold their undeniable truths.

But let's not over-politicise. The point of this diversion is to reinforce the breadth of the claims that can be made for well-founded classroom dialogue: collective as well as individual, civic as well as developmental, an end in itself as well as a means to many ends, a way of being – and perhaps even surviving – as well as doing. More on all this later; meanwhile, I hope I've said enough to justify *A Dialogic Teaching Companion*.

Using this book

Like its predecessor, this book is written for all who are interested in the quality and potential of classroom talk, but especially for those who teach, train others to teach, lead schools or research teaching. It:

- Presents the evidence and case for treating talk not as merely incidental to teaching and learning but as an essential tool whose exploitation and development require understanding and skill, and traces the halting history of efforts to have this case properly reflected in policy and practice (Chapter 2).
- Explores questions of definition and conceptualisation in the realms of dialogue and argumentation in order that similarities and differences between the main approaches are properly understood (Chapter 3).
- Discusses developments and initiatives that have expanded and enriched the evidence and debate about classroom talk, including those relating to argumentation, student voice and philosophy for children as well

as dialogic pedagogy in general and dialogic teaching in particular (Chapters 3 and 4).

- Examines the contingent idea of oracy and explores the vital but complex relationship between oracy and literacy, or the spoken and the written, an insufficiently investigated aspect of research on classroom talk that has important practical implications (Chapter 5).
- Identifies from the research evidence what it is about dialogic teaching that makes a difference to students' understanding and learning (Chapter 6).
- Presents the latest version of the particular approach to classroom talk reform that I call dialogic teaching (Chapter 7).
- Proposes a professional and/or school development strategy for making dialogic teaching happen (Chapter 8).
- Suggests resources from others working in the field which will further support professional study and development (Appendix 2).

In books like this, there can be a tension between providing guidance and opening up issues for discussion. Readers' needs and preferences vary, and while some wish to be shown the way, others expect to make up their own minds. I have stressed that the framework at the heart of this book's account of dialogic teaching (Chapter 7) hinges on professional repertoire and agency rather than procedural formulae, and that the 'towards' in *Towards Dialogic Teaching* meant what it said, so the book as a whole leans towards the second constituency. But because we have independent evidence from the 2014–17 trial that the framework produces desirable results, some may wish to apply it more or less as it stands. However, such application must never be unquestioning, so either way we hope for critical engagement.

In thinking about how the balance might best be struck, it is useful to recall the reactions of those teachers who participated in the 2014–17 EEF trial. For the pilot in London, the dialogic teaching framework was loose and open-ended, and schools were encouraged to use it creatively. That led not just to diversity but also, in some cases, to interaction which was only minimally dialogic, for in the arena of educational improvement there are always those who say 'We do this already' even if they do not. But the following year's main trial in Birmingham, Bradford and Leeds required what our independent evaluators called 'fidelity' to the approach being trialled, so we had to reduce the variation. We did so, as will be more fully explained in Chapter 8, by setting out a sequence of cycles of targeted activity to be implemented as the school year progressed, while combining this 'directed focus' with a 'responsive focus' which acknowledged the uniqueness of each teacher's working situation.

At the end of the trial's first phase, we brought our teachers together to share experiences and review progress. Among other matters, we asked whether they had found our approach too prescriptive. Without exception, they assured us that that they had not, that the level of detail provided was essential to their understanding of what the project was about, and that without this detail they might have floundered.

How you use this book is therefore for you to decide, but if you are a teacher or trainee teacher, do at least try expanding your own and your students' repertoires as outlined in Chapter 7; and, before you form a view on the approach as a whole, do engage with the 'orientation' discussion themes and readings and some of the developmental cycles in Chapter 8. But do also read Chapters 2–6 in order to understand the evidence and thinking that has led to this approach. And bear in mind that we concentrate on *how* you teach, so although the 'how' obviously influences the 'what' as your students experience it (and their attitudes to it), you can implement the programme within the requirements of your school's curriculum as it stands. Having said that, I predict that you will discover that the how becomes the what, because the vocalised dialogues of speaking and listening reflect and articulate the inner dialogues of thinking, learning, knowing and understanding.

Notes

1 Hattie 2009, 25.
2 This problem is discussed in Alexander 2015a. It goes back at least as far as the Flanders Interaction Analysis categories (Flanders 1960).
3 This episode is recounted in Alexander 2012a.
4 E.g. Goody 1987; Wells 1999; Heath 1983. See Chapter 5.
5 Oracy All-Party Parliamentary Group (2019). See Chapters 2 and 5.
6 Alexander 2017.
7 Alexander 2003, 2005a, 2005b.
8 Jay *et al.* 2017; Alexander 2018.
9 Bakhtin 1986.
10 See also the annotated bibliography in the Appendix.
11 Alexander 1988; Alexander and Willcocks 1995; Alexander, Willcocks and Nelson 1996; Alexander 1997.
12 See the chapter 'Beyond dichotomous pedagogies' in Alexander 2008.
13 QCA: Qualifications and Curriculum Authority, the non-governmental public body which from 1997 to 2008 was responsible for England's National Curriculum, national assessment and examinations, and school-level qualifications.
14 Alexander 2001.
15 Alexander, Broadfoot and Phillips 1999; Alexander 2009a.
16 Alexander 2010a, 2012b.
17 Alexander 2008, 2015b. The programmes in question were the District Primary Education Programme (DPEP) and its successor, Sarva Shiksha Abhiyan (SSA) or Education for All.
18 Mills 1996.
19 Alexander 2003, 2005a, 2005b.
20 Alexander 2018.
21 According to Jay *et al.* 2017.
22 Jay *et al.* 2017.
23 Resnick, Asterhan and Clarke 2015.
24 Mercer, Mannion and Warwick 2020.
25 Alexander 2010b, chapters 12 and 15.

26 Alexander 2010b; Alexander *et al.* 2010. The website, which contains a large body of information about both the Review and the Trust, together with numerous downloadable publications, is accessed at www.cprtrust.org.uk.

27 Alexander 2006, 2010b.

28 Alexander 2006. This is now out of print, but the text was revised as chapter 6, 'Pedagogy for a runaway world', in Alexander 2008b.

29 Alexander 2019. For a commentary on this paper, see Andal 2019.

30 I refer particularly to the murder of 13 students and three teachers at the Marjorie Stoneman Douglas High School in Florida in February 2018. This provoked the nationwide demonstration March For Our Lives, the setting up of Never Again MSD, a political action student-led committee for gun control, and campaigns that have continued to this day.

2   Talk for learning

Learning to talk, talking to learn

'When children learn language,' said Michael Halliday, 'they are not simply engaging in one type of learning among many; rather, they are learning the foundations of learning itself.'[1] If that is so, then the scope and character of the language children encounter condition the quality of that learning. For, as Jerome Bruner reminds us, language is both tool and constraint.[2]

Nowadays these propositions seem self-evident, but this has not always been the case. During the 1960s and 1970s, in Britain's primary schools at least, educators were much taken by the idea – attributed perhaps unfairly to Piaget – of the child as a 'lone scientist' whose thinking progresses principally through the manipulation of objects and materials. It was only from the later 1970s, after Vygotsky's and Luria's pre-war works began to be widely available in translation from their original Russian, that this outlook was increasingly tempered by the 'apprenticeship' proposition that the child's cognitive development also requires it to engage, through the medium of spoken language, with other people;[3] that in learning to talk children talk to learn; and that they – and we as adults – go on doing so.

The 'lone scientist' characterisation may be unduly harsh, not just in relation to Piaget's work but also because the language we encounter takes written, read and digitised as well as spoken forms. So if the materials in question include words or images, as books do, then as a matter of course they afford access to other minds – of the author, of the characters portrayed, which in their turn have influenced what is written or illustrated, and so endlessly on and on – and through sustained and repeated study may even do so more searchingly than through face-to-face interaction. Why, after all, and regardless of whether our choice is *The Gruffalo* or *War and Peace*, do we read and re-read? And even when you read this more modest book, are you not entering into a kind of dialogue with the ideas it contains, which though they are mediated and combined by one person ultimately come from many sources? The scientist, in truth, is never lone, and 'the word in language is [always] half someone else's'.[4]

Yet the value of this shift in perspective is that it encouraged teachers to understand development as a social process as well as a biological one: a process through which children construct meaning not only from the interaction between what they newly encounter and what they already know, but also from verbal interaction with others – parents, teachers, peers – and the worlds those others inhabit, and between what Vygotsky called the 'natural' and 'cultural' lines of development.[5] In turn, this interaction is critical not just for children's understanding of the kind of knowledge with which schools deal but also for the development of their very identity, their sense of self and worth. This is the point where the ideas of Vygotsky converge with those of his polymath compatriot Mikhail Bakhtin, social psychologist G.H. Mead and philosopher Charles Taylor.[6]

The others with whom children interact assume a critical role in the process of cognitive 'scaffolding', a term first coined by Wood, Bruner and Ross in the 1970s in the context of mother-child interaction and now more commonly applied to what goes on in classrooms.[7] This is the use of carefully structured interventions to bridge what Vygotsky called the 'zone of potential [or, in most translations, "proximal"] development' (ZPD), or, in his own words:

> The distance between the actual developmental level as determined by independent problem-solving and the level of potential development as determined through problem-solving under adult guidance or in collaboration with more capable peers.[8]

In other words, learning and development are not synonymous, as in the heyday of British progressivism they tended to be treated, while teaching cannot be reduced, as at that time it often was, to applied child development. It is true that children learn regardless of the actions of their parents, carers or teachers, simply by being alive to who and what are around them. But learning to an externally defined purpose requires external intervention. Emphasising the role of linguistic interaction in this process, Vygotsky even went as far as to argue that 'the true direction of the development of thinking is not from the individual to the social, but from the social to the individual.'[9]

This clearly challenges the once popular view of the teacher as a hands-off 'facilitator' who, like Rousseau's benign teacher-as-gardener,[10] nurtures but does not force children's 'natural' growth. However, we should stress that it does not herald a return to what some perceive as facilitation's antithesis, teaching as instructing and telling. Where both of these models implied an active/passive teacher-student relationship – active students and passive teachers in one, passive students and active teachers in the other – the new approach demands both active student engagement *and* constructive teacher intervention. And the principal means by which students actively engage and teachers constructively (or co-constructively) intervene is through talk.

Such talk, as Daniels emphasises in his work on activity theory, is not bounded by the immediacy of the learning task in hand. Classroom talk mediates not only teaching and learning but also the wider culture,[11] and this is powerfully illustrated in the lesson videotapes and transcripts from England, France, India, Russia and the United States that were analysed as part of the *Culture and Pedagogy* project.[12] And, as Bruner again argues, several lines of research – on intersubjectivity, on the nature of the human mind, on metacognition and on collaborative learning – converge on the principle that children must think for themselves before they truly know and understand, and that teaching must provide them with the linguistic opportunities and encounters which will enable them to do so.[13]

These ideas have been given a further boost by neuroscientific research. It is now understood that talk is necessary not just for learning but also for the building of the brain itself as a physical organism, thereby expanding its power. While, as has long been known, the first three years of life are critical to subsequent development, the period between ages 3/4 and 10/11 – the primary phase of schooling, more or less – is one in which the brain in effect restructures itself, building cells, making new fibre connections between cells, pruning old ones, developing the capacity for learning, memory, emotional response and language, all on a scale which decreases markedly thereafter. Between birth and adolescence, brain metabolism is 150 per cent of its adult level, and synaptogenesis (the growth of brain connections) causes the brain's volume to quadruple. Talk actively and vigorously fuels these processes.[14]

Moreover, the periods between birth and ages 3/4 and between ages 3/4 and ages 10/11 are those when the brain's capacity to acquire language is strongest.[15] Apart from underlining the imperative of talk as a rich and pervasive feature of life at home and in pre-school and primary education, this finding raises a separate question about the way in Britain the learning of foreign languages is postponed until the secondary stage of schooling. By then, it may actually be more difficult, not less, to learn a new language. Having said that, brain research also tends to dent the claim that there are all-or-nothing critical periods for learning. Though some kinds of learning are more effective during the early years, synaptogenesis can occur at any period of life, and humans retain the capacity to learn, and to learn extensively and in complex domains, throughout their lives.[16]

Neuroscience also supports the Vygotskian view of teaching as acceleration rather than 'wait and see' developmental facilitation, discussed previously. In some domains – perceptual, certainly, and to a degree social too – implicit and involuntary learning takes place, but higher-order cognitive activities of the kind that characterise formal schooling require both conscious effort and direct intervention. As Goswami notes, responding sceptically to Blakemore and Frith's views on 'learning without awareness': 'Children spend much of their day in classrooms, [but] their brains do not automatically "notice" how to read or do sums. These skills must be directly taught.'[17]

These insights from emerging neuroscientific research are doubly helpful: first in confirming the importance of teaching itself; second, as an endorsement of teaching that capitalises on the collective and interactive environment which classrooms offer. The boundaries may not be precisely delineated: indeed, that's the point, for it seems evident that it is advantageous to the learner if we see implicit social learning and the explicit teaching of higher-order concepts as linked and mutually supportive processes. In the account of dialogic teaching which we explore in this book, the dynamics of talk matter no less than its content, while social and cognitive purposes go hand in hand.

So of all the tools for educational intervention in students' development, talk is perhaps the most pervasive in its use and powerful in its possibilities. Talk vitally mediates the cognitive and cultural spaces between adult and child, among children themselves, between teacher and learner of any age, between society and the individual, between what the learner knows and understands and what he or she has yet to know and understand. Language not only manifests thinking but also structures it, and speech shapes the higher mental processes necessary for so much of the learning which takes place, or ought to take place, in school. So one of the principal tasks of the teacher is to create interactive opportunities and encounters which directly and appropriately engineer such mediation.

The persistence of recitation

Yet though most educators subscribe in broad terms to the arguments I have outlined, and classrooms are places where a great deal of talking goes on, talk which in an effective and sustained way engages learners and scaffolds their understanding is still less common than it should be. Practice – and, even more, policy – all too frequently lag behind research. By and large, teachers rather than learners control what is said, who says it and to whom; and teachers rather than learners do most of the talking. And, as researchers have consistently found, in many settings one kind of talk still predominates: IRF/IRE, or the so-called 'recitation script' of closed teacher questions, brief recall answers and minimal feedback, which requires children to report someone else's thinking rather than think for themselves and to be judged on their accuracy or compliance in doing so.

This script was famously parodied in Dickens's 1854 novel *Hard Times*, where young Sissy Jupe, who spends much of her waking life with horses and has a deep understanding of them, is unable to define a horse with the arid textbook precision the teacher demands ('Quadruped. Graminivorous. Forty teeth, namely twenty-four grinders, four eye-teeth, and twelve incisors . . .'), illustrating a brutal collision between experiential and academic knowledge, and schools' rejection of the former. The tendency, according to childhood sociologist Berry Mayall, has by no means dissipated. She shows just how much young children learn at home and out of school, yet how little use schools make of such learning, preferring instead to 'scholarise' early childhood.[18]

A century passed before recitation began to be systematically investigated, in the first instance by Barnes in the UK and Cazden and Mehan in the US,[19] and it has proved remarkably resistant to efforts to transform it. 'When recitation starts,' observed Martin Nystrand, 'remembering and guessing supplant thinking.'[20] Or, as Resnick asks: 'If adults learned through discussing problems and debating solutions with one another, then why were children expected to learn by listening and repeating what their teachers said?'[21] Synthesising evidence from studies undertaken in British and American classrooms, we find that in recitation:

- Interactions tend to be brief rather than sustained.
- Teachers move rapidly from one student to another to maximise participation, or from one question to another to maintain pace, and therefore rarely develop sustained or incremental lines of thinking and understanding.
- Teachers ask questions about content, but students' questions, on the rare occasions they ask them, are more likely to be confined to points of procedure.
- In Nystrand's words,[22] closed teacher 'test' questions predominate, and there are fewer 'authentic' questions for which the teacher has not specified or implied a particular answer.
- Students concentrate on providing 'correct' answers, and teachers gloss over 'incorrect' answers rather than use them as stepping stones to understanding.
- There is relatively little talk of a kind that encourages speculation, hypothesising or thinking aloud.
- Teachers give students time to recall but not time to think ('wait time').[23]
- Feedback is positively or negatively evaluative, but is less likely to inform, so the full cognitive potential of exchanges may be wasted.
- Students' communicative competence is judged less by how well they reason aloud (which they are given few opportunities to demonstrate) than by their ability to 'play the language games typical of classrooms', as outlined previously.[24]

Consequently:

- Students may not sufficiently develop the narrative, explanatory and questioning powers necessary to demonstrate what they know and understand, or don't know and understand, and to engage in decisions about how and what they should learn.
- Teachers may be unaware of, and tacitly or explicitly discount, students' out-of-school knowledge and experience that has a bearing on the task in hand and their personal ways of making sense.
- Teachers may remain similarly under-informed about students' grasp of what is being taught, and on both counts may be likely to lack the diagnostic purchase which is essential if their teaching is to be other

than hit-or-miss and if their assessments are to be accurate, equitable and useful.

- Students do not learn as quickly or as effectively as they could.
- While some will play the game of 'spot the correct answer', others will become alienated or bored by a process that appears to define learning merely as a process of jumping through linguistic hoops towards a non-negotiable end.

Not so simple

But is it that straightforward? Well, no. For example, a variant on the above is recitation disguised as enquiry: ostensibly open questions that stem from a desire to avoid overt didacticism but which may be no less closed than IRE in their intent. We frequently recorded this in the 1986–91 PRINDEP study, where in one not untypical example a teacher spent 20 minutes repeatedly asking more or less the same ostensibly open question – 'What do you see?' – of children examining fabric with magnifying lenses, glossing over their many and varied answers before eventually running out of time and telling them the 'correct' answer.[25] The more honest question would have been, 'What do I expect you to see?'

As Dillon notes of similar episodes: 'If the teacher repeats the *question* without saying "wrong," it means the answer is wrong.'[26] Conversely, repeating the *answer* – as long as the tone doesn't approach Lady Bracknell's 'A handbag?' for outraged incredulity – usually signals that if not praiseworthy it is acceptable. In speech, the paralinguistic – body language, gesture, tone, pitch, volume – may modify, emphasise or even contradict the linguistic. A decisive 'Yes!' is worlds apart from a tentative 'Ye-es,' and in transcription it's the question mark that reads Lady Bracknell's mind.

Apart from reminding us of the sheer pervasiveness of pseudo-open questions (which perhaps suggests that the matter is more than ethical) and the need to understand the impact of the paralinguistic on the semantic, there's a methodological problem here for systematic analysts of classroom discourse: should the question 'What do you see?' be coded 'open' or 'closed'? Does even that apparently simple question require a higher level of inference than typical coding systems allow?[27] In everyday parlance, we recognise the tension in phrases like: 'She means (or doesn't mean) what she says' or even 'His bark is worse than his bite.' Framing the problem linguistically we can distinguish an utterance's *form* from its *function*,[28] or, referencing J.L. Austin, its *locutionary*, *illocutionary* and *perlocutionary* force:[29]

> An utterance framed in *locutionary* terms as a question – such as 'Who's making all that noise?' – may have the *illocutionary* intention of a command ('stop making that noise') and the *perlocutionary* outcome of producing silence. As speech act it elicits, as move it directs.[30]

This pattern was recorded back in 1969 by Douglas Barnes, and its underlying dilemma was examined in a 1977 article by Atkinson and Delamont entertainingly entitled 'Mock-ups and cock-ups: the stage management of guided discovery instruction'.[31] More recently, and provocatively for those who see dialogue as the way out of this problem, Lefstein and his colleagues have coined the phrase 'exuberant voiceless participation' to characterise discussion observed in Israeli classrooms which is behaviourally dialogic – students enthusiastically explore and build on each other's ideas – but in which 'most student contributions [are] aligned with the official voice of the teacher and the curriculum.'[32] (We return to their work in Chapter 4.)

These examples point to an obvious tension in forms of classroom discourse that strive to avoid a 'teaching as telling' paradigm, for teaching is necessarily directed to particular purposes, and it is the teacher or school, not the student, who defines them. So it might be argued that in this regard recitation at least has the virtue of honesty, however bizarrely it may sometimes emerge, as for instance in this parodic exchange borrowed by Tony Edwards and David Westgate from the inimitable Peter Ustinov:

T: Who is the greatest composer?
S: Beethoven.
T: Wrong. Bach. Name me one Russian composer.
S: Tchaikovsky.
T: Wrong. Rimsky-Korsakov.[33]

We shall return to this problem later, for the dynamics of teaching are not necessarily what they seem, and since every exchange has a minimum of two participants, it may also have a minimum of two meanings. It may indeed be polyvocal, exceeding in its range of voices (in the sense of points of view) the number of voices (that is, speakers) that participate. Researchers have rightly problematised this, but in reality it's the way that much everyday conversation works, as we as everyday conversationalists intuit, and as novelists and dramatists tellingly exploit.

Two further caveats are necessary. First, even the most habitual or dedicated users of recitation/IRE are unlikely to rely on that approach alone. In this book, we commend the principle of *repertoire* not because it is earth-shatteringly novel but because it speaks to the way many teachers actually work, mixing methods not only between lessons but also within them, so our concern will be the nature, extent and use of a teacher's repertoire rather than its presence or absence.

Second, in pedagogy as in all things we should avoid the lure of the binary. We do not propose a simple choice between recitation and dialogue. For too long, education has been plagued by dichotomies of one kind or another – traditional/progressive, subject-centred/child-centred, formal/informal, instruction/discovery (as in the Atkinson and Delamont article cited previously) and many more – and we are not about to add to them, still less give comfort to those who caricature schooling in such polarised terms for the purposes of selling newspapers or winning elections. Like Courtney Cazden, we prefer the inclusive 'both/and' to the oppositional 'either/or',[34] and our preference is empirical as well as philosophical. That is to say, the observable practice of teaching rarely if ever boils down to two contrasting paradigms, especially if what the teacher means is not necessarily what the pupil, or the observer, thinks she means.

On the plus side

As Galton's 1990s follow-up to his 1970s ORACLE classroom research showed, and as was confirmed in other UK studies – for example by Hardman, Smith, Mortimer, Scott, Skidmore, Myhill, Moyles, Hargreaves, Alexander, *et al.* – 'deep structure' pedagogical change is extremely slow, and basic interactive habits are highly resilient.[35]

And yet. . . . We now have robust and replicable evidence that talk that is well-structured and cognitively demanding has a direct and positive impact on student engagement and learning, notably (if only because these are the subjects in which students are usually tested) in language, mathematics and science.[36] And whether independently or in response to this research, teachers have increasingly come to accept that talk makes a unique and powerful contribution to children's development, thinking and learning, and that it must therefore have a central place in their education.

Teachers also know, and frequently testify, that the educational consequences of social disadvantage are compounded by children's difficulties in oral development and communication; and that talk can be an effective means of re-engaging the disengaged and closing the overlapping gaps of equity and attainment (a proposition that our 2014–17 Education Endowment Foundation dialogic teaching project, on which more later, was specifically commissioned to test). And they understand, though not universally, that once they broaden their view of assessment beyond summative written tests, talk is a powerful tool for formative assessment because of the way talk is embedded in teaching rather than separate from it. It enables teachers to combine assessment *of* learning with assessment *for* learning and to shift from *post hoc* judgement of the magisterial but utterly unhelpful 'could do better' variety to meaningful diagnosis and support.[37]

Outside the school, meanwhile, employers insist on the social and economic importance of the skills of articulate communication, in speaking as well as writing; and student voice is nurtured not only as a vital aspect of classroom learning but also as a prerequisite of democratic engagement, now underwritten by the United Nations as a basic human right:

> States Parties shall assure to the child who is capable of forming his or her own views the right to express those views freely in all matters affecting the child, the views of the child being given due weight in accordance

with the age and maturity of the child. . . . The child shall have the right to freedom of expression; this right shall include freedom to seek, receive and impart information and ideas of all kinds, regardless of frontiers, either orally, in writing or in print, in the form of art, or through any other media of the child's choice.[38]

There is growing though again far from universal interest in how far these ideals are compatible with traditional modes of classroom talk (by 'traditional' I mean not only recitation, IRE and questions that *test* children's thinking but don't actually *foster* it, but also the endless round of unfocused open questions and the genial but unstructured, directionless and repetitious conversation that some teachers believe is recitation's antithesis); and in the potential of more rigorous forms in which reciprocity, exploration, speculation, argumentation and carefully structured discussion replace mere recall of predetermined responses, and in which – in Martin Nystrand's words – classroom talk 'requires students to think, not just to report someone else's thinking.'[39]

The six functions of classroom talk implicit above – for *thinking, learning, communicating, democratically engaging, teaching* and *assessing* – are sometimes rather carelessly conflated. They should not be, though in pursuit of whichever of these purposes it is also true that recent years have witnessed a broadening of the observable repertoire of classroom talk among both teachers and students – with, for example, paired and small group discussion taking their places alongside whole class interaction, and teachers showing greater readiness to switch between these. More strikingly, in a significant number of classrooms, and sometimes across whole schools and local authorities, there are now teachers who give high priority to talk in one, two, three or indeed all of the senses previously described and use it with rigour and flair and to impressive effect.

Some of the commensurate growth in research on productive classroom talk has resulted in practical guidance and materials for teachers, in print, video and/or online. Some of this excellent, some of it – unfortunately – pretty poor. The best material comes from non-official sources. So does the worst.

Challenges

Yet despite the growth in interest in talk, employers, university admissions tutors and others regularly complain that applicants' oral communication skills are in decline, that remedial action is needed to bring them up to scratch and that the problem lies squarely with schools and education's 'progressive' wing, which since the 1960s has celebrated cultural and linguistic relativism and unthinking and undisciplined chatter rather than Standard English. This charge has been around for decades, is regularly recycled, and is part of that politico-media 'discourse of dichotomy' to which I refer later.

Note for example the complaint of the right-leaning Hillgate Group that the teacher's proper task of authoritatively transmitting knowledge has been replaced by 'easygoing discussion and opinionated vagueness'.[40] There are two challenges here, then: students' communication skills and the polarisation of the debate about them.

Although there is now more talk about talk, it has a price: the ever-present danger of semantic regression through careless usage. Too often, 'dialogue' is equated with talk of unspecified kinds; and, as with 'assessment for learning', the adoption of the novel term may merely allow old habits to persist unchallenged: 'We do this already. . . .'

Underlining how far we still have to go, speaking in England's state schools is still the poor relation of reading and writing, as it has been since Sir Edward Curtis, nearly 200 years ago, coined the term '3Rs' to define what is supposedly 'basic' to children's education and what is not. Consequently, for many teachers, parents and Ofsted inspectors written work is still regarded as the only 'real' work, and talk may be enlisted to support reading and writing but is less commonly pursued as an educational goal in its own right. In England it is still unusual to witness (outside the teaching of drama) wholly oral lessons of the kind that that can be observed in some other countries, or lessons where talking, reading and writing are brought into a really fruitful interplay.[41] These matters, and the challenge of understanding and taking full advantage of the relationship between oracy and literacy, are more fully explored in Chapter 5.

Significantly, too, in the UK government's report on responses to its call for evidence to inform its revision of England's national curriculum, a mere 41 per cent of respondents 'said that Speaking and Listening must . . . be a central element in the statutory curriculum at every key stage [i.e. up to age 16] and that the ability to communicate effectively is fundamental to all aspects of human development'.[42] Put another way, the majority of respondents, many of whom were serving teachers, did *not* consider speaking and listening sufficiently important to be included in the national curriculum.

Why is this? Well, we start with the remarkably resilient legacy of nineteenth century elementary education, when the 3Rs ruled supreme and talk other than what the teacher invited was castigated as 'idle' (as it was by an education minister in 2012) or subversive of the expectation that students should be voicelessly compliant in school in order to know their place outside it.

No less pervasive has been a tendency to see the function of talk as primarily *social*, as chiefly about the acquisition of confidence in the business of communicating and holding one's own in conversation. Of course, confidence is a precondition for articulating ideas to others, but so too is the formulation of ideas to articulate, so confidence cannot be pursued in isolation. After all, we all know people who speak confident rubbish, and some of them purport to lead. Yet most of the attainment target levels for speaking and listening in the pre-2014 requirements for language in England's national curriculum made heavy and repeated use of the words 'confident', 'confidently' and 'carefully': 'pupils talk confidently . . . pupils listen carefully'. These behavioural modifiers said nothing about the *structure, content, quality* or *meaning* of talk, and indeed they deflected attention away from such attributes. But as psychologists, neuroscientists, anthropologists and classroom researchers have long understood, the function of talk in classrooms is *cognitive* and *cultural* as well as social.

In any event, transforming classroom talk into an instrument of greater rigour is easier for some teachers than it is for others, for it exposes two potential vulnerabilities: classroom control and subject knowledge. When as teachers we move from recitation to genuinely reciprocal talk, we loosen our control over what is said and how, and hence over student behaviour. This ceding of control, of course, is deliberate, for we want to empower students as talkers and decision-makers, but it carries risks. And if we are interested in other than yes/no or factual recall answers, then we must expect students to stray into aspects of the subject where we may be less secure than we would like to be. This second risk underscores the importance of what Shulman calls 'pedagogical content knowledge' and of teachers' ability to offer and open up 'deep representations of subject matter' in the way that Berliner highlights in his reviews of what differentiates expert teachers from the rest.[43]

A cautionary tale

The optimistic rise and premature decline of a succession of talk-focused official initiatives, notwithstanding the kind of evidence I have mentioned, bears witness to the extent to which talk still doesn't have the place in Britain's educational culture that it deserves and requires, and to the challenges facing those interested in genuine and lasting reform. These challenges are both professional and political.

The 1975 Bullock report *A Language for Life* included a powerful and still relevant chapter on the place of oral language in the teaching of English and across the curriculum as a whole. Clearly influenced by the work of Douglas Barnes, James Britton and Harold Rosen (whom it cites), Bullock provoked respect but little action. Yet it remains utterly relevant. Consider, for example, this:

> When we consider the working day in a secondary school the neglect of pupil talk as a valuable means of learning stands out sharply.[44]

School leaders take note. Or this (my italics):

> A curriculum subject . . . is a distinctive mode of analysis. While many teachers . . . aim . . . to initiate students into a particular mode of analysis, they rarely recognise the *linguistic* implications of doing so . . . [or] that the mental processes they seek to foster are the outcome of a development that originates in speech.[45]

Or this:

> Some teachers acquire . . . skill in assessing the spoken language of their
> pupils, but . . . many find it difficult. . . . An explicit understanding of the
> nature of language would extend their ability to influence it.[46]

And this (though the unthinking 'his' dates it):

> The teacher's own speech is a crucial factor in developing that of his
> pupils.[47]

The Kingman and Cox reports of 1988 and 1989[48] repeated Bullock's messages about language across the curriculum, which again originated with
Barnes, Britton and Rosen,[49] but even more forcefully than Bullock. They
judged that a major bar to reform was the paucity – among both teachers and
students – of 'knowledge about language', abbreviated to KAL and covering
the *forms* of language, its modes of *communication and comprehension*, its
acquisition and development and its *historical and geographical variation*.[50]
For students, KAL was to be an essential part of their English curriculum.
For teachers, it was viewed as a prerequisite not only for teaching English
but also for opening up the concepts and discourses of any subject with
anything approaching the necessary competence and commitment. Pressing
its argument, Kingman proposed that the training of all teachers, primary
and secondary, regardless of what subject or subjects they expected to teach,
should include mandatory courses to enable them to 'acquire, understand
and make use of knowledge about language.'[51] A year later, Cox placed KAL
squarely within its proposals for English in the national curriculum.

The call was taken up in the Language in the National Curriculum (LINC)
project,[52] which began to develop materials for teachers before being closed
down in 1991 by the same government that had funded it, on the grounds of
its imputed appeal to cultural and linguistic relativism and its alleged failure to
uphold the cause of Standard English. Next, and back within the more specific
domain of spoken language, the 1987–93 National Oracy Project piloted extensive materials to support the speaking and listening component of National
Curriculum English. It, too, rapidly disappeared almost without trace.[53]

By now it will be evident that language teaching and talk reform were –
and remain – intensely political matters. Carter reckons this is because language study is 'fascinating, complex and ultimately *dangerous*' (his italics),
for, quoting Halliday, 'language reflects and reveals the inequalities that are
enshrined in the social process.'[54] Carter cites a symptomatic 1980s political
intervention by the then Chairman of the British Conservative Party, Norman Tebbit:

> We've allowed so many standards to slip. . . . Teachers weren't bothering
> to teach kids to spell and punctuate properly. . . . If you allow standards

to slip to the stage where good English is no better than bad English, where people turn up filthy at school . . . all those things cause people to have no standards at all, and once you lose standards there's no imperative to stay out of crime.[55]

Thus, Standard English equates with standards of cleanliness and morality, and a failure to teach it leads to crime.

From 1998, the Labour government's National Literacy Strategy (NLS) focused attention on literacy at the expense of oracy, so much so that when in 2003 the Literacy and Numeracy Strategies were merged as the Primary National Strategy (PNS), talk was hardly mentioned in the new strategy's manifesto document *Excellence and Enjoyment*.[56] To its subsequent credit, the PNS worked hard to remedy this deficiency.

The national strategies did, however, make much of 'interactive whole class teaching', an idea imported from the classrooms of Switzerland, Germany and Taiwan. Unfortunately, and despite the efforts of Roger Luxton,[57] whose leadership turned it to impressive purpose in schools in East London, others paid greater attention to the whole class teaching than to the interaction. This, however, spectacularly missed the point, because in interactive whole class teaching as in all teaching, it is the quality of the *interaction* that makes the difference.[58] But for political converts to this cause, 'interactive whole class teaching', like Standard English, spoke to something more visceral: traditional pedagogy, transmission, order, control.

Meanwhile, building on my own international classroom discourse video and transcript data,[59] QCA (the 'arms-length' statutory body at that time responsible for England's national curriculum and assessment) began from 2001 to develop multi-media materials to support a more rigorous approach to classroom dialogue. David Reedy, David Rosenthal and I filmed in classrooms in different parts of Britain, scoped a professional guidance pack, selected our preferred clips and then waited . . . and waited. In the end, the initiative, and the materials, fell foul of turf wars between QCA and the government's national strategies for literacy and numeracy, for having crossed the line set by previous governments – that governments may tell schools *what* to teach but not *how* – the Labour government was not about to relinquish the control of pedagogy that the national strategies enabled it to exert. Echoing the fate of LINC, only a single clip from the dozens of lessons videotaped and edited for the QCA pack was ever released.[60]

But the pathology of pedagogy was not as simple as it seemed. Rose's 2006 review of early reading underlined the essential role of oracy in literacy development[61] but then cited the 2005 Ofsted report which found that teachers gave 'too little attention . . . to teaching the full National Curriculum programme of study for speaking and listening, and the range of contexts provided for speaking and listening remains too limited.'[62]

The resilience of professional culture and habit had been flagged earlier by the CICADA and ORACLE II projects, both of which examined pedagogical change over time and showed how the interactive core of teaching remained largely untouched by the 1990s government reforms of curriculum and assessment.[63] That was why, from 1997, the incoming Labour government judged that it could not leave the 'how' of teaching to teachers if its much-vaunted standards agenda was to have a chance of being realised. Yet studies by Hardman and his colleagues of the impact of the government's national literacy and numeracy strategies, on which that agenda depended, showed that 'traditional patterns of whole class interaction [had] not been dramatically transformed. . . . Teachers spent the majority of their time either explaining or using highly structured question and answer sequences' and that 'far from encouraging and extending pupil contributions to promote high levels of interaction and cognitive engagement, most of the questions . . . were of a low cognitive level designed to funnel pupils' response towards a required answer.'[64] Further, most teacher-student exchanges were very short. They lasted, on average, for 5 seconds and for 70 per cent of the time were limited to 3 words or fewer.[65]

And so to 2011, when the then Education Secretary Michael Gove launched the review leading to the version of England's current national curriculum introduced in 2014 and at the date of this book's first publication (2020) still in force. A four-person 'expert panel' was tasked with coming up with proposals. Chapter 9 of its 2011 report was entitled 'Oral language and its development within the national curriculum' and promisingly began thus:

> There is a compelling body of evidence that highlights a connection between oral development, cognitive development and educational attainment. Over the past four decades successive reviews, enquiries and development projects have also explored the crucial nature of oral capability within education. We are strongly of the view that the development of oral language should be a strong feature of any new national curriculum.[66]

But then, bafflingly in terms of the above but in line with the historical trend I have briefly surveyed, there followed this apparent copout:

> We are aware of and support the pedagogic significance of language and other forms of dialogue in classroom practice across the curriculum. However, this is not the direct focus of this report on a framework for the National Curriculum.[67]

Aside from quibbling about 'language and other forms of dialogue' – it should surely be the other way round – the assertion that we can define talk as pedagogy but not as curriculum is, I suggest, both problematic and symptomatic, so it requires our attention.

Oracy, pedagogy and curriculum

Let us tease out these strands. The term 'oracy' dates back to 1965, when it was coined by Andrew Wilkinson.[68] He used it in an attempt to give educational and pedagogical life to the primacy of speech in human development and culture, and to ensure that teachers treat children's oral development no less seriously than they treat the development of children's ability to read, write and count. Whether we call it 'oracy' (as in the National Oracy Project), 'oral development' (the expert panel's term, quoted earlier), 'communication skills' (the title of a pioneering Schools Council project led by Joan Tough in the 1970s and a no-nonsense term preferred by many)[69] or 'speaking and listening' (as, until 2014, in England's National Curriculum), the field is the same. The primary focus in each case is on the development of the child's capacity to use spoken language. Although Bullock argued for 'language across the curriculum', and Wilkinson insisted that oracy 'is not a subject – it is a condition of learning in all subjects',[70] spoken language thus conceived tended to be subsumed within the teaching of English, as it was in each version of England's national curriculum from 1989 to 2014.

But Wilkinson's 'condition of learning' points us to a second strand, what we might call 'oral pedagogy'. This foregrounds the kind of talk through which teaching and learning – all teaching and all learning, in all subjects, not just English – is mediated, as well as its relationship to students' thinking and understanding. Interest in this strand has also been around for some time, and it is the main focus of the chapters that follow this one. Its proponents have analysed prevailing patterns of classroom talk, assessed their impact on children's learning in specific subjects and indeed on their 'oracy', 'oral development' and 'communication skills', and have proposed alternative patterns which appear to be more effective: reciprocal teaching, accountable talk, interthinking, dialogic teaching and so on.[71]

I accept that these two aspects of talk – the *developmental* and the *pedagogical* – are not synonymous, for much or indeed most of children's oral development takes place outside the classroom, and there's more to pedagogy than talk. So why, when it comes to oracy in the classroom, do I insist that we cannot consider *talk as curriculum* in isolation from *talk as pedagogy*? And why do I say that the UK government's national curriculum 'expert panel' was wrong to fear that if it said anything about oral pedagogy it would have exceeded its curriculum brief?

In all classroom learning, the agency of the teacher is central, but in no aspect of children's learning, or of the curriculum, is this truer than in relation to talk. For unlike reading, writing, calculating, experimenting, drawing, making, moving and physically exercising, all of which the child can pursue independently, *talk by its nature is nearly always contingent upon others*. Talk has to be with someone; that 'someone' may be other pupils, but it is usually the teacher; and because of the power differential which Philip Jackson reminded us long ago is a fact of classroom life,[72] it is mainly through and in response to the teacher's talk that the child's own talk is facilitated, prompted, inspired, probed or otherwise orchestrated; or indeed inhibited, restricted, ignored, prematurely terminated or persistently channelled along the narrow tramlines of recitation and factual recall. What the teacher says partly conditions what the child says. But if we follow the expert panel's self-imposed ruling, then what the student says is 'curriculum' while what the teacher says is 'pedagogy'. There's the categorical difficulty.

In fact, given that curriculum is process as well as content, and that pedagogy necessarily encompasses learning as well as teaching – for teaching is by definition the intention or act of generating learning – one can as readily reverse the equation and argue that what the child says is pedagogy and what the teacher says is curriculum. That would be both true and equally arbitrary, for every exchange between teacher and student manifests both curriculum *and* pedagogy.

In reading and writing, the student's skills are influenced more by the teacher's skills as a *teacher* of reading and writing than by how well the teacher herself reads and writes. Not so with talk. Its essentially interactive nature means, as the 1975 Bullock enquiry (cited earlier) understood, that *the teacher's own competence as a speaker and listener contributes significantly to the developing oral competence of the student.* Hence, once again, 'dialogic teaching'.

Thus, in oracy, the teacher's agency is critical in perhaps unique and uniquely powerful ways. So, arguably, it makes little sense to specify a curriculum for speaking and listening which lists requirements for one of the parties to classroom talk but not for the other, but that is exactly what successive versions of England's national curriculum have done, and the same applies in many other countries and jurisdictions.

In fact, talk is the one area of classroom learning where the familiar distinctions between what and how, content and process, curriculum and pedagogy, break down. Courtney Cazden shows how the classroom 'communication system' combines 'the language of curriculum, the language of control, and the language of personal identity.'[73] Where talk is concerned, the what *is* the how (and indeed the who), and curriculum *is* pedagogy. The most obvious example of this is in literacy itself, for where would phonics be in the reading curriculum without talk? In the teaching of reading, the relationship between grapheme and phoneme, between what is written and spoken, is fundamental, while, in Gordon Wells's words, 'written texts only take on their full meaning in relation to the activities in which they play a part and to the talk that surrounds their composition and interpretation.'[74] This is something that Rose's 2006 report on early reading articulated clearly, and the matter will be explored in greater depth in this book's Chapter 5. Rose argued that raising the profile of speaking and listening would enhance not just the teaching of phonics but also literacy development more widely.[75] That is why the education minister's objection that raising the profile of talk would detract from the teaching of literacy was so bizarre. (See page 2.)

Behind these categorical difficulties is another, the distinction between the curriculum as *prescribed* and *enacted*, and in relation to oracy we once again have a problem, for talk is largely about the enacted curriculum, so much of what is said in classrooms cannot conceivably be scripted in advance in the way that a paper curriculum attempts to do. We can have a shot at prescribing the questions that teachers might ask, but can we prescribe pupils' answers? Well, actually, some teachers attempt to do just that, and it's called the 'recitation script', about which much has already been said.

Of course, in classroom talk, content isn't wholly synonymous with process, for talk actually has two kinds of content or subject matter: first, that which is *subject-specific* to the issue being discussed or the subject being taught and which makes, say, mathematical talk different from scientific talk, historical talk or artistic talk – for mathematicians, scientists, historians, artists ask different kinds of questions, use different vocabularies and think and reason in different ways. This is the force of Resnick's idea that talk should be accountable to knowledge and standards of reasoning, that is to say, to the particular kinds of knowledge and standards of reasoning that each curriculum domain embodies.[76] Second, it is also possible to identify a *generic* content of talk as such, which applies to all subjects and in all contexts, but especially within the teaching of English (or its equivalent national language in other countries) and foreign languages. This is what the pre-2014 national curriculum tried to do; and, rather differently, it is what Carter's work on the 'grammar of talk' and my own work on dialogic teaching have attempted.[77]

But especially the generic content of talk is what is signalled by KAL, which, it will be remembered, relates primarily to the student's knowledge but by extension to the teacher's too. That is to say, how language works: its building blocks from sound and letter to word, sentence and text, or (in speech) from utterance to act and exchange; its formal properties; its grammars (spoken as well as written); the nature, origins and nuances of words; the way language conveys, explores and manipulates meaning; the panoply of rhetorical devices which take the language user from competence to mastery; the many registers and social contexts of spoken language in use; the interplay of speaking, reading and writing; the artistry of spoken language at its best and the knowledge and skill that underpin that artistry.

Idle chatter

To return to our 'cautionary tale' of talk and policy. Shortly after the launch of the 2011–13 UK national curriculum review, I attended an international conference in Pittsburgh, USA at which leading researchers working not on oracy or 'communication skills' but on dialogic pedagogy shared evidence about its nature and impact. From the substantial number of studies by then available, Lauren Resnick, Christa Asterhan and Sherice Clarke, the conference organisers, concluded:

> Students who had experienced . . . structured dialogic teaching performed better on standardised tests . . . some students retained their learned knowledge for two or three years . . . in some cases students . . . transferred their academic advantage to a different domain.[78]

On returning to the UK, I wrote to Education Secretary Michael Gove, summarising the conference's positive finding about the relationship between talk and those educational standards that preoccupy every education minister and about which governments with centralising tendencies (as in England since 1988) know that they are vulnerable. To his credit, Gove immediately instructed his officials to organise an in-house seminar which would hear the evidence and discuss its implications for the then ongoing national curriculum review. The seminar was held a few months later, in February 2012. It included presentations from myself and, by videolink from the US, Lauren Resnick as chief architect of the Pittsburgh conference.[79] It was during the subsequent discussion that the delegated minister, while acknowledging that the evidence was persuasive, made his immortal comments about 'idle chatter', literacy and – the shibboleth that merges student attainment with public morality – 'standards'. As a result, the first draft of the new national curriculum excluded spoken language altogether – a seriously retrograde step, because it had been given reasonable prominence in every previous version since England first introduced a national curriculum in 1988–9.

Clearly, the minister just didn't get it, and his 'expert panel' had provided him with his escape clause: talk, his panel had said, is pedagogy not curriculum, so it has no place in a national curriculum review. In the face of protests from many quarters the minister stuck to his guns and in doing so shot himself in the foot (subverting his intention though not my metaphor), for marginalising oracy weakened rather than strengthened his professed commitment to raising standards in literacy. It was only after sustained pressure during the next 12 months, especially once Neil Mercer, Jim Rose and myself joined forces to lobby ministers and officials, that the government at last agreed to include a programme of study for spoken language in the final draft of the new national curriculum, a task in which we were invited to assist. However, though I count this a victory of sorts – a Freedom of Information request to the government from a doctoral student at the University of York revealed that my paper for the 2012 DfE seminar was what persuaded the government to change its mind[80] – the published requirements[81] remained too brief and generalised to have a significant impact on schools' thinking and practice.

The fallout of this egregious instance of misguided ministerial intervention may be with us for some time, not so much on account of the way spoken language was handled in England's 2014 national curriculum framework as because in venting what seemed like one person's maverick prejudice, the minister was in fact reinforcing a more pervasive mindset. This holds that education is essentially a process of transmitting knowledge from teacher to learner, so the thoughts and words of learners are of little consequence – that is, they are so much 'idle chatter' – until that transmission is complete.[82] In 2019, this view surfaced with a vengeance when 16-year-old Greta Thunberg inspired school students worldwide to strike against the climate crisis and dared to speak knowledgeably about climate science. Many political and media commentators flatly refused to accept that people of her age, being still at school and not yet replete with the required information, could or indeed had a right to know what they were talking about. The fact that Greta Thunberg was female may have had something to do with it too.

This, then, is where policy stands as this book goes to press, in England at least. However, in 2019 an all-party Parliamentary group (APPG) launched an enquiry into oracy education, expressing concern that 'oracy is being undervalued and overlooked within state education, denying the majority of children and young people the opportunity to develop these vital skills and hampering social mobility, educational achievement, wellbeing and future employability.'[83]

Note that the APPG enquiry uses the term 'oracy' and appears to opt for its developmental rather than pedagogical definition as I differentiated these earlier. Whether this initiative succeeds where others have failed remains to be seen. Some may argue that it may not matter much, for by virtue of being both content and process, curriculum and pedagogy, the quality of classroom talk is essentially down to teachers; so if schools wish to raise its profile, they can do so without reference to government edicts or parliamentary enquiries.

Strictly speaking, this is true, but even when ministers insist, as they do, that 'questions about how to teach are not for government to determine',[84] teachers' decisions in a relatively centralised education system are restricted in other ways. So when a statutory national curriculum framework devotes 86 pages to detailed requirements for literacy and barely two pages to oracy,[85] or for the purposes of quality assurance school inspectors define as 'work' what students write but not what they say, then the message to teachers is pretty clear. Conversely, even though it is a central premise of this book that teacher agency is a condition of teaching quality, that agency would be enacted with much greater alacrity and confidence if policy and its instruments were to align themselves with what the evidence on talk for learning and teaching dictates.

On the other hand, agency is surely about autonomy rather than permission, and, following the Cambridge Primary Review, students 'will not learn to think for themselves if their teachers . . . merely do as they are told.'[86] That principle, I should add, is indivisible: it applies as much to this book's framework for dialogic teaching as to the edicts of ministers or inspectors.

Notes

1 Halliday 1993.
2 Bruner 1971, 23.
3 Bruner and Haste 1987; Vygotsky 1962; Goswami and Bryant 2010.
4 Bakhtin 1986, 170.
5 Vygotsky 1981.
6 Bakhtin 1981; Mead 1962; Taylor 1991.
7 Wood, Bruner and Ross 1976.
8 Vygotsky 1978, 86. See also: Vygotsky 1962; Bruner and Haste 1987, 21–22; Vygotsky in Simon and Simon 1963, 21–34. Joan Simon, who studied Soviet psychology and translated Vygotsky's work (Simon and Simon 1963), argues that Vygotsky's colleague Alexander Luria, whom she knew, preferred 'potential' to 'proximal', which has an oddly spatial ring (Simon 1987).
9 Vygotsky 1962, 10.
10 Rousseau's *Émile, ou de l'éducation*, published in 1762.
11 Daniels 2001.
12 Alexander 2001, especially the analysis of transcribed lesson extracts from the five countries in chapter 16. See also the pioneering ethnographic studies by Tobin and his colleagues in pre-schools in China, Japan and the US (Tobin, Wu and Davidson 1989; Tobin, Hsueh and Karasawa 2009).
13 Bruner 1996, 56–60.
14 Johnson 2004; Goswami 2005; Goswami and Bryant 2010.
15 Kotulak 1997.
16 Goswami 2005.
17 Goswami 2005; Blakemore and Frith 2005.
18 Mayall 2010.
19 Barnes 1969; Cazden 2001; Mehan 1979.
20 Nystrand *et al.* 1997, 6.
21 Resnick, Libertus and Schantz 2020, 561.
22 Nystrand *et al.* 1997, 33.
23 Rowe 1986.
24 Edwards and Westgate 1994, 149–162; Mehan 1979.
25 This episode, with transcripts, is discussed in Alexander *et al.* 1995, 183–194.
26 Dillon 1988, 96.
27 There is an excellent discussion of this problem in Park *et al.* 2017.
28 Boyd and Markarian 2015.
29 Austin 1962.
30 Alexander 2001, 433. Emphasis in original.
31 Barnes 1969; Atkinson and Delamont 1977.
32 Segal and Lefstein 2015, 1.
33 Quoted from Peter Ustinov in Edwards and Westgate 1994, 100.
34 Cazden 2001, 56. For a fuller discussion of the dichotomising tendency, see the chapter 'Beyond dichotomous pedagogies' in Alexander 2008b. See also Lefstein, Trachtenberg-Maslaton and Pollak 2017.
35 Galton and Simon 1980; Galton *et al.* 1999; Hardman, Smith and Wall 2003; Smith, Hardman *et al.* 2004; Mortimer and Scott 2003; Skidmore, Perez-Parent and Arnfield 2003; Myhill 2005; Alexander *et al.* 1996; Moyles *et al.* 2003.
36 Many outcome-directed studies with an explicitly dialogic focus were brought together in Resnick *et al.* 2015. Four years later, the Routledge handbook of Mercer *et al.* 2020 extended this field. However, it is important to note that the headline finding about the primacy of interaction rich in cognitive challenge emerged much earlier from studies outside this tradition which used systematic

observation protocols and tracked variables such as time on task as well as discourse. The most important of these, all undertaken in primary schools, were the 1970s ORACLE study led by Maurice Galton and Brian Simon (Galton and Simon 1980; Galton, Simon and Croll 1980), its 1990s follow-up (Galton *et al.* 1999) and the studies by Bennett *et al.* 1986 and Mortimore *et al.* 1988. The 1986–91 PRINDEP and 1991–3 CICADA studies (Alexander 1997; Alexander *et al.* 1996) straddled both paradigms, combining both systematic observation and close-grained analysis of discourse.

37 Assessment Reform Group 1999; Black *et al.* 2003; Harlen 2014.
38 UNCRC 1990, clauses 12 and 13.
39 Nystrand *et al.* 1997, 72.
40 Cited by Edwards and Westgate 1994, 7.
41 See 'Learning to write by talking about writing', Nystrand 2019, 86–92.
42 DfE 2011a, 17.
43 Shulman 1987; Berliner 2004.
44 DES 1975, para 12.5.
45 DES 1975, para 12.4.
46 DES 1975, para 10.9.
47 DES 1975, para 10.9.jk.
48 DES 1988 (Kingman); DES 1989 (Cox).
49 During the 1960s, Harold Rosen produced the far-sighted discussion document *Towards a Language Policy Across the Curriculum* for the London Association for the Teaching of English. Reprinted as Rosen 1971.
50 DES 1988, 17 (my italics).
51 DES 1988, 63.
52 Carter 1990.
53 Norman 1992.
54 Carter 1997, 52. He cites Halliday 1982.
55 Norman Tebbit MP, speaking in 1985 (quoted in Carter 1997, 9).
56 DfES 1993.
57 Luxton 2000.
58 For an account and critique of the 'interactive whole class teaching' movement, see Alexander 2008b, 9–42.
59 Alexander 2001.
60 QCA 2005.
61 DfES 2006.
62 Ofsted 2005.
63 Alexander *et al.* 1996; Galton *et al.* 1999.
64 Smith, Hardman *et al.* 2004, 408.
65 Smith, Hardman *et al.* 2004, 408.
66 DfE 2011b, 52.
67 DfE 2011b, 54.
68 Wilkinson 1965.
69 For example, from the project's many publications, Tough 1979.
70 Wilkinson 1965, 58.
71 These refer, respectively, to Palincsar and Brown 1984; Michaels, O'Connor and Resnick 2008; Mercer 2000; myself and others.
72 Jackson 1968.
73 Cazden 2001, 3.
74 Wells 1999, 147.
75 DfES 2006.
76 Resnick, Michaels and O'Connor 2010.
77 Carter 2004.
78 Resnick *et al.* 2015, 1.

79 The revised conference papers are in Resnick *et al.* 2015.
80 DfE 2013a. The paper that the DfE official said made the difference was Alexander 2012.
81 DfE 2013b, 11, 14–15, 18–19, 83, 104 and 156.
82 Edwards and Westgate 1994, 7.
83 Oracy All-Party Parliamentary Group (2019).
84 Secretary of State Kenneth Clarke in 1991, launching the so-called 'three wise men' primary education. Quoted in the resulting report: Alexander, Rose and Woodhead 1992, 5.
85 DfE 2013b.
86 Alexander 2010b, 496. The Cambridge Primary Review, Britain's most comprehensive enquiry into primary education since the 1960s, was funded by Esmée Fairbairn Foundation, ran from 2006–10 and produced 31 interim reports, a final report and a research compendium. Its work was extended by the Cambridge Primary Review Trust, with support from Pearson Education, until 2017. Publications and other material from both ventures can be viewed/downloaded at www.cprtrust.org.uk.

3   Versions of dialogue

A question of definition

If, as the evidence shows, dialogic teaching really does make a difference, then our mission is clear: spread the word, scale up the practice. But –

> Two major . . . tasks face us. First, we need a larger empirical base for the claim that dialogic teaching is likely to be effective with all kinds of students in various settings and subject matters. Second, we need to find ways of training many more teachers who are willing and able to use academic dialogue as a major component of their teaching.[1]

That was Lauren Resnick's assessment in light of evidence available up to 2015. Dialogic teaching needed to become more inclusive as to students, subjects and contexts, and to secure a firmer place in the mainstream of teacher development, thinking and practice – neither of which conditions, presumably, had at that time been met.

It is fair to say that there has been progress on both fronts since then – the project on which this book's later chapters draw provides one example, the increasing number of teacher education courses focusing on dialogic pedagogy another, the mushrooming of research projects and publications a third[2] – so achieving our objective may be within reach.

But tackling Resnick's nominated tasks presumes something else: agreement on what dialogue is and how dialogic teaching is best conceived. Two major surveys published some years after Resnick's suggest that this goal has yet to be achieved. In their 2019 literature review, Kim and Wilkinson note that 'despite its appeal, or perhaps because of it, the idea of dialogic teaching has been variously interpreted', while Park and her colleagues conclude that there is a 'lack of shared conceptualisations of what [dialogic pedagogy] is and how best to characterise it'.[3]

In relation to Resnick's 'larger empirical base', such authoritative but pessimistic assessments are serious, because if dialogic pedagogy remains ill-defined, it might be presumed that any teaching branded as 'dialogic' is destined to be effective, which on the snake-oil principle is improbable. To come to the heart of dialogic teaching as concept and practice, what we really need to know is what kinds of talk exert greatest leverage over what kinds of learning, however they are labelled. (We investigate this more fully in Chapter 6.) We do know, from successive evaluations, and especially from the 2014–17 EEF dialogic teaching project, that this book's particular version of dialogic teaching has been shown to increase student engagement and raises test scores in English, mathematics and science, and that in spite of its challenges, it is an approach with which teachers are comfortable (a necessary condition, surely).[4] But that doesn't mean that all interventions that call themselves 'dialogic' are thereby validated. The tasks, then, are conceptual as well as evidential and professional.

Educators are no more immune than anyone else to fad, fashion and shibboleth, and 'dialogic' seems to have found its niche in the glossary of eduspeak for upwardly mobile researchers and school leaders, so we might profitably heed Shaw's warning that 'the biggest single problem in communication is the illusion that it has taken place.'[5] His aphorism is doubly apposite when, as now, it is in relation to the idea of communication itself that the illusion of communication may exist. For without explanation, 'dialogic' may be little more than virtue signalling: IRE/recitation (defined) = bad, dialogic teaching (undefined) = good.

It is with definitions, therefore, that we must start, and throughout this book key terms will be explained with what I hope is acceptable clarity. Language being our business, we should also note Locke's distinction between definitions *real* and *nominal*,[6] that is to say, between a definition that strives to get to the essence of a thing and one that uses other words to describe it, notably the *synonymous* definitions that are the business of lexicographers and deal with everyday usage. Since few synonyms provide an exact match, even in English where the language's parallel Germanic and Romance roots offer exceptional synonymic riches, dictionary definitions create space for semantic nuance and ambiguity. This applies especially to abstract and polysemous terms like dialogue/dialogic. A spoon, in contrast, is a spoon is a spoon (or at best a ladle).

Further, once a concept shifts from everyday to more specialised usage, it may acquire or require the kind of definition we call *stipulative*. Stipulative definitions are created in particular contexts and for particular purposes and may or may not have wider currency. To these, from time to time in this book, we add *ostensive* definitions, where direct speech is quoted, on the 'show don't tell' principle, to illuminate the kinds of talk that characterise dialogic teaching.

Finally, all educational terms – including 'dialogue' itself – are nuanced by the culture and history in which their meanings have evolved. Of his project *Keywords*, in which he painstakingly unravels the changing meanings of terms central to discourse about culture, society and politics, Raymond Williams remarks that it 'has been classified under headings as various as cultural history, historical semantics, history of ideas, social criticism, literary history and sociology.'[7] I cannot do this kind of justice to dialogue's keywords, but I hope I can at least encourage awareness that some of them are less straightforward than they seem, or than those who see teaching in purely technical or practical terms would like them to be. We are dealing, after all, with one of every culture's most important and contested themes: education.[8]

Defining dialogue . . .

So to *dialogue*, which in the first instance we define lexically and later, in the context of *dialogic teaching*, stipulatively.[9] With adjustments of spelling and pronunciation, 'dialogue' is conveniently the same in most European languages (though not in Finnish or Hungarian): *dialogue, Dialog, dijalog, diálogo, ∂uaлoг, dialogo, diyalog, dialoog, dialog*. . . . It comes to us via Latin from the Greek *διάλογος/dialogos*, meaning a *conversation*. 'Dia', incidentally, means 'through', so a dialogue can involve any number of participants, whereas a *dualogue* is confined to two. Both are contrasted, though in slightly different senses, with *monologue* (speaking alone). Of course, the very universality of the word 'dialogue' conceals a danger of presuming greater shared understanding than actually exists, for human interaction is mediated through culture, and words like 'dialogue' by which such interaction is signalled bear the unique cultural accretions of societies and their histories.

When we refer to a 'conversation', or use the word 'dialogue' as conversation's synonym, neither the form nor the function of the spoken exchange is embedded in the definition, so to escape vagueness, 'conversation' is qualified by adjectives such as 'casual', 'lively', 'desultory', 'heated', 'productive', 'scintillating', 'boring' or 'pointless' (we could fill a book with such epithets). With culture again in mind, we should note that the unspoken norms of spoken conversation vary between time, place and community, and within cultures as well as between them. That means that if we wish to bring precision to the way we talk about classroom talk, defining dialogue as 'conversation' won't take us very far.

However, also in everyday parlance we find 'dialogue' used to mean the *exchange of ideas* or, when tacitly or explicitly tempered by agreed norms (what some call 'ground rules'),[10] the *juxtaposition and resolution of competing points of view*. Here, then, we have the beginnings of a lexical family or hierarchy. Dialogue as *conversation* may mean much or little, so for that term to be useful it must be qualified: what kind of a conversation and to what end? Dialogue as the *exchange of ideas* shades into another contingent term, *discussion*, whose Latinate root suggests investigation or examination (literally 'shaking up') and in any event something more searching than a chat. When the discussion is considered and attentive, we might call it *deliberation*, the careful weighing of ideas in the way its etymology suggests.[11] And when deliberation marshals reasons or evidence in its quest to build, assess or defend a case, we talk of *argumentation*.

Thus, as interactive form, with function implicit, dialogue may be defined as:

- conversation
- discussion
- deliberation
- argumentation.

. . . and argumentation

For the purposes of lexical definition, I have treated argumentation as a form of dialogue. Yet argumentation may be voiced or silent, an oral encounter or an intellectual one, a meeting of people, ideas or both, so equally it can stand apart from dialogue as talk. For while argumentation may benefit from oral interaction, it does not in every case require this. In the solitary task of writing a book, I argue mostly with myself, while books and screen tangibly counter solipsism and give me access to other minds and voices from which I may be separated by hundreds of years or thousands of miles, and they do so with vivid immediacy; and I argue with them too, and listen to their arguments. Yet, whether voiced through outer or inner speech, argument is essentially dialogic.[12] So in the context of dialogic teaching, I view dialogue and argumentation as contingent rather than synonymous.

Like 'dialogue', 'argument' carries definitional baggage and indeed – as we shall see – is a complex field in its own right. Its basic lexical meanings range from (i) a *statement or proposition*, through (ii) *making and testing a case* and (iii) the more formal process of *proceeding from premise to conclusion supported by reasons*, to, in more adversarial mode, (iv) a *debate between holders of opposing viewpoints*, (v) a *dispute* that is equally oppositional but may involve more than two viewpoints, and finally and most vexatiously, (vi) a *quarrel*.

In many languages other than English, the words for argument in its rational and adversarial senses are different, so there is less room for ambiguity. But since, reportedly, many students whose mother tongue is English think of 'argument' in disputatious and even bellicose rather than rational terms,[13] definition is doubly necessary. In the UK, we are not helped by the high political premium put on the particular form of argument known as 'debate', in which complex issues are reduced to the opposition of just two points of view, each of which may be further oversimplified to fit debate's constraining mould; and through which in the UK's national Parliament Her Majesty's Government and Her Majesty's Opposition physically confront and score points off each other from their benches on either side of the House of Commons. (As we shall see in Chapters 7 and 8, the physical arrangement of classrooms, as of legislative assemblies, is a factor in the fostering of dialogue and argument of a less rebarbative kind.)

The distinction between debate and dispute needs perhaps to be noted. Whereas debate is ritualised and binary, a dispute is more open in its possibilities, processes and number of viewpoints. But both debate and dispute require an outright winner and are therefore to be distinguished from exploratory and deliberative forms of argument which aim to discover the most convincing idea, or what Reznitskaya and Wilkinson call, felicitously, 'the most reasonable answer'.[14]

So to extend our view of dialogic forms, we can make use of the following broadly lexical definitions of argument, grouping them according to whether the intent is to explore/evaluate (deliberative) or to win (disputatious):[15]

Deliberative argument

- proposition
- making and/or evaluating a case
- reasoning from premise to conclusion

Disputatious argument

- formalised debate
- dispute
- quarrel

Dialogic stance

The point at which simple lexical definitions become concepts exhibiting varying degrees of complexity is when they hint at purpose. Purpose manifests attitudes, outlook and values, or *stance*, and every account of dialogue, however commonsense it may seem or claim to be, expresses a stance of some kind.

In relation to the *study* of dialogue, that is to the more or less sedentary activity that keeps a surprising number of academics in what they claim is gainful employment, stance may be *descriptive, prescriptive* or *evaluative*. Thus, some scholars tell us what dialogue is; some specify the purposes it should serve and the form it should take; and others decide how its quality and/or impact should be judged, indicated, assessed or measured. (These modes of evaluation are not synonymous, and indeed each is a stance in itself: we can assess without measuring and judge without doing either.)

In such matters, the differences that are most likely to confound communication are those that stem from the disciplinary affiliations of the scholars in question. The fact that classroom talk, dialogic or otherwise, has attracted the attention of cognitive psychologists, sociologists, anthropologists, philosophers, psycholinguists, sociolinguists, ethnolinguists, psychometricians, pragmatists, comparative linguists, discourse analysts and conversation analysts might justify celebration that its importance is so widely recognised; as might the prescriptive adaptations of dialogue for purposes as varied as teaching and psychotherapy. However, such variety reduces even further the prospects of mutual understanding; for, self-evidently, our disciplinary perspective determines what we look at, how we look at it and what, having looked, we see.

Let us approach the matter differently, from the specific stance of the comparativist. Elsewhere I have proposed that teaching, however, whenever and wherever it takes place, can be reduced to a simple and irreducible proposition:

> Teaching, in any setting, is the act of using method x to enable students to learn y.[16]

If that is so, then we might expect analysis of teaching deemed 'dialogic' to reveal stances on the proposition's basic ingredients: teachers and teaching; learners and learning; the knowledge, understanding, skills and dispositions to be encountered; and, with particular reference to its interactive component, pedagogy.

The *Culture and Pedagogy* international data, from which our proposition arose, revealed complex webs of attitudes, beliefs, assumptions and values in relation to these and other matters that it is not possible to go into here, though from that exercise it is pertinent to record three observations. First, the range of accounts of teaching voiced and witnessed across classrooms and cultures amounted to variations, albeit culturally and situationally nuanced, on a relatively small number of common themes: for example, purposes, content, the management of space and time, routines and rituals, assessment and of course interaction. Second, they revealed differences in emphasis on the main ingredients captured in the proposition: for some educators, what mattered most was the teacher's task, for others, the situation of the learner, for others again, the imperatives of what was taught. Third, because teaching is located within and responsive to culture, the views expressed something deeper and subtler than the merely transactional.

So, noting that 'talk doesn't just communicate something from person x to person y, it also reflects and defines human relations',[17] we recorded that within both the wider context of education and the more specific domain of teaching, stances that we can call *relational* were pervasive. Indeed there are those who say of teaching, 'It's all about relationships' and dig no deeper.

Teachers in England, France, India, Russia and the United States articulated, enacted or steered an uncertain path between *individualism, community* and *collectivism*. These are concerned with that most fundamental human question, the relationship of humans to each other and to the societies they inhabit. They are familiar enough in social and political theory, less so in accounts of pedagogy:

- *Individualism* is manifested in intellectual or social differentiation, divergent rather than uniform learning outcomes, and a view of knowledge as personal and unique rather than framed by publicly approved disciplines or subjects.

- *Community* is reflected in collaborative learning tasks, often in small groups, in 'caring and sharing' rather than competing, and in an emphasis on the affective as much as, or sometimes more than, the cognitive.
- *Collectivism* is reflected in common knowledge, common ideals, a single curriculum for all, national culture rather than pluralism and multiculture, and in learning together rather than in isolation or small groups.

In the *Five Cultures* data these values were pervasive at national, school and classroom levels. Compare them, for example, with Shweder's contrast of 'holistic, sociocentric' cultures like India and what he calls 'Western' cultures – the label is surely much too broad – with their concept of 'the autonomous distinctive individual living in society';[18] or the survey that found that only Britain was within striking distance of US respondents' insistence that freedom is far more important than equality and that personal happiness and welfare far outweigh responsibility to society. German respondents voted a balance of both sets of commitments.[19]

In the *Five Cultures* analysis, we then showed how these 'primordial values' surfaced in the educational practices of each of the schools in which we worked, including not only rituals like school assemblies and curriculum domains such as personal education and citizenship but also that quintessential pedagogical distinction between individualised learning, collaborative group work and whole class teaching. We argued that 'individual, group and class are the organisational nodes of pedagogy not just for reasons of practical exigency but because they are the social and indeed political nodes of human relations.'[20] Group work is fostered not only because it can be highly productive educationally but also because learning to collaborate, co-operate, listen to each other and develop mutual respect are deemed to be socially desirable in themselves. Whole class teaching may be a time-efficient way to convey information to all the students in a class, and as a bonus it may serve as an effective instrument of behavioural control; but it also speaks to social solidarity and cohesion, and to conformity to established norms. Here, then, teaching practices that seem merely *procedural* combine with and express the *relational, cultural* and *ethical*.

Alongside these three stances on human and pedagogical relations, there emerged from our cross-cultural data a second set. Where individualism, community and collectivism start with the relationship of individuals to society and each other, and move thence into the classroom, the following six stances start with the purposes of education, the nature of knowledge and the relationship between teacher and learner. So to the procedural, relational, cultural and ethical, they add the *epistemic* and *ratiocinative*.

- Teaching as *transmission* sees education primarily as a process of instructing students to absorb, replicate and apply basic information and skills.

- Teaching as *initiation* sees education as the means of providing access to, and passing on from one generation to the next, the culture's stock of high-status knowledge, for example in the sciences, literature, the arts and humanities.
- Teaching as *negotiation* reflects the Deweyan idea that teachers and students jointly create knowledge and understanding rather than relate to one another as authoritative source of knowledge and its passive recipient.
- Teaching as *facilitation* guides the teacher by principles which are developmental (and tacitly Piagetian) rather than cultural or epistemological. The teacher respects and nurtures individual differences and waits until children are ready to move on instead of pressing them to do so.
- Teaching as *acceleration*, in contrast, implements the Vygotskian principle that education is planned and guided acculturation rather than facilitated 'natural' development, and indeed that the teacher seeks to outpace development rather than follow it.[21]
- Teaching as *technique*, finally, is more neutral in its stance on society, knowledge and the learner. Here the important issue is the efficacy of teaching regardless of the context of values, and to that end, imperatives like structure, economic use of time and space, carefully graduated tasks, regular assessment and clear feedback are more pressing than ideas such as democracy, autonomy, development or the disciplines.

In Britain, transmission was and remains the legacy of mass elementary '3Rs' education, with cultural initiation as its loftier, more Arnoldian counterpart in public and grammar schools and the universities. That is, transmission for the masses, initiation for the elite. It is also the stance of the political right. Teaching as negotiation, or democratic pedagogy, was fleetingly glimpsed in the 1931 Hadow report on primary education, then more overtly combined with facilitation and its adjunct 'readiness' in the 1967 Plowden report, reaching its apogee in the 1970s progressive movement and its US 'open education' counterpart.[22] It stands in conscious antithesis to both transmission and induction, and if it has a political home this is slightly to the left of centre, though to its detractors it is not so much centrist as rabidly left-wing or, worse, 'liberal'.[23] Then, deriving from Vygotsky's maxim that 'the only good teaching is that which outpaces development',[24] acceleration sits as uncomfortably with facilitation as negotiation does with transmission. Finally, the idea that teaching is first and foremost a technology, guided by principles of structure, economy, conciseness and rapidity, and implemented through standardised procedures and materials, reaches back to a much older European tradition, that initiated in the mid seventeenth century by Jan Kamensky (Comenius) in his *Great Didactic*.[25]

In the same way that our three primordial values of collectivism, community and individualism have their organisational counterparts in the classroom, stance thus expressed is readily translated into teaching approaches. Transmission is most effectively achieved through rote and recitation, and initiation through recitation and discussion. Dialogic pedagogy, being in a rather different manner interventive, is unwilling to stand back and 'facilitate', but instead may combine the epistemic stance of negotiation with the developmental and procedural stance of acceleration. Yet – following Argyris and Schön[26] – it is important to distinguish between the stances as 'espoused' and 'in use'. If the aspiration of cultural and disciplinary induction is pursued largely through the recitation script of closed question and recall answer, it becomes in effect no-questions-asked transmission. Indeed, however hard we try to escape its clutches, IRE's hold on our collective memory, and its sheer simplicity, forever drag us back.

My argument, then, is that ostensibly instrumental approaches to classroom dialogue as practice reflect, sometimes explicitly though more usually implicitly, broader stances of a normative kind that can be summarised thus:

- *Developmental*: concerning the nature and processes of human development and learning.
- *Relational*: concerning classroom relationships and how these should be conceived and fostered.
- *Procedural*: concerning the ways, instrumentally, that interactions should be managed.
- *Ratiocinative*: concerning the ways that ideas, propositions and arguments should be handled.
- *Epistemic*: concerning how knowledge, both generic and domain-specific, is conceived and its claims are validated.
- *Ethical*: concerning the moral basis for classroom decisions and relationships and the values by which they should be underpinned.
- *Cultural*: concerning the nature of society, the groups and values that it comprises, and the extent to which dialogue should reflect or even foreground these (for example, in relation to gender, class, race, majorities and minorities).
- *Ontological*: concerning the extent to which dialogue is viewed as a way not only of teaching but also of being and doing, a way of life.

In giving practical form to particular values concerning education, its purposes and its contribution to culture and society, dialogue may well be *ideological* too (for example, directed to promoting talk of a kind that advances a particular political outlook or cause).

These eight conceptual categories compare with the two – epistemological and ontological – offered by Wegerif, Mercer and Major, in what might seem an excessively reductive mapping of the dialogic territory.[27] Where, in their account, are ethics, culture, relationships – and learning? Further, the categories are not mutually exclusive. That is to say, accounts of dialogue can and do combine standpoints on, say, the nature of knowledge and how students should treat each other.

The three analytical categories with which this section started (descriptive, prescriptive, evaluative) are equally slippery because, while they may purport to be distinct, they may in practice elide. In particular, the ostensibly objective account may tacitly privilege some versions of dialogue over others or fallaciously slide from description to prescription, from what *is* to what, in someone's opinion, *ought to be*.

From definition and stance to dialogue: versions and variations

Adam Lefstein and Julia Snell have picked their way through some of the foregoing territory, selecting conceptions of dialogue and in each case, though not as framed previously, identifying key questions, goals and 'indicative thinkers'.[28] Thus, they say, Socrates offers dialogue as *critique* underpinned by doubt and questioning. From Mikhail Bakhtin, they deduce the notion of dialogue as *voice*, an interplay operating and competing not just in oral exchange but also in our thoughts and ideas and the culture and history we inhabit.[29] Lev Vygotsky informs the idea of dialogue as *thinking together*, an essential tool for developing the child's higher mental functions; but it is also a dialogue between personal and collective knowledge, between what Vygotsky called the natural and cultural lines of the child's development.[30] (Some dialogists mistakenly merge this with the cognitive/social axis of talk for learning, which is not the same and downplays culture outside the classroom.) Martin Buber gives us dialogue as *relationship* which, if it is to generate other than instrumental or competitive interactions, is predicated on respect, mutual concern and communality. Buber, indeed, defines reality itself as dialogic.[31] Finally, Paulo Freire starts with society's endemic inequalities and injustices and proposes a corrective role for dialogue as emancipation and *empowerment*.[32]

The emphases here can be mapped, though again without implying exclusivity, onto our conceptual stances: developmental (Vygotsky); relational (Buber, Freire, Bakhtin, Vygotsky); ethical (Buber, Freire, Bakhtin); ratiocinative (Socrates, Vygotsky, Bakhtin); epistemological (Bakhtin, Vygotsky); cultural (Bakhtin, Freire); ontological (Buber, Bakhtin); ideological (Freire). All are to a degree prescriptive – Freire notably so – as well as descriptive. Bakhtin's stance on dialogue is perhaps uniquely all-embracing in its focus.

Lefstein and Snell then describe four well-known models of dialogic classroom practice. First, Martin Nystrand's *dialogically organised instruction* highlights 'authentic' rather than 'test' questions. For Nystrand and his colleagues, an 'authentic' question is one 'for which the questioner has not specified an answer' and which therefore encourages the learner to think for himself/herself, which they view as the bottom line in effective teaching.

From event history analysis, Nystrand offers other high-leverage concepts – 'question events', 'dialogic spells' and 'dialogic bids', on which more later.[33] Next, Mercer's *exploratory talk* – a term borrowed from the earlier work of Douglas Barnes and Frankie Todd[34] – aims to break away from teacher-dominated recitation and the high premium placed on what Barnes calls 'presentational talk'[35] by maximising the potential of small group discussion in which students 'engage critically but constructively with each other's ideas', allowing themselves to think aloud and as tentatively as need be in pursuit of new insights.[36] The *accountable talk* initiated by Lauren Resnick and developed with Sarah Michaels and Cathy O'Connor applies three criteria – made explicit to students as well as teachers – to the task of making talk 'academically productive': accountability to the learning community, to standards of reasoning and to knowledge.[37] This appears to aim for a more disciplined, less conversational form of talk than that promoted by Mercer and his colleagues. Finally, Lefstein and Snell summarise my own version of *dialogic teaching*, as it was a few years ago. The current version is described in Chapters 7 and 8, so I shall say no more about it here.

In terms of our conceptual categories, all four frameworks are explicitly procedural, so for readers interested in the practicalities of classroom talk, they repay study. But to different degrees and in different ways they are also relational, ratiocinative and epistemological: all invoke preferred relationships between teacher and student and among students themselves, all prioritise certain kinds of reasoning, and some presume particular accounts of knowledge. So they all manifest a stance. Perhaps most striking in this regard is Martin Nystrand, whose 2019 autobiography post-dated the analysis of Lefstein and Snell and is a useful corrective to the impression that their chosen four models of dialogic practice are merely technical. Nystrand ontologically reveals the way that, over a 40-year period, his work as teacher and researcher dialogically interweaves with his responses to the 20-acre family woodlot on which he lives and where he set about building a Japanese-inspired teahouse. 'These narratives', Nystrand tells us, 'increasingly meet, inspire and . . . "re-enlighten" each other.'[38]

Stance, then is inescapable: we acquire skills for teaching or research that others have used and refined, but in that elusive amalgam of the personal and the professional we make them our own. Professional development is also a personal journey.[39]

A study by Kim and Wilkinson complements Lefstein and Snell's analysis while differing from it in the way it uses my own account of dialogue teaching as its point of departure and comparison rather than as one model among several. They tease out, in chronological order of publication, the features of eight other approaches to dialogic pedagogy, concentrating on stance as well as method. They then review six further approaches that explicitly use the term 'dialogic teaching'.[40] That yields 15 versions of dialogue (to compare perhaps with Empson's Seven Types of Ambiguity) and raises the definitional stakes still further.

The first group includes: Freire (see earlier discussion); Nicholas Burbules[41] (strongly relational); Nystrand (see earlier discussion); Resnick (see earlier discussion); Gordon Wells's 'dialogic inquiry', in which 'inquiry' is less a procedure than a frame of mind directed towards the co-construction of knowledge;[42] the 'dialogic/authoritative' matrix devised by Mortimer and Scott for framing talk in science lessons;[43] Rupert Wegerif's 'dialogic space', which references Burbules's emphasis on the relational but injects as a prerequisite for true dialogue in small group discussion the tensions of perspective difference;[44] and Eugene Matusov's 'dialogic pedagogy', which is more ontological than epistemological and like Bakhtin sees dialogue as a way of being as well as doing.[45]

The six approaches that Kim and Wilkinson nominate in their second group 'have substantial programmes of research on classroom dialogue and . . . routinely invoke the term "dialogic teaching" in framing their research and scholarship.'[46] Inevitably, advocates of the selected approaches use 'dialogic teaching' in different ways. This definitional plurality may be in itself commendably dialogic, but it adds to the challenge of helping teachers make sense of the field and gives weight to the need for definitions that both have stipulative clarity and are sufficiently detailed for us to understand how they might work in normal classroom settings. And, as I noted at the beginning of this chapter, it may confound the task of proving that dialogic teaching makes a difference.

Kim and Wilkinson first cite Mercer, who has taken up the term 'dialogic teaching' relatively recently to repackage and extend his earlier work on 'interthinking' in small group discussion, with its progression from 'disputational' and 'cumulative' talk to 'exploratory'[47] (see earlier discussion – we also note in passing, to be picked up later, that both Mercer and I use 'cumulative' as a classifier but do so differently). Next comes Maureen Boyd, who emphasises a relational stance that highlights the centrality of the student's role in framing and shaping classroom discourse, and who is less concerned with the precise forms of talk than with their cognitive and epistemic function; and indeed Boyd is concerned that in their preoccupation with dialogue's procedural and relational aspects, some advocates may wrongly attribute to it significant ratiocinative or epistemological gains – or, put more bluntly, give such talk more educational credit than it deserves just because it looks and sounds good.[48] Alina Reznitskaya's account of dialogic teaching prefigures the important work on argumentation she has done with Ian Wilkinson (to which we return later), but like that later work, her account is firmly ratiocinative as well as procedural.[49] She advocates an 'inquiry dialogue' 'in which students collectively work towards the most reasonable answers to complex questions.'[50] Mary Juzwik uses 'dialogic teaching' to connote any talk that engages multiple student voices in the construction of knowledge, so it is more relational and indeed ethical than procedural, but also, in its emphasis on co-construction, epistemological.[51] Lefstein's approach is eclectic, subsuming some of my own principles but more prominently emphasising the tensions, dilemmas and even contradictions of dialogue and voice in the context of conventional schooling.[52] These and his ethnographic approach to classroom culture and knowledge tend to foreground dialogue's relational, epistemological and indeed ontological aspects. Finally, Kim and Wilkinson cite Klara Sedova, who is particularly exercised by the challenge of professional development in dialogic teaching, and like Lefstein notes the monologic/dialogic tension. Her account seems to tend more towards the procedural and relational.[53]

By now, I fear, readers may be somewhat confused. Howe and Abedin hope to reassure us when they conclude from their earlier research review that the literature on dialogic pedagogy – or at least that segment of it on which they choose to focus – has a 'shared conceptual core', albeit with 'divergence around the edges'.[54] However, my reading of this and other literature prompts me to suggest that once we move beyond merely technical accounts of classroom discourse, the consensus may be more limited and the divergence more extensive than Howe and Abedin allow, especially once we start to unpick stance in the way suggested previously. Indeed, as the dialogic field expands and the number of its academic furrows multiplies, consensus could well diminish further, and each account of dialogic teaching will probably require its unique stipulative definition. As Kim and Wilkinson noted in the quote at the beginning of this chapter, the term 'dialogic teaching' has been variously defined 'despite its appeal, *or perhaps because of it*' (my italics).

Dialogic teaching, dialogic pedagogy, dialogic education?

While we are on the matter of definitions, it will not have escaped readers' notice that though the preceding pages refer to dialogic *teaching*, 'dialogic' is also used, in this book as elsewhere in the literature, to qualify the words 'pedagogy' and 'education'. The terms are not synonymous, and in this book they are not treated as such.

Teaching is the intention and act of bringing about learning, usually but not exclusively in institutions established for that purpose. Its elements have been variously adumbrated, and there are many models of teaching in the literature, some of them deceptively simple and others soporifically complex,[55] but however teaching is conceived it is always directed towards specific goals and underpinned by assumptions, values and ideas, even when it becomes routine and the goals and ideas recede from view or are justified by no more than habit. ('But miss, *why* do we have to do this?' 'Because you do.') Those who speak aggressively, defensively or proprietorially of the 'coal-face'/ 'chalk-face'/ 'nitty-gritty' of teaching, as if the work were practical (which it is) to the point of being mindless (which it must never be), or who impatiently dismiss discussion of educational ideas with 'never mind the theory, let's get down to the practice' are deluding themselves about the nature of teaching, for all practice is in some way 'theory-soaked' and teaching especially so.

Pedagogy brings the ideas firmly into focus and commands that we give them our attention, not just dutifully in pre-service training or in professional masters' programmes but willingly as part of our everyday planning, thinking and discussion. Pedagogy gives us the bigger picture of both *what* is done in classrooms and *why*. So in line with the continental European tradition that reaches back to Jan Komensky (Comenius),[56] I define pedagogy as the practical and observable act of teaching *together with* the purposes, values, ideas, assumptions, theories and beliefs that inform, shape and seek to justify it. In acquiring this penumbra, pedagogy also connects teaching with the wider culture. Elsewhere, I have attempted to map pedagogy as both teaching act and, through categories of ideas that enable, formalise and locate that act, as discourse.[57] (See Chapter 7.)

Education forms the outermost of our three circles and embraces the entire enterprise, not just because alongside law, rights, justice, democracy, community, religion and so on education is one of every society's grandest cultural narratives but also because it extends outwards from the individual classroom to constitute a system of hundreds or thousands of schools, colleges, universities and other institutions and is a major recipient of public expenditure. The system has physical, administrative and fiscal structures and is framed by law; it has its own professions and subcultures; and again it can be mapped conceptually.[58] But however the system is configured, and whatever idea or ideas it promotes (for there are many to choose from), education expresses itself through pedagogy and is enacted and achieved through teaching. And at the heart of the enterprise is interaction: between and among teachers and students; between these and the texts, screens and other media and materials by which teaching and learning are supported.

Properly speaking, therefore, this book is about dialogic pedagogy, because it advances a view of teaching that attends as closely to ideas, values and evidence as to practice. Hence the discussion of evidence on the relationship between spoken language, thinking and learning in Chapter 2, our mapping of definitions and conceptualisations of dialogue and argumentation in the present chapter, and the discussion in Chapters 4–6 that leads into the repertoires in Chapter 7; not to mention the list of references at the book's end. Yet, once we have looked in detail at the book's take on dialogic teaching, it will be apparent that it is also about dialogic education.

Why, then, have I opted for 'dialogic teaching' rather than 'dialogic pedagogy'? There are two main reasons.

When my journey towards dialogic teaching started during the 1980s, there was a need for a corrective to the view that while the development and quality of the student's talk were manifestly of critical importance in relation to his or her learning, the teacher's agency in respect of that talk was somehow incidental. Professional sentiment, especially in primary education, framed the teacher's role as *facilitator* of the child's 'oracy' or 'speaking and listening' (and much else) and frequently missed the point that in 'facilitating' student talk, what the teacher says, and how he or she says it, is actually rather important.

This, as we saw earlier, was part of the abiding legacy of the Hadow and Plowden reports of 1931 and 1967,[59] as misinterpreted by several generations of teacher educators who equated teaching with mere telling and paraded adversarial and logically untenable dichotomies like 'child *versus* curriculum', 'process *versus* content', 'skills *versus* knowledge', 'informal *versus* formal', 'progressive *versus* traditional' and, of course, 'practice *versus* theory' and 'learning *versus* teaching'.[60] Each of these managed to play down the Vygotskian principle that through the teacher's intervention education accelerates rather than follows the child's 'natural' line of development.[61]

By calling my approach dialogic *teaching*, I believed that I might help to correct the still discernible imbalance in discussion of teaching in general and classroom talk in particular, and encourage more equitable attention to the talk used by all parties in classroom exchanges, and especially the kinds of talk the teacher might use in order to open up the talk, and hence the thinking, of the student. In any case, it would have been odd to advocate something called 'dialogue' by exploring one side of the interaction and leaving the other to chance, though that, regrettably, has been a tendency in some accounts of oracy. So 'dialogic teaching' it was, and 'dialogic teaching' it has remained, because while since then the professional discourse has accommodated to a more rounded view of teaching, my name and 'dialogic teaching' have become so firmly linked that changing the brand to 'dialogic pedagogy' would have caused confusion. Or so – to pre-empt accusations of hubris – I have been advised.

There was a second reason for appending 'teaching' to 'dialogic' rather than the more accurate 'pedagogy'. I first wrote about pedagogy in a book published in 1984,[62] inspired in part by a now celebrated article by the great educational historian, internationalist and campaigner Brian Simon, who with his fellow-historian and wife Joan Simon had brought the work of Vygotsky, Leontiev, Luria and their colleagues (and indeed Luria in person) to the UK. Joan herself speedily learned Russian so that she could translate their second volume of papers by Russian psychologists and pedagogical theorists.[63] (My own link is more tenuous: in Moscow in 1995 I met and interviewed Leontiev's son Alexei Alexeivich in connection with the *Culture and Pedagogy* research.) At that time the word 'pedagogy' was rarely heard, but Simon's 1981 paper, 'Why no pedagogy in England?', was about something more fundamental than terminological frequency. He deplored and cogently explained the absence in English educational discourse of anything comparable to the long-established continental European 'science of teaching'.[64]

Twenty years later, I published my own *Culture and Pedagogy* (and post-Soviet Russia was one of the countries where the fieldwork was undertaken) and shortly afterwards my first article using the term 'dialogic teaching'. Yet in Britain at that time, the word 'pedagogy' was still rarely heard or used, so although I wrote about dialogic pedagogy as I have defined the latter word, 'teaching' was deemed, as they say, more 'user-friendly'. I revisited Simon's critique in 2004 in light of the then-government's interventions in teaching via its national literacy, numeracy, primary and secondary strategies, which when judged as pedagogy, were deeply flawed,[65] so I was probably right to be cautious.

So: this book's key term is 'dialogic teaching', but as used here, the term, and the book as a whole, are equally about dialogic pedagogy and dialogic education. I said earlier that in defining an apparently universal word like 'dialogue' we must acknowledge the unique cultural accretions of societies, their histories and their manners. The same applies to 'teaching', 'pedagogy' and 'education'. Had I been working in the Czech Republic – which, after all, has an excellent pedagogical museum dating back to 1892[66] and images of Comenius everywhere – I would have used 'pedagogy' from the outset, without reservation or explanation.

Conclusion

This chapter started by warning that the now widespread and unqualified use of the terms 'dialogue' and 'dialogic' in educational contexts masks a problem of definition, and that if we are to capitalise on the evidence that dialogic teaching makes a difference, we need to use these and related terms with greater discrimination.

Accordingly, we distinguished between dialogue as *conversation, discussion, deliberation* and *argumentation*, marking the last of these as both intrinsic and extrinsic to dialogic teaching, and differentiating *deliberative* and *disputatious* forms of argument, three in each case.

Moving from definition to *stance*, we distinguished between descriptive, prescriptive and evaluative modes of analysis of dialogue – what it is, what it should be, and what it achieves – and, in the preoccupations of such analyses, between dialogue's *developmental, relational, procedural, ratiocinative, epistemological, ethical, cultural* and *ontological* aspects. We showed how dialogue as transaction both reflects and is shaped by broader social and cultural values.

We then compared two exercises in mapping the conceptual territory of dialogic teaching. Lefstein and Snell contrasted the broadly dialogic stances of Socrates, Bakhtin, Vygotsky and Buber, and then compared the models of dialogic practice proposed by Nystrand, Mercer, Resnick, Michaels and O'Connor, and myself. Kim and Wilkinson approached the task differently, using my own work as the point of comparison for eight other approaches they deemed generically 'dialogic' (Freire, Burbules, Nystrand, Resnick, Wells, Mortimer and Scott, Wegerif, Matusov) and six more that have explicitly coined the term 'dialogic teaching' (Mercer, Boyd, Reznitskaya, Juzwik, Lefstein, Sedova).

Next, we considered the three words that 'dialogic' most frequently precedes and qualifies – *teaching, pedagogy* and *education* – arguing the self-evident but still necessary point that these are not synonymous. I then explained why, in the country whose educational culture prompted Brian Simon to ask 'Why no pedagogy?', I adopted the term 'dialogic teaching', when my own work is equally about dialogic pedagogy and dialogic education.

In the next two chapters we continue our exploration by reviewing four fields of enquiry where the vocabulary of dialogue is less insistent but where goals, premises and processes may overlap and sometimes even coincide with those we have discussed here.

Notes

1 Resnick 2015, 448.
2 At the time of writing, the most substantial edited collections of studies of dialogue in education are Resnick *et al.* 2015 and Mercer *et al.* 2020. Between them they report on a large number of initiatives from many countries.
3 Kim and Wilkinson 2019, 2; Park *et al.* 2017, 17.
4 Alexander 2003, 2005a, 2005b, 2018; Jay *et al.* 2017.
5 George Bernard Shaw (1856–1950), eminent Irish playwright, essayist and activist. It should perhaps be '*alleged* warning', since some think the quotation is apocryphal.
6 In *An Essay Concerning Human Understanding* (1689).
7 Williams 1998, 13. This seminal work has now been updated and extended by MacCabe, Yanacek and the Keywords Project 2018.
8 See Alexander 2001, and Alexander 2008b, 97–99 for an exploration of the 'shifting linguistic sands' of some of education's keywords as they are used in different cultures.
9 Wegerif, Mercer and Major (2020) differentiate 'dictionary or everyday', 'epistemological' and 'ontological' definitions of dialogue, but then treat the terms 'definition', 'conception' and 'version' as synonymous, which they are not, so it is not clear whether they are dealing with definition or stance.
10 Notably Mercer and his colleagues: Mercer 2000; Dawes, Mercer and Wegerif 2004. As I explain in Chapter 7, I am not entirely happy with the term 'ground rules'. Rules are usually (a) explicit, (b) imposed, (c) compulsory, (d) inflexible, whereas behavioural norms are often tacit and, to be true to dialogue, they should surely be subject to negotiation and agreement.
11 From *deliberare* (Latin), to consider well, and *libra* (Latin), scales or a unit of weight (and, later in Britain, of currency, hence £).
12 Walton 2013.
13 Kuhn, Wang and Li 2011; Osborne 2015.
14 The title of Reznitskaya and Wilkinson 2017.
15 Schwarz and Baker 2017, 187. They draw on Asterhan, Schwarz and Butler 2009: argumentation as deliberation aims 'to reach a better and deeper understanding of the topic under discussion', while argumentation as dispute aims 'to convince one another of the correctness of one's own solutions.'
16 Alexander 2001, 323–325, 2008b, 77–78.
17 Alexander 2008b, 100.
18 Shweder 1991.
19 Wattenberg 1991.
20 Alexander 2008b, 101.
21 Alexander 2001, 424–426, 2008b, 78–81.
22 Board of Education 1931; CACE 1967; Silberman 1973.

23 O'Hear 1991, but see also Richard Pring's critique: Pring 2017.
24 Vygotsky 1963, 31.
25 Comenius, J.A. [1657] 1896, especially 312–334.
26 Argyris and Schön 1974.
27 Wegerif, Mercer and Major 2020, 2–3.
28 Lefstein and Snell 2014, 14–19.
29 Bakhtin 1981, 1986. For an excellent exposition of Bakhtin's thinking, see Holquist 1990.
30 Vygotsky 1978. On the second aspect, not covered by Lefstein and Snell: 'The very essence of cultural development is the collision of mature cultural forms of behaviour with the primitive forms that characterise the child's behaviour' (Vygotsky 1981, 151).
31 Buber 1937.
32 Freire 1986.
33 Nystrand *et al.* 1997, 2003; Applebee *et al.* 2003; Nystrand 2019.
34 Barnes and Todd 1977, 1995.
35 Barnes 2008, 5.
36 Dawes *et al.* 2004, 4; also Mercer 2000; Mercer and Littleton 2007; Mercer and Dawes 2008.
37 Resnick *et al.* 2010; Michaels *et al.* 2008; Michaels and O'Connor 2015.
38 Nystrand 2019, (iv).
39 An idea I first explored in a 1980s research project with a group of mid-career teachers: Alexander 1988.
40 Kim and Wilkinson 2019.
41 Burbules 1993.
42 Wells 1999.
43 Mortimer and Scott 2003.
44 Wegerif 2007, 2013.
45 Matusov 2009.
46 Kim and Wilkinson 2019, 8.
47 Mercer 2000; Mercer and Littleton 2007.
48 Boyd and Markarian 2011, 2015.
49 Reznitskaya 2012; Reznitskaya and Glina 2013.
50 Reznitskaya 2012; Reznitskaya and Glina 2013; Reznitskaya and Wilkinson 2017, 14.
51 Juzwik *et al.* 2013.
52 Lefstein and Snell 2014.
53 Sedova 2017; Sedova *et al.* 2014.
54 Howe and Abedin 2013. All such reviews, comprehensive – in the case of Howe and Abedin – though they may claim to be, are selective, some inexplicably so. Thus, while the review of Dysthe, Bernhardt and Esbjørn 2013 makes much of the work of Mercer and Wegerif, it ignores that of Resnick, Michaels, O'Connor and Lefstein – contributions that in my view are no less significant – and indeed the pioneering studies of Barnes and Todd in which Mercer's approach to small group discussion is grounded, and which Mercer himself is careful to acknowledge.
55 The problem of models of teaching is discussed in Alexander 2001, 269–276 and 320–325.
56 J.A. Comenius, 1592–1670. His *Didactica Magna* (Great Didactic) of 1657 sets out 'universal principles of teaching' that still repay a visit, as does the Comenius Pedagogical Museum in Prague. See Alexander 2001, especially pp. 310, 425 and 542–547.
57 Alexander 2001, 540–563; Alexander 2008b, 45–50 and 180–183.
58 See, for instance, the comprehensive framework developed to map the territory to be covered, and the evidence to be gathered, in the 2006–10 Cambridge Primary

Review of England's public system of primary education. The Review had three overarching perspectives, ten themes and 23 sub-themes, and for every theme there were descriptive/evidential questions about the current situation and predictive/speculative/normative questions about the future, yielding nearly 100 questions in all (Alexander 2010b, 522–526).

59 Board of Education 1931; CACE 1967.

60 See 'Beyond dichotomous pedagogies' in Alexander 2008, 72–91.

61 Vygotsky 1963.

62 Alexander 1984.

63 Simon 1957; Simon and Simon 1963.

64 Simon 1981. 'Science' here in the older sense of *scientia* – any branch of knowledge coherently delineated. Compare the German *Wissen* and *Wissenschaft*.

65 Alexander 2004.

66 Well worth a visit, http://pedagogicalmuseum.com/permanent-exposition, as is the museum in the Franckesche Stiftungen in Halle, www.francke-halle.de/about-us.html (both accessed June 2019). There are pedagogical museums in Belgrade and Kiev too, but I haven't visited them yet.

4   Dialogue in other words

If we wish to take full advantage of the rich seam of evidence and ideas yielding insights into dialogic pedagogy, we should broaden our search to include contingent fields where the terminology of dialogue may be less prominent but premises and processes are no less germane. The next two chapters consider four of these: *voice, philosophy for children, argumentation* and *oracy*. The latter – too often considered in isolation, or as a junior partner to literacy, or even in opposition to it – raises important questions not only about the place of talk in human development and education but also, culturally, linguistically and pedagogically, about the relationship between speech and writing, talk and text.

Voice

Like our other keywords here and in the previous chapter, 'voice' has several meanings. In life we speak, shout, scream, whisper or sing, and these contrasting physical exercises of our vocal cords express intentions, opinions, ideas, emotions, wants and needs: indeed, who we are. Grammarians distinguish the active and passive voices of verbs, and stylists argue over their proper use. Writers explore the vocal interplay of author, narrator and character and the different writer/reader relationships afforded by using the first, third or second person pronoun to subjectify voice, to objectify it or – as with Bakhtin on the novels of Dostoevsky and Rowan Williams on both of these cultural giants – to render it elusive, many-layered and teasingly ambiguous.[1]

Campaigners for oracy tend to use 'voice', as one might expect, to mean the act of speaking; but they may also tend to confine the opportunities afforded by that act to communicative confidence and competence, which they call 'communication skills'. But 'voice', as we have seen, is as much a stance as an act, and specifically it speaks – in both senses – to the right of students to express their ideas, opinions and concerns, and to the obligation of teachers and fellow students to listen to them and treat them with due seriousness.

In the UK, the leading figure in this movement was, and by reputation and influence remains, the late Jean Rudduck. Much of the published work on voice by Rudduck and others is concerned with what, in relation to a wide range of issues including schooling itself, students say when given the opportunity. The contexts of these investigations have tended to be consultation exercises conducted for research purposes, or perhaps school-level student councils, rather than everyday classroom practice.[2]

Latterly, the UN Convention on the Rights of the Child has strengthened the idea of voice as moral right by stimulating materials and awards for 'Rights Respecting Schools'. In this UNICEF-endorsed scheme, schools commit themselves to advancing students' 'wellbeing, participation, relationships and self-esteem' and to learning *about* rights, in part through participative practices that enact them.[3]

However, Carol Robinson's survey of evidence on student voice commissioned by the Cambridge Primary Review (which she later updated for the Cambridge Primary Review Trust) warns:

> If teachers and pupils are to genuinely work together on . . . teaching and learning, there needs to be a reconceptualisation of [their] roles. . . . This reconceptualisation should of course pervade life inside as well as outside the classroom, and it underlines the need for more genuinely dialogic approaches to pedagogy.[4]

A series of papers by Adam Lefstein and his colleagues, working in Israeli classrooms, responds to this challenge and shows its resolution to be problematic.[5] They differentiate four senses of student voice: having the opportunity to speak; expressing one's own ideas; speaking on one's own terms; and being heeded. These stages in the progress of the classroom exchange, from permission to speak to acknowledgement of what is spoken, are again about ownership and rights. Together, they prompt four questions. What do we do to encourage our students to speak? How do we ensure that what they say is treated equitably and respectfully? When they speak, whose voices do we hear? And how do we handle the contributions that do not follow our agenda?

Given the widespread assumption that classroom dialogue constitutes a positive response to at least the first two of these questions and thus addresses Robinson's concern, the analysis of Segal and Lefstein gives pause for thought. The students in their study

> enthusiastically contribute to lively classroom discussion and often frame these discussions as dialogical responses that build on each other's ideas . . .

So far, so dialogic. However:

> . . . at the level of *voice* the discussion is mostly univocal, since most student contributions are aligned with the official voice of the teacher and

the curriculum and in the rare instances where they emerge, independent student voices fall out of the conversation.[6]

The authors call such encounters 'exuberant voiceless participation', using voice in the last three of their four senses – expressing one's own ideas, speaking on one's own terms and being heeded – for clearly their students were given, and seized, the opportunity to speak. The problem arises because, while Segal and Lefstein acknowledge Bakhtin's much quoted maxim that 'the word in language is half someone else's', they find their observed teachers and students caught between the principle of co-construction and the 'official knowledge' of the school curriculum. This dilemma, say Segal and Lefstein, is translated into teaching that is likely to be dialogic in form but monologic in function. Discussion, however lively and apparently dialogic, yields what the teacher expects and is therefore, in the authors' second, third and fourth senses, 'voiceless'.

This is not the same as the voicelessness experienced by students in Sherice Clarke's study.[7] Here, students were physically rather than semantically silent because they felt they did not have the *right* to speak. That right, they believed, stemmed from their having concluded from their teachers' reactions on previous occasions that the knowledge they possessed was 'correct' or 'incorrect'. This is similar to Edwards's account of 'communicative competence', or the conditions under which students judge from precedent and the teacher's signals what they may say or indeed whether they should say nothing.[8] So while Lefstein's students were vocal but voiceless, Clarke's students, nearly half of those in her study, were both voiceless and silent.

Given the nature of teaching, these tensions are up to a point inevitable, though most of us would regard its extreme manifestation in Clarke's study – in solidarity with this book's mission, hopefully, as well as with the students in question – as unacceptable. Even so, matters are rarely that clear-cut. For teachers do not create the 'official knowledge of the school curriculum' but mediate knowledge whose origins are more remote in both time and place, and their own voices, too, may be muted. Equally, it is surely possible to be both goal-directed and dialogic in a way that enables students, within the established framework, to 'express their own ideas' and 'speak on their own terms'.

Further, and drawing now on the *Culture and Pedagogy* research, the analysis of classroom discourse in our five cultures included an exploration of the balance of discourse control between teachers and students and the degree to which the teacher's authority was absolute to the extent that student 'voicelessness' implies; or whether, taking our cue from Dewey's view that democracy is the proper antithesis of authoritarianism, in classrooms as in society, it could be judged tolerably democratic.[9] In practice, we found – even in those Russian and Indian classrooms whose discourse was most overtly and tightly steered by the teacher – that the normal conduct of teaching was always located somewhere between 'directed' and 'negotiated', and that it was seldom at a fixed point on the continuum and rarely if ever tipped towards its 'autocratic' or 'anarchic' extremes.[10] Judged in these terms, the adjective 'voiceless' may overstate the condition to which it refers.

In any event, voice – like all aspects of pedagogy – needs to be located culturally rather than viewed as a function of classroom dynamics alone. Here, Basil Bernstein's later work is relevant, for it reminds us to differentiate – as intimated previously – between how the curriculum is 'classified' for classroom mediation and the way the teacher 'frames' that curriculum as pedagogic discourse.[11] Classification and framing do not necessary follow the same trajectory: the relationship between a curriculum as specified nationally and as transacted and experienced locally is rarely isomorphic, and all teaching entails a greater or lesser degree of curriculum translation and indeed re-creation. In the *Culture and Pedagogy* research, the most extreme example of classification/framing incongruence was in some of the Indian classrooms, where highly authoritarian teaching delivered by rote a curriculum over which the teacher had no say whatever. It was in this context that Indian educationist Krishna Kumar referred to his rural elementary school teacher compatriots as 'meek dictators'.[12] But this was indeed an extreme.

In a further study, Lefstein's group identify a second tension relating to voice. They examine a lesson dealing with the particularly sensitive theme of social ostracism, which the teacher aimed to illuminate through the obligatory recounting of personal experiences or 'confessions'. The process made some of the students uncomfortable, and the authors conclude:

> As educators, we have been committed to enlarging the space in classroom discourse for student voice. . . . Such a commitment can backfire, and safeguarding voice also requires maintaining the right to be silent.[13]

I suspect that this will resonate with every reader except the most resolutely insouciant or unquenchably verbose. In many countries, the right of adults to remain silent is enshrined in law, in some cultures loquacity is frowned upon, and in some religions, silence is counted a virtue or even an obligation. In Ireland, I once passed a place of worship with '*Vide, audi, tace*' – see, hear, be silent – sternly inscribed above the doorway, a scholarly echo of the taciturn Yorkshire maxim 'See all, hear all, say nowt.' (The Latin version, apparently, is also a Masonic motto, and in that context may have less to do with reticence than secrecy. Not being a Mason, I wouldn't know.)

But despite the UN Convention on the Rights of the Child and 'Rights-Respecting Schools', the right to silence does not necessarily extend to school classrooms. There, for some students, being *required* to speak can be an excruciating experience: they may be shy, their ideas may be slow to coalesce, they may consider their opinions not worth voicing or likely to be judged 'wrong', their natural proclivity may be more towards inner speech than outer, or their thoughts may lie too deep if not for tears then for words assembled as aptly and speedily as the teacher requires.[14] ('Quickly now, what is the meaning of life? Hurry up, I haven't got all day.')

Other students may have specific language and communication difficulties that have not been recognised or correctly diagnosed, so that they lack the specialised support to which diagnosis would have entitled them and find themselves floundering in a classroom culture where they are expected to 'speak up'. But, as we note in Chapter 5, the 2009 Bercow report on provision for children with speech, language and communication needs (SLCN) found considerable geographical variation in the availability and quality of support services for such children and a pervasive problem of late diagnosis.[15] It is therefore a reasonable supposition that in many classrooms there will be students who are reluctant to speak, or who have difficulty in articulating their thoughts, for reasons which on the basis of proper diagnosis would be judged as clinical, yet of this their teachers will be unaware. (Bercow noted symptoms such as 'difficulties with fluency, forming sounds and words, formulating sentences, understanding what others say, and using language socially.')[16] Yet ten years on from Bercow, and notwithstanding the systemic amelioration his review recommended, a follow-up report found a continuing lack of awareness and information about speech, language and communication in general and more specifically about SLCN, and highlighted the severe personal, social and economic impact of not meeting these students' needs.[17]

Yet many teachers view speaking up and instantly as the proper measure of participation, deeming the silent or hesitant student unengaged or uncommitted. Thus, a familiar comment on children's school reports is, 'Must learn to participate [i.e. speak] more' (which might reasonably prompt the riposte, 'OK, but what are you doing to help me to do so? Why is literacy your responsibility but oracy mine?'); while one of the most frequent responses by British teachers to my advocating extended teacher-student exchanges rather than quick-fire question-and-answer round the class has been, 'Yes, but what do the other students do?', as if those students who for the moment are not speaking are doing nothing. The answer, of course, is that they are, or should be, listening and thinking, which when the habit has been developed is a form of participation every bit as intense as speaking: *tace, atque vide et audi*.

So far, I have referred to 'students' collectively, but every child and adult knows, often from the bitterest of experience, that the right to speak and be heard is granted to some more than others, in classrooms no less than in society. Britain, the United States and many other countries remain deeply divided by inequalities of income, opportunity, education, class, race and gender. One of the promises of dialogic teaching is that it distributes classroom talk more equitably, first between teacher and students collectively, then among students themselves; and that this redistribution contributes to the larger cause of reducing social inequality. That is why the UK Education Endowment Foundation was keen to support our trial of dialogic teaching with children meeting its criteria of social and economic disadvantage.

Yet while dialogic teaching can be shown to shift the balance of classroom talk towards students collectively, we must ask how far it equalises the voices of different groups of students, and of the individuals within those groups. If the word is indeed 'half someone else's', does this maxim apply to every student equally, or is it the case that for some students theirs is a wholly 'silenced dialogue',[18] while others view their right to speak and be heard as a matter of entitlement, regardless of what they say?

These days the silencing of those deemed unentitled is increasingly brutal, especially in relation to gender and race. The office scenario gently captured in Riana Duncan's cartoon – 'That's an excellent suggestion, Miss Triggs. Perhaps one of the men here would like to make it'[19] – remains commonplace, but the reality for many girls, women and members of ethnic minorities is much darker. In 2016, Britain's *Guardian* – hardly a tabloid and always careful to avoid inflammatory language – published an analysis of the 70 million comments left on its website during the previous ten years. They reported that although most of their regular opinion writers were white men, those who experienced the highest levels of abuse and dismissive trolling were not:

> The ten regular writers who got the most abuse were eight women (four white and four non-white) and two black men. Two of the women and one of the men were gay. And of the eight women in the 'top ten', one was Muslim and one Jewish. And the ten regular writers who got the least abuse? All men.[20]

Similarly, of those recipients of misogynist, racist, homophobic or anti-Semitic hate mail who are elected Members of the UK Parliament (MPs), most are women; and in 2016, after a long online campaign against her for her views of Brexit and human rights, one female MP, Jo Cox, paid the ultimate price and was murdered in broad daylight outside her constituency office. Other female MPs then came forward and spoke of their own experiences. One reported receiving 600 online rape threats in one night.[21] Yet in response to complaints from women MPs about the way online and physical violence were being stoked by violent language from political leaders, the then Prime Minister Boris Johnson merely retorted, 'I've never heard such humbug in all my life.'[22]

Unsurprisingly in light of these trends and the Prime Minister's effrontery, the UK Home Office reported a 10 per cent increase in police-recorded hate crime in 2018–19 compared with the previous year, with reported incidents rising from 42,255 in 2012–3 to 103,379 in 2018–19.[23] Meanwhile, US President Donald Trump singled out for abuse four Congresswomen of colour and encouraged his followers to do likewise;[24] and in Britain, middle-aged male politicians and media barons competed in their efforts to silence

16-year-old climate campaigner Greta Thunberg, prompting this tart but apt comment:

> A society that cannot bear to be lectured by its children, even when they've got a point, while the adults are behaving like toddlers refusing to clean up their own mess, can never progress.[25]

This, of course, is not confined to adults, though the public verbal pillorying of children by adults has added a disturbing dimension to child abuse, even if – in this case – the verbal assault on Thunberg is a clear case of *ad feminam* by those who know the evidence is against them. But NSPCC, the UK's largest child-protection charity, also reports an upsurge in cyberbullying, sexting and grooming *among adolescents*,[26] and every teacher knows both the harm this causes and – of particular relevance to the task of this book – the impact it can have on life inside the classroom as well as outside it. Similarly, in 2019, the Equality and Human Rights Commission reported that in British universities 24 per cent of ethnic minority students and 9 per cent of white students had experienced racial harassment since starting their courses. That is, 13 per cent of all students, both UK and international. One in five victims had been physically attacked.[27]

There is one more twist to this tale: the silencing of teachers themselves. Controversial speakers at universities find themselves 'disinvited', 'no-platformed' and even physically threatened because of the views they have expressed or written, and formal complaints are lodged against teachers of literature who treat as the object of study writing that uses language that some find offensive, provoking concern about the erosion of free speech generally and academic freedom in particular.[28] On which, lest it be thought that this lets overt racism, misogyny, homophobia or xenophobia off the hook, PEN America commented: 'There is a distinction to be made between a racial slur wielded against someone and a quote used for pedagogical purposes.'[29] But is it really as straightforward as that?

There is an older subtext to all this, a variation on what in the philosophy of education literature used to problematise as the tension between the logical and psychological aspects of teaching: that is, the tension between the nature of the subject as collective cultural artefact and the individual natures, needs, capacities and interests of learners.[30] Mayer, O'Connor and Lefstein give the tension a dialogic and indeed polyvocal nudge towards reconciliation:

> The generative relationship that Dewey first theorised between individual thriving and the common good implies a need for classroom practices to attend to divergent voices, even when confusing or potentially disruptive to the disciplinary content. At the same time these classroom practices must also serve to give all students access to established understandings and practices. A teacher's successful negotiation of the tension . . . can

provide all members of a classroom with opportunities to feel seen and accepted. And it is through such recognition that historically margin-alised students are most likely to be drawn into the work and life of their schools and the broader societies they represent.[31]

While taking due account of what the evidence shows about the dominance of the teacher's voice in typical classroom settings, we should avoid con-cluding that voice, whether as physical utterance, expression of meaning or moral right, whether as sound or silence, speaking or listening, is always and wholly on the teacher's terms. We should be equally aware of the extent to which, in what they say or do not say, students respond to that part of school and classroom culture over which they, rather than their teachers, exert control. Peer culture and adolescent self-consciousness may combine to set limits to what individual students are prepared to venture. Equally, some will delight in transgressing the norms – their own or the teacher's – that others dutifully accept.

Voice in the various senses discussed in this section is an essential ingredi-ent of dialogue, but it is an acutely problematic one too. In the interests of equity as well as pedagogy, it demands our vigilance.

Philosophy for children

Grounded in the frustration of American academic Matthew Lipman[32] with the less than adequate reasoning capacities displayed by his students at Columbia University, philosophy for children (commonly abbreviated to P4C) has developed into a significant international movement. In the United States, it has been spearheaded by the Institute for the Advance-ment of Philosophy for Children (IAPC), and in Britain by the charity Sapere, which sustains its work by publishing P4C materials and running training courses for teachers. The basic training aims to enable teachers to 'encourage philosophical questioning and dialogue . . . facilitate P4C enquiry . . . identify resources to stimulate rich discussions.' The advanced training explores the ethics, politics, language and pedagogy of P4C in greater depth.[33]

P4C is structured round the notion of classrooms as 'communities of enquiry' in which, during one or two dedicated P4C sessions each week, students discuss questions that they or the teacher have identified but over which, in any event, students feel they have ownership and in relation to which – harking back to the previous section – their voice counts. The teacher then acts as 'facilitator', arranging students in a circle or horseshoe (this being the most inclusive and ostensibly democratic arrangement), intro-ducing written, visual or auditory stimulus materials (notably novels written for this purpose), establishing a culture of mutual respect, listening and turn-taking, and prompting Lipman's three kinds of thinking: critical, creative and caring.[34] About this approach IAPC insists that 'the most effective stimulus materials may be ineffectual without the central practice of Philosophy for Children: the community of inquiry'.

> Participating in a community of inquiry engages young people in impor-
> tant cognitive moves such as creating hypotheses, clarifying their terms,
> asking for and giving good reasons, offering examples and counterex-
> amples, questioning each other's assumptions, drawing inferences, and
> following the inquiry where it leads. But inquiry is also a social enter-
> prise, which requires students to share their own perspectives, listen to
> one another, read faces, challenge and build on one another's thinking,
> look for missing perspectives and reconstruct their own ideas.[35]

Robert Fisher lists the kinds of question that lend themselves to this approach. They range from the eternal and perhaps unanswerable to the everyday and practical: 'What is a good person?' 'What is thinking?' 'What is government for?' 'What is truth?' 'What is mathematics?' 'What is a friend?' 'If you find something should you keep it?' and many more.[36] With younger children in mind, IAPC instances: 'When Dad tells me to be good, what does he mean?' 'What do people mean when they say they love me?' 'Mom said I didn't have a good reason. What did she mean?' 'Where did grandpa go when he died?'[37]

Fisher categorises questions such as these as *conceptual, empirical, logical* and *evaluative* (though, curiously in light of his examples, not *ethical*), and he identifies interactive strategies through which the teacher/facilitator can help students to address them. Several of these are close or even identical to those used in dialogic teaching, especially the 'talk moves' developed by Michaels and O'Connor:[38] thinking time,[39] 'think-pair-share', inviting the whole group to express agreement or disagreement, playing devil's advocate and so on.[40] To help teachers assess the quality of the discussion, Fisher offers a checklist of 'discourse skills' in areas such as questioning, collaborat-ing, initiating, extending, countering, reasoning and reviewing.[41] Given how explicitly such talk moves are highlighted, it is therefore odd to encounter the rather exclusivist claim by Mercer and his colleagues that P4C is unhelpful to the teaching of oracy because 'it does not focus on the use of talk itself, but on the more abstract notion of a community of enquiry.'[42]

The synergy with dialogic teaching is even more obvious when we consider P4C's outcomes as claimed by Sapere:

- improved educational attainment through enhanced thinking and rea-soning skills;
- gains in oral communication skills, literacy and numeracy, particularly for the less able;
- social and emotional development, and more collaborative relationships with others;
- improved articulacy and confidence in speaking and listening;

- students become more able to challenge and question, within the rules of respectful dialogue.[43]

Among the 'benefits for schools' Sapere includes 'dialogic teaching skills', though these are not defined.

Sapere's claims, like those of this book's version of dialogic teaching, are supported by both positive teacher feedback and a randomised control trial commissioned by the Education Endowment Foundation (EEF). A first trial, in 48 schools, recorded significant test score gains (like ours, with upper-primary students and yielding gains of up to two months overall in reading and mathematics – ours also included science) and even higher gains among disadvantaged students.[44] EEF rated the results 'moderately secure', though no security rating was provided for the disadvantaged students. On that basis, Sapere was invited to participate in a larger effectiveness trial which, as this book goes to press, is in its third year. This time, the outcome measure is confined to reading, and the incongruence of such a narrow measure with the broader goals of P4C exposes one of the problems of the way EEF applies the randomised control trial, and perhaps its broader limitations. For it has been objected that randomised control trials are not well suited to an arena as complex, idiosyncratic and ephemeral as teaching, and that their claim to represent the 'gold standard' in educational and social research is overstated, misguided and perhaps even imperialist.[45]

Yet notwithstanding such methodological reservations, the significance of P4C is undeniable, and its synergy with dialogic teaching is helpful to the higher cause of talking to think, learn and – next – argue.

Argumentation

In the previous chapter, I positioned argumentation alongside conversation, discussion and deliberation as one of the forms of dialogue of particular relevance to educators, while noting that argumentation is also a major philosophical field in its own right. I then suggested a continuum of deliberative and disputatious forms of argumentation ranging from a *proposition*, through *making and testing a case*, and *reasoning from premise to conclusion* to *debate*, *dispute* and *quarrel*.

One of the more substantial accounts to date of the educational role and relationship of argumentation and dialogue is the study by Baruch Schwarz and Michael Baker.[46] They confirm that there is no single, agreed definition of argumentation 'other than that in all cases it involves means for attempting to make claims or discourses more acceptable to people than they were initially' and that in the English language the word can be compromised by its belligerent overtones. Paying particular attention to 'real world' argumentation in law and science (as opposed to its more abstract pursuit by logical philosophers such as Russell, Whitehead, Ayer and Wittgenstein), they then seek to set the main theories of argumentation within a matrix whose axes are conceived as the dichotomies of argument as (i) 'discursive vs structural' and (ii) 'monological vs dialogical'.[47] Here, argumentation as discourse is about forms of persuasion; argumentation as structure focuses on the different kinds of statement that can be made in support of a claim.

However it is defined, argumentation is an acquired skill, so helping students to move from mere disagreement to evidentiary discussion and reasoning is one of education's essential tasks. Mercer and Dawes are among those who believe norms for argumentation should be made explicit and translated into ground rules,[48] while Osborne's work is particularly helpful in elucidating the nature and pursuit of argument in science education,[49] where he builds on studies going back to Rosalind Driver's ground-breaking 1983 book, *The Pupil as Scientist?*.[50] It is a pity that this admirable work does not have counterparts in every subject.

Argument and rhetoric, uses and abuses

It is hardly surprising if students view argument as conflict. They witness the media turning complex issues into battling binaries. They enter a Twittersphere that thrives on intolerance. They see politicians asserting cases rather than demonstrating them, using evidence selectively, wrongly or not at all, and cynically stoking disagreement into conflict. But the manipulation and selective use of evidence are the oldest tricks in the political game, so it is important that rather than throw up their hands in horror, students understand that political and academic argument have different goals and conventions. When argument is about persuasion and power rather than truth, evidence gives way to rhetoric, for as Cicero, master of political rhetoric, said, 'Wisdom without eloquence does little benefit'; though he did have the grace to add, 'But eloquence without wisdom does much harm.'[51]

Appropriately, there has been a revival of interest in classical rhetoric and its modern variants, especially in university English departments.[52] The last great flowering was during the Renaissance, when the key texts of Aristotle, Cicero and Quintilian were rediscovered, and in schools and universities the practice of rhetoric was as essential as the study of arithmetic, geometry and astronomy.[53] Rhetoric, too, guided and framed renaissance poetic discourse. Some of Shakespeare's greatest speeches and bouts of oral fencing can be properly understood only if one has a grasp of the rhetorical devices and figures of speech with which many in Shakespeare's audiences were familiar.[54]

Rhetoric has historical resonance and longevity; social media less obviously so. But Tom Standage, writing of Cicero's classicism in relation not to his rhetoric but his networking, argues from analysis of Roman techniques of publication and dissemination that 'many of the ways we handle, consume and manipulate information, even in the internet era, build upon habits and conventions that date back centuries'; and that 'modern social media is, in fact, merely the latest example of a deep and rich tradition of media sharing.'[55]

Historical echoes notwithstanding, argument is multi-dimensional and complex, so to keep it firmly within this book's dialogic purlieu it is helpful to draw on the analytical framework of Douglas Walton. This is particularly pertinent because Walton conceives of argument itself as a dialogic process in which participants take turns in making moves which he characterises as speech acts of various kinds: asking a question, making an assertion, and so on. He posits seven types of argumentation dialogue:

- *Persuasion*, which starts with a conflict of opinion about which each side aims to persuade the other or to resolve.
- *Inquiry*, which requires and searches for evidence in order to verify or disprove.
- *Discovery*, which looks for explanation and to achieve it finds and tests a hypothesis.
- *Negotiation*, where a conflict of interests requires a reasonable settlement with which both parties will be content.
- *Information-seeking*, which seeks, obtains and exchanges information in pursuit of answers.
- *Deliberation*, which starts with a dilemma or practical choice and works collaboratively towards deciding the best course of action.
- *Eristic*, where personal conflict is not resolved but exacerbated, because that is its goal.[56]

The first six are reasoned and rule-bound, and only eristic argument (from the Greek word for 'strife') aims to win by whatever means are available. Political argument can and often does entail negotiation, inquiry, deliberation and – we hope – a search for information, but the eristic is always there as the last resort or, for some, the first. From that point onwards, all bets about the other six are off.

Prominent in eristic argument are fallacies, which for Walton include one or more of 'a failure . . . in what is supposed to be an argument . . . a deception or illusion . . . a violation of . . . maxims of reasonable dialogue . . . wrongly applied technique of reasonable argumentation.'[57] He differentiates between accidental and deliberate fallacies: 'In some cases a fallacy is merely a blunder or an error while in other cases it is a sophisticated tactic used to try to get the best of a speech partner in dialogue unfairly, typically by using verbal deception or trickery.'[58]

Especially prominent are the well-known fallacies of syllogistic reasoning: equivocation, or exploiting ambiguity; begging the question; ad verecundiam, or citing an 'authority' who may be nothing of the sort; ad hominem/ad feminam, attacking the person rather than the argument; ad baculum, or threatening dire consequences if one's views aren't accepted; the delightfully named 'poisoning the well' (making challenge to a position impossible by discrediting its basis); and so on.

Some of these classic fallacies are numbered among Schopenhauer's '38 ways to win an argument',[59] which start from the proposition that logic pursues truth but eristic aims only for victory. Schopenhauer's list, published in 1831 but in 2020 still resonant, includes alongside the familiar syllogistic fallacies some depressingly contemporary echoes: 'make your opponent angry', 'generalise from the specific', 'claim victory despite defeat', 'persuade the audience, not the opponent', 'interrupt or divert the dispute if you think you are losing', 'puzzle or bewilder your opponent by mere bombast' and 'be personal, insulting and rude.'

The relevance of efforts to expose fallacious reasoning and unsubstantiated claims is evident in the current interest in 'fake news'. Daily and assiduously, websites on both sides of the Atlantic check political pronouncements for factual accuracy. The best of them do not confine their investigations to the populist right but investigate a spreading virus of deliberate misinformation infesting all sides.[60] Many such pronouncements are unashamedly eristic in language and intent: most egregiously, of course, those from US President Trump, but also from a string of other national and political leaders who – perhaps feeling themselves liberated by his dubious example – have raised the stakes for truth and democracy with rhetoric that is not only mendacious but also, and calculatedly, divisive and threatening.[61]

What we have witnessed in the public sphere in recent years is the ascendancy of the eristic over the deliberative. As I note elsewhere, this trend exposes the inadequacy of traditional models of civic education and the severity of the challenge for those educators who believe, following John Dewey, that democracy starts with a deliberative pedagogy.[62] For, as Kakutani says, 'Without commonly agreed-upon facts . . . there can be no rational debate. . . . Without truth, democracy is hobbled.'[63] Equally, when in 1946 George Orwell warned that 'The present political chaos is connected with the decay of language',[64] he foreshadowed our own present, for the misuse and abuse of language are conspicuous indicators of the current political malaise. And in considering where all this might lead, many have revisited Hannah Arendt's warning in *The Origins of Totalitarianism* that:

> The ideal subject of totalitarian rule is not the convinced Nazi or the convinced Communist, but people for whom the distinction between fact and fiction (i.e. the reality of experience) and the distinction between true and false (i.e. the standards of thought) no longer exist.[65]

Educational responses

Several educational responses to these trends have been proposed. Since digital media are now the main channel for conveying and distorting information for public consumption, there is a strong case for extending the idea of literacy to include digital media. In 2018, a UK parliamentary select committee published *Disinformation and Fake News*. After outlining evidence of attempts to use digital media to 'play to the fears and prejudices of people and to influence their voting plans and behaviour', notably in the 2016 US presidential election and the UK Brexit referendum, the committee's report concluded that 'urgent action needs to be taken . . . to build resilience against misinformation and disinformation into our democratic system. . . . Our democracy is at risk.'[66]

Much of the report documented the activities of tech giants like Google and Facebook, and the media, political parties, pressure groups and others who, for better or worse, were implicated in the processes under scrutiny, but there was one recommendation about education:

> Our education system should [equip] children with the necessary tools to live in our digital world, so that their mental health, emotional well-being and faculty for critical thinking are protected. . . . Digital literacy should be the fourth pillar of education, alongside reading, writing and maths.[67]

The need is aptly expressed – children must acquire the knowledge and skills necessary for coping in a digital world – but I am less sanguine about the wording of the recommendation, for it merely bolts digital literacy onto a curriculum that in all other respects remains unexamined and untouched. Most conspicuously unexamined and untouched, in that statement about 'the fourth pillar of education', is the belief that the so-called '3Rs' of reading, writing and reckoning (i.e. maths) are what basic education is all about; and that this antiquated definition which guided Victorian schools for the urban industrial masses, and indeed goes back much further to St Augustine's 'legere et scribere et numerare', can be brought up to date by adding digital literacy but not by challenging the assumption that talk doesn't matter. We know better: children's spoken language, and their capacity to use it to think, reason, find their way in a dangerous world and play their part as citizens in a democracy, are of the highest priority. There are words out there as well as algorithms.

A second response, more broadly conceived, is to arm students with the tools for testing the truth claims of politicians and the media. Coining the hybrid banner 'civilytics', Robert Janke and Bruce Cooper propose a new approach to civic education that combines

> media literacy in identifying potential sources of information, data literacy in understanding and analyzing quantitative information, and critical thinking skills in evaluating potential evidence and alternative explanations and actions.[68]

Their approach includes helpful guidance for teachers and students on news sources and terms, both accurate and fake; an anatomy of the typical vocabulary of fake news and the way it works its appeal; and ways to source, collect, analyse and interpret the material in question.[69] Interestingly, their list of 'fake news techniques'[70] has exactly the same number (38) as Schopenhauer's 'ways to win an argument' referred to previously, and several of the techniques appear in both lists.

Yet both of these approaches are essentially reactive: a trend has been detected and education must respond. But while in the present case we may not disagree with the diagnosis or goal, we should also note that this is how, historically, a curriculum becomes overcrowded and incoherent. When I led the Cambridge Primary Review from 2006 to 2010, we were lobbied by hundreds of organisations making equally persuasive cases for earmarking school time to address their concerns, often – as with digital and news literacy – taking advantage of the educational unassailability of the word 'literacy'. Consequently we warned that constructing a curriculum on this basis was a logistical nightmare, for:

> The national curriculum risked overload from the start. More elements were subsequently added but none was removed, for what lobby would be happy to relinquish the claims of a subject in whose educational importance it so passionately believed [in order to make room for another]. Meanwhile, the school day, week and year remained the same length. Something had to give, and it did.[71]

A third approach, then, is to look to ways to embed the necessary student capacities across the *existing* curriculum, taking the opportunity to re-examine both its content and its pedagogy. Can the print-based traditional account of literacy education and language arts be reconfigured to accommodate media 'literacy'? Are digital and data 'literacy' matters for the mathematics curriculum, for ICT, or both? If mathematics, is it the concept of numeracy that needs updating? Do these new 'literacies' also have implications for how we conceive and teach civic and citizenship education?

Similarly, and noting that in its claims about truth and evidence fake news is a species of argumentation, albeit a debased one, we might look at the way argument and argumentation are handled in every curriculum domain, noting immediately that just as academic and political argument are not mutually exclusive but overlap on a continuum, so academic argument is not one mode but many.

Scientific, mathematical and historical reasoning, to take three obvious paradigms, are manifestly different, though all have recourse to tests of evidence and/or proof. Less frequently considered in the research on either dialogue or educational argumentation is argument in the artistic and literary spheres. How do we make or test the case for a work of art, music or literature? Between the 1930s and 1970s, the influential Cambridge literary critic F.R. Leavis taught his students to investigate and assess the technical, linguistic and stylistic ingredients of prose, poetry and drama and locate them in historical context, so that they could distinguish the technically original and inventive from the mediocre or routine and assign dates to samples of writing without knowing the author, which, like 'blind' student grading, certainly aids objectivity.

But moving from assessments of artistic technique and style to judgements of artistic merit is more problematic. Here Leavis relied on his famous question, 'This is so, isn't it?', which puts a literary work's moral seriousness and psychological or experiential authenticity on the line alongside its technical and imaginative mastery. Leavis also believed in literary canons and the redeeming power of high culture, but such now unfashionable notions[72] are not the issue here; nor do they undermine the heuristic value of his critical approach. In any case, 'This is so, isn't it?' was always followed by 'Yes, but . . .', an obligatory rejoinder that commands both convincing justification and rigorous scepticism about every judgement ventured, the literary equivalent of Popper's theory of scientific conjectures and refutations, perhaps,[73] though it does not deal with the objection that the formula appears to ascribe to the reader or critic, *a priori*, the maturity, experience and psychological insight needed to judge the correspondence between life as lived and portrayed.

Of course, this process interrogates evidence of a kind and in a way that would be unlikely to satisfy a physicist, but that's the point: the modes of argument and justification in the arts, humanities, social sciences and physical sciences – not to mention mathematics, philosophy and theology – are different but not necessarily of unequal validity. Yet, for many, accepting anything approaching equivalence here requires a leap of faith, especially at a time when educational policy-making, in the UK at least, is steered by the possibly chimerical absolutes of economic utility, objective knowledge and scientific proof. These days, as Helen Small shows, demonstrating the public value of the arts and humanities – and, in this context, of the educational value and validity of their discourses and modes of argumentation – requires resilience and honesty:

> One of the most damaging effects of a sense of embattlement, periodically evident in our cultures of debate, is that it can prevent advocates for the humanities doing one of the things they may legitimately claim to do best – submitting claims of value to proper scrutiny: rhetorical, historical, philosophical.[74]

This is the course on which Small then embarks, scrupulously testing and ultimately validating five claims to the humanities' public value, namely that they:

> Preserve and extend distinctive kinds of understanding (broadly, qualitative understanding of the meaning making of the culture), and possess a distinctive relation to the idea of knowledge as being inextricable from human subjectivity. . . . Assist in the preservation and curation of the

culture, and of the skills for interpreting and reinterpreting that culture to meet the needs and interests of the present. . . . Make a vital contribution to individual happiness. . . . Make a vital contribution to the maintenance and . . . health of the democracy [resting] on their role as centres for the . . . study and practice of the skills of reasoning, debate and the evaluation of ideas. . . . Have value in themselves.[75]

Stephen Toulmin offers a measure of reconciliation, granted that evidence and authenticity, or proof and judgement, do not represent categorically matching sides of the same coin, and that 'authenticity' is particularly difficult to pin down. So we must ask whether, following Dewey, authenticity is truth to lived communal experience[76] or, acceding to Rousseau, Sartre and Camus, truth to oneself regardless of external conventions, which Taylor warns can too easily slide into the 'soft relativism' of 'doing your own thing'?[77]

For those wedded to a notion of argumentation that pivots on the provision and testing of evidence and proof, the arts and humanities present an awkward case. Not only is their content – culture and what it is to be human – frustratingly elusive (though perhaps less so for the theoretical physicist than the materials scientist), but also at the heart of the way they are approached for the purposes of interpretation and critical evaluation resides 'an ineliminable element of subjectivity . . . [so that] truth claims will not, and cannot, be founded only on positivistic appeals to evidence; rather they will necessarily entail the exercise of judgement.'[78] Which is why 'Yes, but . . .' is a mandatory rather than optional rejoinder to 'This is so, isn't it?' and requires analysis that is no less stringent.

For readers working within the disciplinary frameworks of secondary and higher education, it would therefore seem essential that their exploration of the pedagogical possibilities of dialogue be embedded in discussion of the relationship between the conceptual and methodological questions their discipline entails and the oral questions and patterns of classroom exchange to which these are best suited. Meanwhile, Toulmin shows how, although different kinds of question or claim call for different treatment, he is able to propose a generic 'layout' of six elements of argumentation that work in most circumstances:

- *claim* (what has to be established or proved)
- *ground* (facts, evidence, data or reasoning in support of the claim)
- *warrant* (justification for the grounds cited)
- *backing* (additional or alternative support)
- *qualifier* (limitations on the claim)
- *rebuttal* (counter-arguments).

This, arguably, applies as well to literary judgement as to the scientific and mathematical examples that Toulmin cites, such as 'whether . . . Fröhlich's theory of super-conductivity is really satisfactory, when the next eclipse of the moon will take place, or the exact nature of the relation between the squares on the different sides of a right-angled triangle.'[79]

One of the more promising translations of some of these ideas into principles and strategies for developing students' ability to use and analyse argument in the classroom comes from Alina Reznitskaya, Ian Wilkinson and their colleagues. Over several years, they worked with 49 teachers and 935 students to develop the kind of classroom discussion that would improve students' 'argument literacy' in response to the US Common Core State Standards Initiative, the US equivalent of England's National Curriculum and Scotland's Curriculum for Excellence.

In this matter, the US specifications are strikingly more prominent and better developed than those promulgated for England, where the emphasis from Years 1 to 9 (US grades K-8) is largely confined to technical understanding and skill, even in the area of reading comprehension. In contrast, the US standards highlight, overall, 'critical-thinking, problem-solving, and analytical skills that are required for success in college, career, and life',[80] while by grade 12 the Common Core requirements for speaking and listening include, within the Language Arts:

> Work with peers to promote civil, democratic discussions and decision-making, set clear goals and deadlines, and establish individual roles as needed. . . . Propel conversations by posing and responding to questions that probe reasoning and evidence; ensure a hearing for a full range of positions on a topic or issue; clarify, verify, or challenge ideas and conclusions; and promote divergent and creative perspectives. . . . Respond thoughtfully to diverse perspectives; synthesize comments, claims, and evidence made on all sides of an issue; resolve contradictions when possible; and determine what additional information or research is required to deepen the investigation or complete the task.[81]

Acknowledging that such requirements both mark a significant change of direction for US language arts teaching and that they are likely to place heavy demands on teachers, Reznitskaya and Wilkinson define 'argument literacy' as 'the ability to comprehend, formulate and evaluate arguments through speaking, listening, reading and writing'. They then propose a user-friendly pedagogical framework which starts with analysis of the nature and workings of argument and proceeds via exemplar lessons to an 'argumentation rating tool' ('ART'). This identifies four criteria of 'quality argumentation' and tracks these through 11 'facilitation practices' with a view to using them to evaluate videotaped lesson segments featuring argumentation.[82] The tool itself has been evaluated and judged valid and valuable, though not always easy to use.[83]

Central to the process is 'inquiry dialogue', or 'a type of talk in which participants engage in argumentation to collectively formulate the most reasonable judgements.' The term is also used by Walton, who stiffens it by requiring proof rather than a 'reasonable judgement'. He defines inquiry dialogue as

> A collaborative type of dialogue in which a group of agents – in the simplest case two – work together to prove a central claim at issue by drawing on a knowledge base that contains a set of propositions representing the evidence in the case.[84]

Walton notes that 'inquiry dialogues are especially useful in domains such as health care and science that are essentially co-operative in nature.'[85] To these we might add the domain of teaching. However, Walton also differentiates inquiry dialogue from 'discovery dialogue', on the important grounds that

> in an inquiry dialogue, the proposition that is to be proved true is designated prior to the course of the argumentation in the dialogue, whereas in a discovery dialogue the question whose truth is to be determined emerges only during the course of the dialogue itself.[86]

There is probably sufficient latitude in the Reznitskaya and Wilkinson definition of inquiry dialogue – 'a type of talk in which participants engage in argumentation to collectively formulate the most reasonable judgements'[87] – to accommodate discovery as well as inquiry and hard proof as well as the 'most reasonable judgement.' Bearing in mind our earlier consideration of the use and evaluation of argument in curriculum domains as strikingly different as physics and English literature, there needs to be.

Be that as it may, inquiry dialogue in this iteration is underpinned by principles not unlike those of P4C (as the authors acknowledge): giving students control over the flow of talk, making talk cumulative, searching for alternative ideas, developing students' meta-level understanding of talk, and the 'community of enquiry'. As we shall see, three of these also resonate with the principles underlying this book's approach to dialogic teaching, which foregrounds, among others, *collectivity* (cf. the community of enquiry in P4C and Reznitskaya and Wilkinson), *reciprocity* (their alternative ideas and perspectives) and *cumulation* (in which they adopt our definition). Their approach also endorses this book's commitment to repertoire, citing the five main paradigms of teacher talk that emerged from the international *Culture and Pedagogy* research: rote, recitation, exposition, discussion and dialogue.[88] (In the revised dialogic teaching framework set out in Chapter 7, this list has been extended from five to eight.)

Reznitskaya and Wilkinson use texts to stimulate their inquiry dialogue and propose three criteria by which such texts can be selected: *dialogic* ('is rich in conceptual content and deals with issues that lend themselves to multiple interpretations, perspectives, explanations or opinions . . . is thought-provoking and invites several readings'); *accessible* ('students have sufficient background knowledge to understand the topic and issues addressed');

engaging ('students can identify with the characters portrayed and their life circumstances').[89] One might suggest that 'accessible' and 'engaging' should pertain to the style and quality of writing as well as its content, and that – as Ferretti and Fan note – all text is inherently dialogic 'because it involves communication between real or imagined interlocutors'.[90] Indeed, in light of Bakhtin's work and our earlier discussion of voice, we can extend the intrinsically dialogic properties of writing well beyond this.

But what is relatively unusual about this approach is that it appears to make text subordinate to talk, whereas, as we shall see in the next chapter, it is usually the other way round, and text tends to rule. While the goal of Reznitskaya and Wilkinson is to foster 'argument literacy' (a slightly confusing use of 'literacy' in this context because despite the focus on talk, it may suggest to some that text is the default after all), its actual preoccupation is more with argumentative talk, or 'inquiry dialogue', and the authors approvingly cite Neil Mercer's 'interthinking',[91] a concept that connotes talk that unites the cognitive and the social in pursuit of learning and understanding.

Less clear is how far the ideas of Reznitskaya and Wilkinson address my concern about the conceptual and logistical risks of a 'bolt on' approach to curriculum development and renewal. Is argument literacy yet another 'literacy' for which time must be found? Is it a partial re-positioning of literacy as traditionally conceived, an ability to 'read' literary texts in new ways? Is it confined to the English/language arts curriculum, or does it accept the imperative that every curriculum domain embodies argument of some kind; and that, following our discussion of the relevance of Leavis and Toulmin, helping students to become instinctively and comprehensively 'literate' in relation to argument is a task for teachers of all subjects?

So, by analogy with the 1960s/1970s idea of 'language across the curriculum', and in line with this book's insistence that dialogic pedagogy is a pervasive educational stance rather than a mere teaching technique, I would suggest that the proper outcome of this discussion is an educational commitment to the study and pursuit of 'argument across the curriculum'. There is also a case for attending particularly closely to argumentation as an aspect of teaching about language, but this is of limited value if in other curriculum domains students are expected not to question the ideas they encounter.

There is one more loose end. It is as yet unclear how far 'argument literacy', however conceived, does justice to what is distinctive about oral argumentation on the one hand and written argumentation on the other. I shall return to this question in light of the last and in some ways most problematic of our contingent themes, oracy. It is to this that we turn next.

Notes

1 Bakhtin 1984; Williams 2008.
2 As in the ESRC project *Consulting pupils about teaching and learning* (Rudduck and McIntyre 2007). See also Rudduck and Flutter 2000.

3 UNICEF Rights Respecting Schools website: www.unicef.org.uk/rights-respecting-schools/the-rrsa/what-is-a-rights-respecting-school/ (accessed June 2019).
4 Robinson 2014, 19.
5 Segal and Lefstein 2015; Segal, Pollak and Lefstein 2016; Lefstein, Pollak and Segal 2016.
6 Segal and Lefstein 2015, 1.
7 Clarke 2015.
8 Edwards 1992.
9 Dewey 1916.
10 Alexander 2001, 521–523.
11 Bernstein 1990.
12 Kumar 1991, 71–93; Alexander 2001, chapter 4.
13 Lefstein, Pollak and Segal 2018, 14.
14 Cf. Wordsworth in *Intimations of Immortality*: 'Thoughts that do often lie too deep for tears.'
15 DCSF 2008.
16 DCSF 2008, 13.
17 ICAN/RCSLT 2018.
18 Delpit 1988; Edwards 1989.
19 In *Punch*, January 1988: https://punch.photoshelter.com/image/I0000eHEXGJ_wImQ (accessed July 2019).
20 *The Guardian*, 12 April 2016. www.theguardian.com/technology/2016/apr/12/the-dark-side-of-guardian-comments (accessed July 2019).
21 *The Guardian*, 18 June 2016. www.theguardian.com/technology/2016/jun/18/vile-online-abuse-against-women-mps-needs-to-be-challenged-now (accessed July 2019).
22 www.youtube.com/watch?v=vz87TAeKdLY or www.theguardian.com/politics/2019/sep/25/pm-branded-a-disgrace-after-saying-best-way-to-honour-jo-cox-is-to-deliver-brexit (accessed September 2019).
23 HM Government 2019. The official hate crime categories in England and Wales are race, religion, sexual orientation, disability, transgender.
24 *The Guardian*, 15 July 2019. www.theguardian.com/us-news/2019/jul/14/trump-squad-tlaib-omar-pressley-ocasio-cortez (accessed July 2019).
25 Hinsliff 2019.
26 Protecting children from online abuse. https://learning.nspcc.org.uk/child-abuse-and-neglect/online-abuse/ (accessed July 2019).
27 Equality and Human Rights Commission 2019.
28 At the time of writing, the case of poet and professor Laurie Scheck is a prominent example. She was disciplined but then exonerated for inviting her literature students to discuss James Baldwin's use of the n-word (Flood 2019). See also Bernard 2015.
29 Jonathan Friedman, quoted on PEN America website: https://pen.org/press-release/professor-new-school-discipline/ (accessed August 2019).
30 Hamlyn 1967; Hirst 1967.
31 Mayer, O'Connor and Lefstein 2020, 205.
32 Lipman 2003.
33 www.sapere.org.uk (accessed June 2019).
34 Smith 2010.
35 IAPC: www.montclair.edu/iapc/what-is-philosophy-for-children/what-is-a-typical-p4c-session-like/ (accessed June 2019).
36 Fisher 2003, 257–258.
37 www.montclair.edu/iapc/what-is-philosophy-for-children/why-philosophy-for-children/ (accessed June 2019).
38 Michaels and O'Connor 2012.

39 That is, Rowe's 'wait time' (Rowe 1986).
40 Fisher 2003, 161–162.
41 Fisher 2003, 263–266.
42 Mercer *et al.* 2020, 300.
43 Sapere *Going for Gold* programme: https://sapere.satorimm.com/Content/Media/
   SAPERE%20Going%20for%20Gold%20Brochure%202017%20CURRENT.
   pdf (accessed June 2019).
44 https://educationendowmentfoundation.org.uk/projects-and-evaluation/projects/
   philosophy-for-children/ (accessed June 2019).
45 The problems of the RCT as applied to the 2014–17 dialogic teaching project are
   discussed in Alexander 2018 (especially 587–588). For more sustained critiques,
   see Berliner 2002; Prideaux 2002; Norman 2003; Sullivan 2011; Ginsburg and
   Smith 2016. As a matter of record, I should mention that at the conclusion of
   the 2014–17 trial of this book's approach to dialogic teaching in 78 schools,
   we were invited to plan a bigger trial involving up to 200 schools and 12,000
   students. The proposal was prepared, negotiated, costed and accepted by EEF,
   evaluators were appointed and the project was ready to start in 2019. However,
   despite our best efforts, the trial methodology remained in our view so rigid, the
   outcome measures so narrow, and the explanatory potential so puny in relation
   to the project's scale and demands that we had no alternative but to withdraw
   our proposal. In contrast, Sapere decided to accept reading as its sole outcome
   measure, presumably after weighing this restriction against the benefits of dissemination that the trial would bring.
46 Schwarz and Baker 2017.
47 Schwarz and Baker 2017, 67–68.
48 Mercer and Dawes 2008.
49 Osborne *et al.* 2010.
50 Driver 1983.
51 Kennedy 1999, 94.
52 Welch 1990.
53 Simon 1966.
54 Adamson, Alexander and Ettenhuber 2007.
55 Standage 2014.
56 Walton 2013, 7–10.
57 Walton 2013, 213–214.
58 Walton 2013, 216.
59 Schopenhauer 2004.
60 In the UK, Full Fact: https://fullfact.org. In the US: FactCheck.org: www.factcheck.
   org, MediaBias/FactCheck: https://mediabiasfactcheck.com/washington-post/
   and several others. Poynter's International Fact-Checking Network brings them
   together: www.poynter.org/ifcn/ (accessed July 2019).
61 Brexit Britain comes to mind, as do Russia, Hungary, Turkey, Italy, Brazil, Ven-
   ezuela, India, the Philippines . . .
62 Alexander 2019; Dewey 1916.
63 Kakutani 2018, 172–173.
64 Orwell 1968, 139.
65 Arendt 2004, 474.
66 House of Commons 2018, 3.
67 House of Commons 2018, 62–63.
68 Janke and Cooper 2017, 139.
69 Janke and Cooper 2017, chapters 2–9.
70 Janke and Cooper 2017, 127–128.
71 Alexander 2010b, 240.
72 See the critique of Leavis in Eagleton 2016, 146–147.

73 Popper 1963.
74 Small 2016, 21.
75 Small 2016, 174–175.
76 Dewey 1916.
77 Taylor 1991, 12–23.
78 Small 2016, 23.
79 Toulmin 2003, 12–13.
80 www.corestandards.org/ELA-Literacy/ (accessed July 2019).
81 www.corestandards.org/ELA-Literacy/SL/11-12/ (accessed July 2019).
82 Reznitskaya and Wilkinson 2017, 29–32 and 183–194.
83 Reznitskaya *et al.* 2016.
84 Walton 2013, 69.
85 Walton 2013, 69.
86 Walton 2013, 200.
87 Reznitskaya and Wilkinson 2017, 14.
88 Reznitskaya and Wilkinson 2017, 8–13; Alexander 2008b.
89 Reznitskaya and Wilkinson 2017, 137–139.
90 Ferretti and Fan 2015, 302.
91 Reznitskaya and Wilkinson 2017, 12; Mercer 2000, 1.

5 Grand dichotomy

Oracy politicised

Now to our final take on 'dialogue in other words', oracy. It may seem odd that a book on classroom talk has taken four chapters to get to it, but beyond its disarmingly simple lexical definition, 'oracy' raises questions that required our earlier discussions as grounding.

In Chapter 2, we noted Andrew Wilkinson's coining of 'oracy'[1] during the 1960s and the rise and fall of the National Oracy Project and Language in the National Curriculum (LINC) during the 1990s. Some may feel that 'assassination' more accurately describes the fate of these projects than the unfortunate mishap of 'fall', for we also saw how, in praiseworthy pursuit of educational improvement, they managed to rouse ancient political prejudices about the relationship between speaking, morality and authority, and no doubt subliminal and darker unease about the wisdom of teaching the masses to talk rather than listen; and how they paid the price for doing so.

In 2019, we witnessed the attempt by an All-Party Parliamentary Group to breathe new life into oracy. At the time of writing, it remains to be seen whether oracy's co-option by a small band of politicians will enable it to fare any better, for they are predominantly from the oppositional left rather than the right-wing party in power,[2] and it is the latter that historically has appointed itself as the scourge of 'idle chatter' and guardian of Standard English.

Is oracy synonymous with dialogue? In the weakest lexical sense considered in Chapter 3, almost, because it may entail conversation. But Mercer and his colleagues sharpen Wilkinson's definition, making oracy education 'the direct, explicit teaching of speaking and listening skills as part of the curriculum',[3] as opposed to 'the best, evidence-based talk strategies for teaching an understanding of any subject',[4] which is their definition of dialogic teaching and raises the interesting possibility that oracy teaching does not need to be dialogic. So the pre-eminent focus of oracy is *student* talk, and such talk by its nature does not always receive or require a response and can be about anything; whereas dialogue as understood in this book is inherently reciprocal in trajectory, pedagogical in intent and epistemic in substance; and it gives considerable if not equal attention to the talk and thinking of the *teacher*. Thus, as we noted in Chapter 2, *oral development* (oracy) may be distinguished from *oral pedagogy* (dialogic teaching).

From international comparison, we glean other differences:

> Close analysis of the lesson videotapes, transcripts and teacher interviews from the *Five Cultures* project . . . [leads] to the conclusion that in English primary classrooms, although much may be made of the importance of talk in learning, and a great deal of talking goes on, its function is seen as primarily social rather than cognitive, and as helpful to learning rather than as fundamental to it.[5]

In this context, the 'social' and 'cognitive' were viewed by our UK teachers not as an essential partnership, as in the 'interthinking' of Mercer in his pre-oracy phase ('the dynamic interaction of *minds* that makes language possible . . . the joint . . . *intellectual* activity which people regularly accomplish using language')[6] but as alternative and not necessarily reconcilable pursuits. The preoccupation with only one of these, it will immediately be recognised, again diverges from this book's notion of dialogue which, in the tradition of research stretching back through Douglas Barnes to Lev Vygotsky, views the social and the cognitive as interdependent and speech as the mediator.[7] It is also at odds with the thinking of Wilkinson himself, who stressed the interdependence of 'oracy as competence' and 'oracy for learning'.[8] Mercer, Mannion and Warwick, in contrast, are at pains to distance oracy from dialogic teaching, which raises the question of whether it is actually possible for the teaching of talk to be only about itself.

The other side of the comparative coin was not so much the modesty of the official vision of oracy in England's national curriculum at that time as its authoritarian tone:

> Pupils should be taught . . . to express themselves correctly and appropriately and . . . to recognise and use standard English.[9]

In UK academic circles, oracy may well enjoy a higher profile in 2020 than it did in 2000, though the ascendancy of the National Oracy Project during the late 1980s and early 1990s, and the prominence given to 'speaking and listening' in the 1989 and 1999 versions of England's national curriculum, reflected a genuine grass-roots blossoming of interest in classroom talk that should not be underestimated, and it may have helped to condition the positive response with which UK teachers greeted dialogic pedagogy a decade or so later. Thus, in 1992 the National Oracy Project's leaders recalled that

> Teachers joining the Project began to listen with increased attention to their pupils' talk. . . . They were amazed, delighted and sometimes

chastened by what they heard. They discovered the wide range of functions and forms of talk in the repertoire of every child.[10]

(Mark, in anticipation of Chapter 7, that 'repertoire'.) But politically, as we saw in Chapter 2, there has been little progress, and the minimal requirements for spoken language in the 2014 version of England's national curriculum were wrung from government ministers and officials with extreme and grudging difficulty,[11] and even then, they were applied to primary schools but not secondary.[12] Indeed, the government elected in 2010 effectively plunged the system into reverse. The 1999 version of the national curriculum had devoted equal attention, as measured by numbers of pages, to speaking and listening, reading and writing at both primary and secondary stages.[13] But of the 88 pages devoted to English in the 2014 national curriculum framework, reading and writing occupied 86, and just two were left for spoken language.

On the other hand, in the latter we did at least manage to secure a statement whose message was recognisably dialogic. It began with the familiar mantra from the 'back to basics' phrase book apparently passed from one minister to the next:

> Pupils should be taught to speak clearly and convey ideas confidently using Standard English.[14]

But, prompted by non-governmental drafters[15] whose efforts somehow evaded the ministerial red pen,[16] it continued:

> They should learn to justify ideas with reasons; ask questions to check understanding; negotiate; evaluate and build on the ideas of others; and select the appropriate register for effective communication. They should be taught to give well-structured descriptions and explanations and develop their understanding through speculating, hypothesising and exploring ideas. This will enable them to clarify their thinking as well as organise their ideas for writing.[17]

Ministers appear not to have spotted the tension here between their ritualistic obeisance to 'Standard English' and our smuggled reference to selecting the 'appropriate' register, which might of course include non-standard forms. That tension has dogged the debate about English in England's national curriculum since its first iteration in 1989 and has tainted much of the public discussion about oracy ever since.[18] But whereas the 1999 version of the national curriculum included requirements for teaching students to understand 'how language varies according to context and purpose . . . between standard and dialect forms . . . between spoken and written forms',[19] by 2014 all that remained in this domain was that cryptic reference to 'the appropriate register', which might be interpreted as having less to do with understanding than with etiquette. In England, at least, oracy has always been an intensely political matter.[20]

Oracy re-branded

Alongside the APPG parliamentary enquiry, two further initiatives at the time of writing have flagged the aspiration towards an oracy revival: Voice 21, a project of the London-based School 21; and Oracy Cambridge, based at Hughes Hall in Cambridge and led by Neil Mercer.[21] The initiatives have been linked through projects supported by the Education Endowment Foundation.

Voice 21, following Mercer (earlier), defines oracy as 'the speaking curriculum' and glosses it as 'the ability to communicate effectively', asserting:

> one of the biggest barriers to young people getting on is a lack of eloquence. Employers put good oral communication at the top of their requirements for employees. Yet we rarely teach it systematically in schools.[22]

Pausing momentarily to ask whether 'eloquence' was what Voice 21 really meant, we find that Oracy Cambridge defines the oracy agenda in almost identical terms:

> In the world of work, the value of effective spoken communication is almost universally recognised. Job adverts emphasise the importance of being a confident communicator, or a strong 'team player'.[23]

Such re-branding of oracy's scope and value will no doubt have instrumental appeal, but they barely scratch the surface of its potential and are more limited than the visions of Andrew Wilkinson, the begetter of the term 'oracy', and the National Oracy Project. The latter nailed its colours firmly to a Vygotskian mast – 'Talking together, with adults and with peers, is the most important means by which children learn to think'[24] – and its publications ranged across the fields of cognition, learning, teaching and social development.

Of course, the communication skills/workplace focus may be strategic, though educators should always be wary of capitulating to commercial criteria of relevance. For note how, in the Oracy Cambridge statement, being a 'strong team player' is presented via the conjunction 'or' as the concomitant of being a 'confident communicator', as if the prime purpose of learning to communicate is to ready oneself to submit to what is required by others. Mercer appears thereby to have created something of a dilemma for himself as well as a curiously conflicted notion of what a 'team player' can and cannot do, for elsewhere he says:

> The notion of 'communication' does not capture the special quality of the joint intellectual activity I am concerned with. . . . 'Communication'

encourages the view of a linear process whereby people exchange ideas, think about them individually and then exchange the products of their separate intellectual efforts. This does not do justice to the dynamic interaction of minds which language makes possible.[25]

Be that as it may, the two projects' preoccupation with workplace-directed communication has yielded a four-stranded 'oracy skills framework' for 11–12-year-olds. The 'skills' are:

- physical (voice, body language)
- linguistic (vocabulary, language variety, structure, rhetorical techniques)
- cognitive (content, clarifying and summarising, self-regulating, reasoning, audience awareness)
- social and emotional (working with others, listening and responding, confidence in speaking).[26]

Here, then, we learn what is entailed in 'the direct, explicit teaching of speaking and listening skills as part of the curriculum'.[27] But, like the definition of oracy that it elaborates, this categorisation is open to question. Voice, it will be recalled from Chapter 4, has several dimensions other than the physical; the 'skills' defined here as 'social and emotional' could equally be classified as 'cognitive', just as 'audience awareness' could be classified as 'social and emotional'. Equally, 'rhetorical techniques' are not exclusively 'linguistic'. And conspicuously absent from this stance on spoken language are cultural, epistemic and ethical considerations of the kind we encountered in Chapter 3. Compare the above list, too, with the eight justifications of classroom talk and the eight kinds of learning talk in Chapter 7 (pages 130 and 142).

Part of the problem is the word 'skill' itself, for this framework appears to follow a reductive and arguably corporate trend that during recent years has redefined much or most of the educational endeavour as marketable skill. Of this the Cambridge Primary Review was sharply critical:

> The concomitant to the elevation of skill . . . is the downgrading of knowledge, understanding, enquiry and exploration. But to set them in opposition is foolish, unnecessary and epistemologically unsound, for all but the most elemental skills – and certainly all those that in educational circles are defined as 'basic' – require knowledge in their application.[28]

And:

> Although the generic skills approach purports to address the claims of lifelong learning, it actually sells such learning short, for it elevates being

able to do something over knowing, understanding, reflecting, speculating, analysing and evaluating, which arguably are no less essential to the fulfilled, successful and useful life. Indeed, without these capacities the exercise of skill becomes in a very real sense meaningless. Skills are vital. We cannot survive without them. But, educators should use the term more discriminatingly, otherwise we shall carelessly lose not only knowledge and understanding, but also skill itself.[29]

In which objections, in view of this typical morsel from the World Bank a decade later, we were surely right:

> Research [no sources given] . . . is increasingly looking at the value of non-cognitive *skills* (also often referred to as socio-emotional *skills*). . . . Demand for these *skills* will continue to change as economies and labor market needs evolve, with trends such as automation causing fundamental shifts. . . . Non-cognitive *skills* cover a range of abilities such as conscientiousness, perseverance, and teamwork. These *skills* are critically important to student achievement, both in and beyond the classroom. They form a critical piece of workers' *skill* sets, which comprise cognitive, non-cognitive and job-specific *skills*. . . . The Bank's . . . survey work . . . found concrete payoff for *skills* such as 'grit' . . . conscientiousness and decision-making in the labor market.[30]

In the face of this assault, some might suspend academic etiquette and dare to invoke terms like 'corporate bunkum'. Granted that knowing *how* cannot be entirely reduced to knowing *that*, and, conversely, that many skills can be exercised without knowledge of their underlying mechanics, the 'social and emotional skills' listed earlier and the 'non-cognitive skills' exemplified by the World Bank are not of this kind and all carry the cognitive charge of intelligent use. So in this context the very phrase 'non-cognitive skills' is an oxymoron, and, in relation to what it purports to describe, a somewhat demeaning one. (Those with long memories will recall similar objections to the opposition of 'cognitive' and 'affective' in Benjamin Bloom's 1950s taxonomy of behavioural objectives, and of this there is perhaps another echo in the way 'skill' too, as currently used, reduces education to supposedly measurable behaviours.)[31]

In any event, it is inconceivable that one can listen and respond (Voice 21) or be a team player (Oracy Cambridge) or make decisions (World Bank) without knowing something, thinking and thinking deeply – unless, that is, one is merely a cipher. The same goes for the ultra-fashionable 'skill' of 'grit', which elsewhere I have traced to its American roots only to find 'serious thinking about what it takes to cope with today's world all but swamped by corporatism, psychobabble and John Wayne.'[32]

This 'oracy skills framework' and a linked 'oracy assessment toolkit' for students aged 11–12 have been piloted and evaluated twice for the

Education Endowment Foundation (EEF). On both occasions, EEF allowed the toolkit's conceptualisations of oracy and oracy skills to pass without comment, for its principal concern is the pragmatic 'what works' rather than whether 'what works' is conceptually sound and educationally worthwhile. After the first pilot, EEF reported that independently administered tests showed no impact on students' 'reasoning skills', though when used internally by the project team, the toolkit produced more positive results.[33] However, EEF admits evidence from independent external evaluations only, so it judged that 'neither of these tests were [sic] able to provide conclusive evidence of the impact of the intervention' and that the project should be viewed as merely formative. The evaluation of the second pilot found that teachers valued the approach, welcomed the assessment toolkit and perceived improvements in students' oracy. But again EEF added:

> Given the limited reliability of the assessment, and the lack of a comparison group, we cannot conclude from these results that the programme improved oracy. The pilot did not measure impact on academic attainment.[34]

This, then, remains work in progress, conceptually as much as empirically.

Oracy denied

We return next to a matter raised under 'voice' in Chapter 4. In 2007, John Bercow MP – later an ebullient and controversial Speaker of the House of Commons – was invited by the then government to chair a review of services for children and young people aged 0–19 years with speech, language and communication needs (SLCN). In 2008 the review concluded:

> There is insufficient understanding of the centrality of speech, language and communication among policy makers and commissioners nationally and locally, professionals and service providers, and sometimes parents and families themselves. It follows that insufficient priority is attached to addressing SLCN.[35]

And:

> Although there are some skilled professionals and good facilities, the overall position in terms of speech, language and communication services is highly unsatisfactory. Access to information and services is often poor, services themselves are very mixed, continuity across the age range is lacking, effective joint working between the health and education services is rare and there is something of a postcode lottery across the country.[36]

What is the scale of this version of the challenge of oracy? The Bercow report calculated that 7 per cent of 5-year-olds entering school have significant difficulties with speech and/or language which are likely to need specialist and/ or targeted intervention at key points in their development; and that one per cent have 'severe and complex' SLCN. However, in areas of social disadvantage, the proportion rises dramatically, so that in some areas and populations up to 50 per cent of children and young people may have speech and language skills that are 'significantly lower than those of other children of the same age.'[37]

The impact of the late or non-existent diagnosis that Bercow criticised can be severe. A follow-up report published in 2018 found that children with SLCN seriously underperformed from the moment they entered school, so that 'just 15 per cent of pupils with identified SLCN achieved the expected standard in reading, writing and mathematics at the end of their primary school years compared with 61 per cent of all pupils', and 'only 20.3 per cent of pupils with SLCN gained grade 4/C or above in English and maths at GCSE, compared with 63.9 per cent of all pupils.'[38]

Meanwhile, language difficulties were strongly associated with emotional and behavioural disorders:

> Young people referred to mental health services are three times more likely to have SLCN than those who have not been referred. . . . Children with poor vocabulary skills are twice as likely to be unemployed when they reach adulthood . . . 60 per cent of young offenders have low language skills.[39]

Ten years on from Bercow, in 2018, modest improvements in some areas appeared to be heavily outnumbered by the damaging consequences of the government policy of austerity in public services that followed the 2008 financial collapse, with a severe cutback in specialist speech and language therapy posts in local authorities. As if to deflect attention from this loss of provision, the 2018 follow-up report to Bercow noted – as of course have we – government efforts to marginalise spoken language in the 2011–13 review of England's national curriculum, the removal of judgements of oral communication from the Ofsted school inspection framework, and the loss of any assessment of the student's spoken language after age five.[40]

On two fronts, then, recent UK government policy has compromised the progress of some – possibly many – of the 1.4 million children in the UK who in 2018, according to the second Bercow report, had speech, language and communication needs of a kind that required diagnosis and special provision: first, by cutting back on funding for their support; second, by seeking to downgrade the importance of oracy in education and teachers' consciousness.

Oracy and literacy

So: oracy politicised, re-branded and, for some children, compromised or denied. There is a further angle. Even if it is deemed necessary for campaigning purposes, positioning oracy in contradistinction to literacy, let alone confining its outcomes to communication and defining these as 'non-cognitive', is to risk reducing rather than elevating its status and perpetuating what anthropologist Jack Goody calls the 'grand dichotomy'.[41] This presents the oral and the written as mutually exclusive and hierarchical. Cultures are deemed to progress inexorably from the oral to the written, writing becomes both a privileged pursuit and the proclaimed measure of education and, as Goody tellingly adds, 'Where writing is, class cannot be far away'.[42]

For it is in relation to public justifications for oracy and literacy that we see how severely the balance is skewed. On the one hand, as historian Harvey Graff provocatively catalogues in his monumental *Legacies of Literacy*, literate persons are held to be empathetic, innovative, achievement-oriented, cosmopolitan, politically aware, urban and technically adaptable; and literacy is said to correlate with economic growth, productivity, political stability, participatory democracy, urbanisation, consumption and contraception.[43] On the other hand, oracy is advocated, as we have seen and even as I write these words, on the grounds that it confers 'non-cognitive' workplace 'skills', no less and certainly no more. That, I suggest, amounts not to advocacy of talk but to its denigration, and is really little better than our minister's 'idle chatter in class.'

In fact, Graff cites sources that show how some of the claims for literacy that he quotes can be sustained, and since 1987, when his book first appeared, we have come to understand the critical importance, in both developed and developing countries, of the relationship between increased literacy, lowered fertility and female emancipation. Evidence on this score informed the framing of the United Nations Millennium Development and Sustainable Development Goals and since 2002 has been documented annually in UNESCO's Global Education Monitoring Reports.[44]

What is also beyond dispute is that literacy is a passport to jobs, social advancement and national economic progress,[45] and that a vast array of information, and a massive amount of cultural capital of different kinds, are stored in written and now digital forms. The ability to read, and to read fluently, discriminatingly and in different genres, is a truly vital skill. Of that there can be no question. In societies where literacy, traditional and/or digital, has acquired this kind of currency, public education has no alternative but to give it the highest priority, however debatable the arguments may be about the precise relationship between literacy and cognition, and especially about the claim that literacy promotes 'higher forms' of thought. For this and several other claims in Graff's list are much less convincingly demonstrated, while a glance back at the history of the twentieth century will show that some are entirely fallacious.[46]

Moreover, citing the late British educationist G.H. Bantock, Graff points out that the consequences of literacy may be mixed and even contradictory:

> Books . . . cause self-consciousness and social distance; they also reinforce privacy and individualism, inwardness and detachment. Print

results in a . . . narrowing of experience, but . . . it also broadens horizons. . . . Literacy and print simultaneously increase problems of identity and rootlessness while they aid in their solution.[47]

So without wishing to deny for a moment the power and importance of universal literacy, we cannot allow its claims either to be disproportionately hyped or to submerge those of oracy, provided that the latter is understood in a way that respects the visions of Wilkinson and the National Oracy Project rather than more recent manifestations. However, given that so much talk in classrooms relates to and/or centres on written texts, and that students, especially in secondary schools, spend the larger part of their classroom time reading and writing,[48] perhaps a more profitable question to pursue would be the nature of the relationship between the oral and the written and, for teachers, the way this relationship might be explored and fostered to the benefit of both.[49]

The spoken and the written: contrasts and commonalities

Lexically and syntactically, written and spoken registers may take very different forms and operate in different time frames. Written English uses longer words, greater lexical variety, is more Latinate, has more nouns, passive verbs, attributive adjectives and subordinate clauses, and is more formal, explicit and elaborate and less elliptical and embedded in context than talk.[50] Oral communication relies on shared knowledge and meanings. Written communication, being in the first instance solitary, can make no such assumptions.[51] In writing, the prototypical units are the phrase and sentence, both of them complete at least in as far as completeness is defined by grammatical conventions. Their equivalent in speech, the utterance, is infinitely variable: it may be monosyllabic, extended or prolix; curtailed or complete; fragmented and hesitant or fluent; liberally punctuated by discourse markers ('so', 'right', 'I mean', 'like', 'well', 'kind of', 'you know', 'anyway', 'mind you') or entirely devoid of them.

We speak about 180 words a minute but write between 20 and 40, though proficient touch-typists expect to achieve between 60 and 100, and one seasoned texter from Brazil earned a Guinness record with an astounding 75.[52] But even at these higher speeds our thoughts when writing may leap ahead of our means to express them, while in speech it is the other way round and we may 'lose the thread'.[53] In writing, transitions are marked by punctuation, sentences and paragraphs; in speech by turn-taking. The latter may be orderly and sequential, as in writing; or they tumble over each other in what, in the trade, are called 'overlapping turns'. Writing allows the writer's ideas, albeit drawing on the ideas of others, to flow unimpeded, but talk – vitally – is co-constructed. And so on.

In his aim of making talk more 'visible', Ron Carter has developed a 'grammar of talk' to counterbalance the grammars that ostensibly apply to all forms of language but are more commonly applied to writing.[54] Thus his grammar of talk is not so much a set of rules governing how talk should be framed as a corpus-based description of the way talk works, starting from three key characteristics: (i) it involves speakers and listeners in orienting to context by means of various kinds of signalling; (ii) it takes place in a context of real time and space so it is relatively unplanned and transitory; and (iii) it involves face-to-face communication and so entails non-verbal as well as verbal communication, incorporates ongoing feedback, and is of course collaborative.[55] The purpose of such a 'grammar' is to make talk as reflective and worthy of study in classrooms, in its own right, as are reading and writing.

The significance of Carter's third feature should not be underestimated, for it has been suggested that a speaker's paralinguistic behaviour doesn't just aid oral communication but also to a greater or lesser extent conditions how it is received. 'This fact', said the Bullock report many years ago, 'is tacitly recognised by most people, who know they can be charmed by nonsense and bored by sense.'[56] Politicians know that they are as likely to be judged by how they look and sound as by what they say, which makes all the more pressing the need not just to promote talk in education but also to make it the object of study, for it comes to the heart of democratic engagement, and at this troubling time for so many of the world's so-called democracies, Carter's aim of 'making talk *visible*' acquires added urgency. 'That one may smile, and smile, and be a villain.'[57]

But the key observation in this context is that literacy and oracy are best understood, as Shirley Brice Heath has argued, not as the dichotomy that Jack Goody deplores but as overlapping continua with structures and functions that are both distinct and shared.[58] There are many kinds of writing and many kinds of talk. Some talk is consciously literary, and some writing – popular journalism, for example – is deliberately conversational. Some talk exhibits the archetypal features of Carter's grammar of vernacular talk, and some is constructed with every maxim of correct written English punctiliously observed. And narrative writing, in particular, works hard to include between inverted commas the idiosyncrasies and nuances of speech, accent and inflection.

A lecture is spoken, but unless it is impromptu or based on PowerPoint slides, it is usually prepared as a written-out text which may then be adjusted so that as heard it recovers some of the cadences of speech, and of course the very word 'lecture' cements the complexity of the relationship because etymologically it means something that is read. The transcripts of political speeches, artfully devised to be read from autocues while seeming to have the spontaneity of talk, are particularly instructive in this regard. They are full of rousing non-sequiturs ('Let me be absolutely clear. . . . I passionately believe in x. . . . So I pledge to you today that we are going to do y. . . . And that's why I am instructing my ministers to do z') that propel cheering party stooges and loyalists to their feet but when read in tomorrow's newspapers look threadbare or ludicrous. Occasionally, text-intended-to-sound-as-talk gets its speaker/reader in a tangle: in 2015 a hapless British politician and autocue novice failed to distinguish between his speech-writer's text and paralinguistic stage directions, heartily proclaiming 'Strong message here!' as he approached his peroration, to the bafflement of his audience.[59]

The relationship is indeed far from straightforward. Queen Victoria famously complained of Prime Minister Gladstone that 'he speaks to me is if I were a public meeting' (that is, he was unable to match register to audience and context), while in electronic communication it is never wholly clear whether emails, which are written texts, should abide by the conventions of writing or are spoken utterances that just happen to be written down. So elderly academics whose manners were implanted when epistolary and social boundaries were clearer may wince when they receive messages from strangers jauntily prefaced 'Hi Prof . . .' or 'Hiya Tony', while in their own messages they doggedly persist with 'Dear Ms X/Dear Dr Y'. Meanwhile, their American counterparts try to steer a line between the stuffy, the conversational and the unwarrantedly familiar by dropping both 'Dear' and 'Hi' and beginning abruptly with the recipient's name: 'Tony: . . .', which on this side of the Atlantic manages to sound not so much friendly as peremptory. As to the Trumpian use of tweets to conduct American domestic and foreign policy, this is as far from Gladstone as can be imagined, for it applies to the realm of what should be carefully considered, painstakingly enunciated and scrupulously qualified the restricted vocabulary, careless syntax and boorish sentiment of speech at its most unbuttoned. But that, for many, is its electoral appeal.

Very occasionally, one encounters people whose oral confidence, command and fluency produce talk that when transcribed is entirely devoid of hesitation, ellipsis, discourse markers and other characteristics of normal conversational speech, and who voice in a single spontaneous take the clausal elaboration, precision and balance that most writers achieve only after much drafting and redrafting. As a school student I was fortunate to be taught by one such person, the remarkable Douglas Brown, here described by his friend Donald Davie:

> For it was when he spoke rapidly in his quiet voice, that everyone was astonished. I have never, before or since, encountered such a gift for articulation, and in the strictest sense; for his vocabulary was wide, fastidious and choice, but what was remarkable was the marshalling of that vocabulary in spoken syntax, the leaping and springing clauses that unwound luxuriantly, crossed over, and yet drew unerringly home. It was daunting, and finding it in a fellow-student I was daunted indeed.[60]

Interestingly, that clause beginning 'for his vocabulary . . .' works as well when visually savoured on the page as when it is read aloud, perhaps because its author was a poet.

Whose oracy?

Oral command and fluency of the kind described above are not the monopoly of Standard English (or its equivalents in other languages), though the current (2014) version of England's National Curriculum does appear to equate them – 'Pupils should be taught to speak audibly and fluently with an increasing command of Standard English'.[61]

The pragmatic arguments for teaching the standard or standardised form of a language are that it enables speakers or writers from widely varying backgrounds to communicate with each other (which is why this book uses it); and that its patina of formality makes it the language of choice in settings where protocols are observed, power is exercised or decisions are made. Mastering the standard form becomes a prerequisite for learning to cope and succeed in such settings. There, standard language is what we need for getting on, not merely getting by. And one of those settings is education.

This is not the place to attempt the probably impossible task of compressing the vast, complex and contested topic of standard and non-standard language forms, or the related fields of language styles, registers and codes. However, in the context of dialogic teaching, four observations are merited.

First, most people do not speak Standard English, a fair number of authors do not write it and those who speak it do so only some of the time. So although there is, as noted, a strong pragmatic case for teaching it, it is neither desirable nor realistic for educators to ignore other forms, still less to belittle or try to eradicate them as has happened in the past. For such a small country, and given the extent of its geographical and social mobility during the past two centuries, Britain is still surprisingly rich in regional dialects (Standard English has evolved from one of them) or at least in the dialect survivals contained in particular words and phrases. To these must be added the many lively cultural, social and ethnic dialects, some of them of more recent origin. Non-standard English is omnipresent, vibrant and here to stay. It is also constantly changing.

Second, although spoken Standard English tends to be associated with Received Pronunciation (RP), the link is not essential. Standard English can be spoken in any accent, and whereas the BBC used to require its announcers and presenters to use the much-parodied RP vowels familiar from 1950s films and 2020s royal impersonators ('flet' for 'flat', 'trite' for 'trout', 'orff' for 'off', 'may' for 'my' and so on), it now takes a more relaxed and inclusive view. In a typical edition of BBC Radio 4's flagship current affairs programme 'Today', one hears more or less Standard English spoken by presenters and newsreaders in the accents of Scotland, Northern Ireland, South Wales, Manchester, Yorkshire and Tyneside, and by interviewees from many other UK regions and indeed from countries where English is the obligatory second language.

Third, the link between linguistic code and social class, for which Basil Bernstein's work has been both admired and criticised, is now less confidently argued, and we are warier of imputing cognitive or educational deficit on the basis of the language that children bring from home to school.[62] The middle class affectation of 'mockney' and the migration of cockney's signature glottal stop far beyond its working-class London borders complicate matters further. Nevertheless, the linguistic gap between home and classroom can cause problems on both sides: children may feel perplexed, intimidated or alienated by what they hear, and from the way children speak teachers may wrongly judge their capacity to think and learn in the ways the school requires. Further, where the teacher's linguistic and cultural referents are close to those of the student, the latter has an obvious advantage. That advantage may increase as the school year progresses because the two, even if unconsciously, will reinforce each other.

More than Bernstein's theoretical studies, Shirley Brice Heath's vivid ethnographic-historical study of white 'Roadville', black 'Trackton' children and the 'townspeople' in the Carolinas shows this process at work and summarises its consequences thus:

> Long before reaching school, children of the townspeople have made the transition from home to the larger societal institutions which share the values, skills and knowledge bases of the school. . . . Long before school, their language and culture at home has structured for them the meanings which will give shape to their experiences in classrooms and beyond.[63]

Finally, if 'language varieties may be "different but equal" from a linguistic perspective and yet be very unequal in the social worlds to which they give . . . access',[64] there are various responses that schools can make. One is to follow Heath and 'draw from the ways of speaking that students use in their lives beyond the classroom into oral and written language opportunities in school . . . to center communication on the here and now.'[65] Another is to heighten children's awareness of code, register and social context and help them learn when and how to match linguistic form to social need and circumstance. Code-switching – between informal and formal, personal and official, everyday and academic, home and school, non-standard and standard – is both commonplace and an acquired skill.

Talk and text: one-way traffic?

In the classroom context, as we saw earlier, the relationship between talking, reading and writing has tended to be one in which talk is viewed as assisting the study or creation of text, but not *vice versa*; what Myhill and Newman call (their italics) 'talk *for* writing . . . to help generate ideas for writing, rather than . . . talk *about* writing which develops . . . understanding of the complex ways in which writing creates meanings'.[66] Lively discussion may precede 'Now write about it' (which signals, not so subliminally, that talk is merely preparation for something more important and, especially, worthier of assessment). England's school inspectorate found in secondary schools a typical lesson pattern of exposition, recapitulation and record, with increasingly febrile student behaviour as the obligatory moment of writing approached.[67]

In English lessons, discussion may serve to illuminate a play – which paradoxically is treated as text for silent reading and analysis even though it is written to be spoken, heard and seen. Lovers of poetry insist that it comes alive, and its meaning becomes clear, only when it is read aloud. Poetic devices such as rhyme, meter, rhythm, consonance, alliteration and onomatopoeia exist to be *heard*: 'Poetry happens between the ears.'[68] Similarly, studying a Shakespeare play in the classroom but never seeing it performed is not only unsatisfactory; it may also inoculate students against Shakespeare for life. Read the words, and they may look archaic and make little sense; hear them, and they acquire sense and contemporary resonance – and beauty too.

And yet the immense value of text is that it can be endlessly revisited, explored and interpreted, and while the language and force of a poem or play are best appreciated when heard or viewed as performance, unlayering their meaning or meanings can take longer and may require not just oral repetition but also sustained study and discussion of the words on the page. Talk illuminates text, and text illuminates talk. Yet it is a paradox of poetry and drama, and of the complexity of the talk/text relationship, that what is meant to be spoken starts as writing, and its apparent spontaneity as heard is often proportionate to the hours of labour with pen or keyboard that have been devoted to it.

Here there may be cultural variation in the extent to which teachers understand and exploit this subtle and rewarding relationship. In the *Culture and Pedagogy* research we contrasted the tripartite lesson structure of a lengthy writing spell sandwiched between brief oral introduction and plenary, which was common in our English and American classrooms, with the episodic structure which interspersed several brief spells of reading or writing with talk that reflected on these as they progressed, which we more frequently observed in Russia and France.[69] The latter structure, arguably, makes more effective use of talk for writing, and I mention it here in anticipation of our argument in Chapter 7 that the repertoires of talk must encompass more than talk alone, in this case the structure of lessons and the apportioning of time. We also observed variation not only in the balance and relationship of speaking, reading and writing but also between curriculum domains. So, in our English primary classrooms:

> In spite of the importance . . . attached to the spoken word . . . language lessons were dominated by reading and writing. Children were offered few opportunities to talk in a structured way, and most of the . . . oral work that took place involved talking by the teacher and listening by the pupils. . . . Science was far more interactive than either language or

mathematics, involving more collaboration between pupils and much more conversation with the teacher. . . . In contrast with all three, the tasks set in art were characterized by an almost total absence of . . . conversation [and] . . . collaboration.[70]

Similarly in secondary schools: some years earlier, England's school inspectors reported 'an over-quick move to writing, reducing time for discussion and preparation . . . reading and talk were crowded out, either as activities in their own right or as linked with the writing.'[71] They also suggested that, like recitation as discussed elsewhere, this was partly about behavioural control: 'One school's advice to young teachers was plain: "Switch to writing if you find them turning restless."'[72]

Talking and writing at the interface

Gordon Wells marks the essential differences between spoken and written discourse in terms partly of form and partly of function, setting out the dimensions of each in contrasting pairs:

Spoken	*Written*
Action	Reflection
Dynamic	Synoptic
Concrete	Abstract
Spontaneous	Scientific
Narrative	Paradigmatic
Social	Individual
Dialogue	Monologue[73]

Wells acknowledges that this is a somewhat stereotypical characterisation, so there is room to quibble (for example, is all writing abstract and paradigmatic?). However, the only one of the pairs that I think is completely unacceptable is the final one. It appears to rest on narrowly lexical definitions of both 'dialogue' and 'monologue', and as a result ignores the monologic in a great deal of talk (outside as well as inside classrooms) and the dialogic in a great deal of writing. Acknowledging the dangers, and in effect demolishing his final pairing, Wells adds:

> What such an . . . account fails to capture . . . is the more dynamic manner in which talk and text can complement and enrich each other through an exploitation of the intertextual relationships between them. For it is when participants move back and forth between text and talk, using each mode to contextualise the other, and both modes as tools to make sense of the activity in which they are engaged, that we see the most important form of complementarity between them. And it is here, in the interpenetration of talk, text, and action in relation to particular

activities, that . . . students are best able to undertake . . . the semiotic apprenticeship into the various ways of knowing.[74]

Something of this is captured in the argument of Myhill and Newman that what is needed is not just 'talk *about* writing' rather than the more familiar 'talk *for* writing', but also what they call 'metatalk about writing', which focuses on language use and choice as a higher-order pedagogical pursuit within which both oracy and literacy can be located. And they suggest that dialogic teaching is particularly suited to this task.[75]

Pursuing the social as well as the cognitive, a meta-analytic review commissioned by the Carnegie Foundation listed collaborative writing as one of 11 'elements of current writing instruction found to be effective for helping adolescent students learn to write well and to use writing as a tool for learning', with a high effect size of 0.75.[76] More specifically, Ian Wilkinson and his colleagues report on their meta-analysis of studies which combine to show that 'dialogue-intensive pedagogies can produce sizeable gains in students' literal and inferential comprehension as well as in their higher order thinking about text.'[77] They find evidence that 'discussion enhances students' understanding of the texts that are read and discussed' (as surely it should, otherwise what kind of discussion is it?) but are less sanguine, evidence-wise, about 'whether students acquire the dispositions and habits of mind to transfer their comprehension abilities to new texts and tasks.'[78]

On the basis of the wider evidence, building students' capacity to transfer reasoning from one curriculum context or domain to another is one of the cited benefits of dialogic teaching (including our 2014–17 EEF study), so this particular meta-analysis appears to buck the evidential trend that Resnick extrapolates from the Pittsburgh studies[79] and which we shall consider in Chapter 6. On the other hand, McKeown and Beck show how, if discussion is conceived not as 'retrieving information' about a text – that is, retrieving the information that the teacher chooses to regard as germane – but as a process of 'enacting the comprehension process' by summarising, predicting and asking questions, then transfer is more likely:

> Through such interactions, students acquire a mental model of the process that habituates their manner of dealing with text. Thus we think of this type of structured talk as *being* reading comprehension instruction (authors' italics).[80]

It depends, then, on what is meant by text 'comprehension'.

The retrieving/enacting distinction resonates with Nystrand's contrast of 'test' and 'authentic' questions – those that permit only one answer and 'allow the student no control over the flow of the discussion' (test) and those 'for which the asker has not pre-specified an answer . . . [and which] invite students to contribute something new to the discussion that can change or modify it in some way' (authentic).[81] Nystrand initially explored this distinction in the context of university students' writing, setting up groups that wrote with fellow-students rather than their teachers in mind and followed drafting by peer discussion. He found that

> The quality of writing for students who wrote only for their teachers declined slightly over the course of the seminar, whereas the quality of writing for students writing for each other improved slightly; the difference was statistically significant. The same was true for editing skills, grammar and usage. . . . The overriding conclusions were that (a) students writing for their teachers came to see their readers as judges, while students writing for their groups came to see their readers as collaborators; (b) students writing for their teachers came . . . to see revision as a matter of editing, whereas students meeting in groups came to see revision as a matter of reconceptualisation; and (c) students writing for each other developed more positive attitudes towards writing.[82]

Dysthe reports comparable outcomes from her cross-cultural study of the interaction of talk and text with 11th/12th grade students in California and Norway. The overarching finding was a multiplication of voices – of students, in talk, in the examination of texts and through the interaction of all three. Talk-with-writing boosted the confidence of those students previously demoralised by assessment based on their writing alone, engendered more intense levels of participation in the task in hand and pushed thinking forward by encouraging reflection in action rather than at one stage removed.[83]

The advancement of oracy *per se*, as we have seen, was the aim of Voice 21, Oracy Cambridge and the 2019 All-Party Oracy Parliamentary Group, but in opening up 'the interface between the written and the oral'[84] we can pursue a task that is no less necessary and uncover possibilities for student engagement and learning that will take us and them considerably further. And we would do well to leaven our efforts with historical consciousness, starting perhaps with Homer, whose epics *Iliad* and *Odyssey* are believed by most scholars to have originated as oral improvisatory poetry framed by well-established metrical conventions; and then leapfrog the intervening two thousand or so years to explore the most recent and ambivalent additions to the oral-written continuum: email, texting, twitter and popular journalism. And that's before we get to philosophy, whether for children or adults. For (Harvey Graff again):

> The oral and the literate, like the written and the printed, need not be opposed as simple choices. Human history and human development did not occur in that way. Rather, they allowed a deep, rich process of reciprocal interaction and conditioning as literacy gradually gained acceptance and influence. . . . The poetic and dramatic word of the ancients was supplanted, if not replaced, by a . . . religion . . . rooted in the book, but propagated primarily by oral preaching and teaching. . . . Analogously, education long remained an oral activity. The written and

then the printed word were spread . . . via oral processes, and far more widely than purely literate means could have allowed. For many centuries, reading itself was an oral, often collective activity and not the private, silent one we [now] consider it to be.[85]

Similarly, David Crystal reminds us that as late as the sixteenth century, long after the invention of printing, there were no English-medium grammars of English or English-language dictionaries.[86] His reminder also prompts a caveat about Carter's grammar of talk, in as far as it might be thought to over-emphasise the oral-written gap. After all, languages, including those that are highly inflected, develop the regularities that their users *orally* internalise long before the arrival of concepts such as case, tense, voice, mood, verb, noun and so on by which such regularities are later named in pedagogical grammars of their *written* form. And, as the development of English illustrates well, descriptive mapping of standard oral tendencies can lead to prescriptive standards for the written form in which such tendencies are rejected or codified as 'rules'. Then, in a return loop, these feed back from the newly minted grammars for writing into notions of 'correct' or 'polite' speech and – this time capitalised and set in tablets of educational, social and political stone – as Standard English.[87]

Reciprocity and segregation

The educational status of talk and the balance and relationship between the oral and the written is one of the more illuminating though under-researched arenas for cross-cultural pedagogical comparison.[88] Thus, on one side of La Manche/the Straits of Dover, we find England's traditional and unyielding definition of the educational 'basics' as reading, writing and calculation, but emphatically not speaking:

> (1861) The duty of a state in public education is . . . to obtain the greatest possible quantity of reading, writing and arithmetic for the greatest number.
> (1993) The principal task of the teacher . . . is to ensure that pupils master the basic skills of reading, writing and number.
> (1997) The first task of the education service is to ensure that every child is taught to read, write and add up.[89]

Across the water, *le langage oral* is firmly positioned both in its own right and as an essential ingredient of reading and writing and indeed maths: 'C'est dans l'oral que l'on apprend à lire et à écrire, mais aussi à compter'.[90] Here, literacy; there, language. And while in England literacy is defined as a 'basic skill', in France *l'oral* reflects a more elevated nexus – admittedly somewhat frayed at the edges in recent years – of literacy, linguistic skill, literary knowledge, republican values and civic virtues.

Further, until recently England has had nothing comparable to the tradition of oral pedagogy which is fundamental to public education in many continental European countries. Or indeed oral assessment: contrast the private and restrained British PhD viva, terminated by a handshake, with the public and almost theatrical French *défense de thèse de doctorat*, which is attended not only by *le jury* – a phalanx of examiners – but also by friends, family and even casual passers-by, and is rounded by applause and, all being well, is broadcast to the world on social media.

So in England the default learning activity has been writing, writing and more writing, and when Ofsted inspectors ask to check students' 'work' they mean their written work. (In one of my dialogic teaching projects a school head tried to buck the trend by insisting that the inspector treat as evidence a videotape of his students talking. The inspector at first refused, then took the tape with evident reluctance. He returned it if not converted then certainly impressed.) Consequently, when parents hear that their children have, unusually, spent an hour in class discussion, they may well frown and say, 'So you weren't working then.'

The 'vast output' of writing required of England's secondary school students, much of it in the form of mechanical copying of 'notes', was computed and criticised by school inspectors in the late 1970s.[91] Judging by students' complaints, the required output has not diminished since then. And it has consequences: Hargreaves and Galton found a significant drop in students' interest in mathematics and science after transfer from primary schools to secondary. Students themselves put this down to a sudden and striking increase in the time spent on writing compared with what they were used to. Probing this through observation, Galton found Year 7 (US 6th grade) classroom talk in maths and science dominated by closed questions and factual recall answers, with little questioning of an exploratory kind that opened up students' thinking or of discussion that tested their ideas.[92]

Yet, as employers and universities also complain, all this writing practice does not make anything approaching perfect. In 2006, a report from the Confederation of British Industry (CBI) deplored poor standards of spelling, grammar and handwriting among school leavers and the low level of 'functional skill' generally, and found that one in three businesses was obliged to send staff for remedial lessons in the basic literacy and numeracy skills they had failed to acquire in school.[93] That kind of criticism has surfaced on many occasions since then and will no doubt continue to do so, not least because the political party in opposition can use it as a stick with which to beat the party in power.

In as far as there is a problem it must be assumed to be rooted in poor teaching of reading and writing *per se*. But it is also worth asking whether the pedagogical segregation of reading and writing from talk may have contributed to the difficulties that students experience in translating their thoughts into writing, indeed in marshalling their thoughts in the first place. It may also be worth asking how far the perceived decline in the standards of school leavers' written English is related to the loss of oral precision and articulateness of which the CBI study also complains. Certainly, comparative classroom study shows clear differences not just in the way reading and writing are taught but also in the balance of reading, writing and talking, the different capacities which speaking and writing are believed to develop, and the way these relate to each other.[94] And, when we juxtapose the evidence from the large primary-secondary transfer study of Hargreaves and Galton referred to above with the complaints from CBI, we might reasonably deduce that the familiar secondary diet of writing plus recitation not only turns students off but is far from efficient too.

This is a crucially neglected area in British educational debate. Instead, Goody's 'grand dichotomy' between the oral and the written too often persists unchallenged, and opportunities to explore these as Heath's 'overlapping continua' are missed. So, for example, when describing their proposals for oracy education, Mercer and his colleagues are of course right to assert that 'the teaching of speaking and listening skills . . . requires different approaches than those used for literacy'.[95] However, having asserted the difference, they do not mention reading and writing again, and the latter appear to play no part in oracy education as they conceive it.[96]

If, as the evidence strongly and consistently shows, talk contributes to learning and understanding, *a fortiori* it is likely to contribute to learning and understanding *in the domains of reading and writing*. We need a clearer grasp of how this process works. But in dialogue's spirit of reciprocity, we also need to know how reading and writing might in their turn contribute to talk.

Argument literacy: problem solved or perpetuated?

In the United States, this exploration has been encouraged, as we saw in Chapter 4, by the prominence given in the 2010 Common Core Standards to argument literacy, which has no counterpart in England's National Curriculum or Scotland's Curriculum for Excellence. However, in relation to Wells's vision of 'participants mov[ing] back and forth between text and talk, using each mode to contextualise the other, and both modes as tools to make sense of the activity in which they are engaged',[97] much of the new US literature joins the historic one-way traffic from talk to writing and treats the latter as the proper destination. Making texts the objects of oral enquiry, exegesis, discussion and debate, as Schwarz and Baker observe, echoes long-established Islamic and Talmudic practices, and here again what matters is the text rather than the talk,[98] not surprisingly when these are 'religions of the book'. Significantly, Schwarz also reports a study of the impact of *oral* argumentation where teachers monitored the resulting quality of *writing* more frequently and systematically than the talk that was the object of study. Text remains the centre of gravity.

In the US, this is probably inevitable because teachers and researchers are responding to the emphasis on argumentative writing in the Common Core

Standards. Thus, Shi and her colleagues use oral dialogue as a 'bridge from the conversational exchanges that come naturally to children to the written production that does not.'[99] They believe that what can make argumentative writing particularly difficult for students is the absence of audience or inter-locutor (writing what the student thinks the teacher expects to read is not the same), so they treat dyadic/paired student-student oral argumentation as preparation for writing that similarly seeks to persuade other students, in both cases aiming to develop argumentative autonomy by cutting out the teacher, an approach that echoes the university-level studies by Nystrand discussed earlier in this chapter. The Shi study somewhat positivistically makes successful argument conditional on evidence (other tests of an argument's strength are available, and see our earlier discussion of authenticity). However, the study is valuable in the way it requires students to take the role of the other:

> If students are to achieve the balanced, two-sided essays that educators want to see, they must be able to envision the evidence that would bear on the alternative they do not advocate, as well as the one they do.[100]

This appears to presume that all arguments are binary, but this epistemic objection is, I think, probably outweighed by the broader learning gain.

A study by VanDerHeide and colleagues seems at first sight to reverse the direction of travel, but in the end does not. Noting that in the teaching of argumentative writing students may be tramlined by traditional forms like the five-paragraph essay, the tripartite argument format of thesis-antithesis-synthesis or the binary agree-disagree of debate, they show how if argument is approached instead as 'multi-voiced conversational turn', it becomes a more genuinely reflexive process.[101] By this they mean not that students rehearse an argument orally before committing it to paper, but that the template for written argument emulates the to-and-fro of its oral counterpart. Here, the formal or idealised structures of argument – claim, warrant, evidence, counter-claim, rebuttal and so on (see previous chapter) – recede into the background and are replaced by the imperative of each participant listening and responding to the other. Writing is viewed as a 'fundamentally social activity . . . characterized by reciprocity among readers and writers', as proposed by Bakhtin and exemplified by Nystrand, and 'What I say in writing, depends on what others have already said and might say in response to my writing.'[102]

The authors' punctuation is ambiguous here, but re-casting written argument as a social activity is helpful. Yet dependence on the thoughts of highly localised others may constrain as much as extend, while our own capacity to respond to what others have said – or rather, written – depends in turn on who and what we happen to know. In this book, I attempt to develop arguments about the importance of dialogic teaching using conventions of classical argumentation – citing evidence or warrant, investigating claim and counter-claim and so on – but I also enter, hopefully in the spirit of Bakhtin, into a conversation with some of those who have also explored this territory, and that is why I do not merely parade unexamined references in support of assertions but quote and discuss them. But while the conversation about education in general and dialogic teaching in particular is infinite, my own contribution to it is finite, because despite my advanced years I have experienced, read and understood only so much.

Transposed to classrooms, this limitation reminds us that oral discussion and argumentation may be reciprocal but it can also be circular, whereas the value of combining both talk and text in developing students' argumentation capacities is that it exploits the motivational immediacy of oral interaction while allowing participants to venture, through text, beyond the information given. This, for its time, was the revolutionary insight of Lawrence Stenhouse's 1970s Humanities Curriculum Project, which used discussion as the forum for secondary school students' exploration of inherently controversial themes – war and society, family, relations between the sexes, people and work, poverty, law and order, living in cities, and education itself – but constantly refuelled and advanced that discussion by dropping into the pool a succession of text extracts and short articles which were read and interrogated before the discussion moved on. The teacher meanwhile combined the role of neutral chair with, through his or her choice of these texts, judicious prompting towards alternative lines of reasoning in order to maintain balance and ensure progress.[103]

Conclusion

The focus on argumentation in the 2010 US Common Core Standards, and its promotion to the status of a 'literacy', raise interesting questions and concerns of relevance to this chapter's consideration of versions of oracy, the relationship between the oral and the written, and the 'grand dichotomy' to which all too often this is reduced.

First, adding argumentation to today's expanding catalogue of 'literacies' – digital, media, news,[104] financial, creative, emotional, gestural, spatial, physical[105] – has taken 'literacy' well beyond its lexical meaning. The word now serves merely as a banner of educational significance and may have little or nothing to do with reading or writing; except in so far as literacy in its strict sense remains the priority of education systems worldwide, so if we wish to raise the educational status of something, we call it a 'literacy'.

This is analogous with the way the arts have re-branded themselves 'creative industries'. (With this strategy and the planet's precarious condition in mind, we might make 'climate literacy' compulsory in every school, government department and business, while at the same time making it an entry test for aspiring heads of government. Most would fail.) But with 'argument literacy', the second word retains more of its lexical meaning because it entails talk but pivots on reading and writing. Consequently, because the latter two remain high status and high priority activities, *oral* argumentation arrives at the finishing post a poor third, even though in other contexts the importance and pedagogical power of talk are confidently acknowledged. In the interests of argumentation as well as oracy, we need to counter this trend.

Second, we might take 'argument literacy' as a cue to investigate the scope of written material used with students in our schools – stories, novels, poetry, plays, factual books, textbooks and so on; for Newell and his colleagues point out that in US classrooms, texts in narrative or explanatory mode are more commonly used than those that foreground argumentation, perhaps in part because the latter are more difficult to handle conceptually and, in classrooms, socially.[106] That may well be true in UK schools too. Newell's finding suggests that if we are interested in promoting argumentation literacy, we may need to audit the kinds of text to which our students are introduced, not only with argumentation in mind but also and routinely in support of their broader capacity to engage with text and use writing to generate and explore ideas. Here, as we have seen, Reznitskaya and Wilkinson propose helpful selection criteria, as, with P4C in mind, does Robert Fisher.[107]

Third, the argument literacy movement prompts us to consider differences between oral and written arguments. Here I do not mean by oral argument the definitional extreme (see Chapter 3) of argument as quarrel, but something more measured in talk as well as text. Newell and his colleagues note the frequency with which Toulmin's 'layout' of claim, ground, warrant, backing, qualifier and rebuttal is used to frame the teaching of argumentation in US schools, but warn that it tends to elevate the structural and logical over the social, and that 'structural notions of argumentation are necessary but insufficient for analyzing the complex argumentative social practices in specific literacy events.'[108] VanDerHeide and her colleagues elaborate that position when – see above – they contrast argumentative writing on 'formalist' and 'dialogic' lines and suggest that while the former is an intellectually detached exercise, the latter is better able to persuade students of 'the social, ethical and other work that argument talk and writing does in the world'.[109]

Put more simply, a written argument – or its oral counterpart, a prepared solo speech – may be linear, gradated and cumulative. In contrast, an oral argument among two or more people is likely to be less ordered, predictable or sequential; more responsive and tangential; more concerned with persuading or achieving consensus or compromise than with proving something beyond dispute; and of course punctuated by interruptions as participants react to claims when they are made and contribute to the argument as it develops. It may be helpful, therefore, to keep the framework of Toulmin in equilibrium with Walton's typology of dialogic argumentation – persuasion, inquiry, discovery, negotiation, information exchange, deliberation and eristic – for the latter is more attuned to argument as interpersonal process. (Both Toulmin and Walton were discussed in Chapter 4.)

Fourth, these developments should sharpen interest in the wider relationship between talk and text, this chapter's main concern. Exploring and exploiting that relationship, I suggest, is partly what dialogic teaching is about; it is certainly essential to the wider dialogue about teaching itself. However, although Reznitskaya and Wilkinson comprehensively define argument literacy as 'the ability to comprehend, formulate, and evaluate arguments through speaking, listening, reading and writing',[110] and although they show how collaborative classroom discussion is an ideal medium for unpicking and developing argument, much of this burgeoning literature continues to cloak the new 'literacy' in its strictly lexical garb of reading and writing because that remains the priority of basic education.

Thus the major research review by Newell and his colleagues[111] exhaustively trawls the literature on 'argumentative reading and writing' and tantalizingly exposes divergence between cognitive and social perspectives (another 'grand dichotomy'):

> The study of argumentative reading and writing . . . requires an interactive theory . . . that combines the study of argument as cognition with argument as a set of social practices. Currently, literacy research assumes competing images of argumentation that reflect a cognitive/social practices polarization.[112]

The authors then look for common ground between these 'images' or paradigms in the important realm of transfer of the learning acquired in one context to its application in another. However, although they highlight the value of small group discussion and report research that demonstrates effective transfer of this to students' capacity to handle competing claims and arguments in their writing,[113] the direction of travel remains the same: oral argumentation is valued not because it is significant in its own right but because it enhances argumentative writing. Yet in real life, oral argumentation is the form in which most of us, most of the time, engage; and it is undoubtedly an essential capability. That being so, schools should surely use every resource at their disposal, including text, to teach students how to use it themselves and analyse its use by others.

Of course, since the Newell review pretty convincingly shows the power of talk in developing *generic* argumentation capacities – for example, uncovering competing perspectives, assessing an argument's audience impact and believability, clarifying claims and counter claims, developing rival hypotheses, and brainstorming about all of these and more – it adds to our stock of ammunition against the UK government minister's 'idle chatter' put-down and, perhaps equally important, against the somewhat impoverished definitions of oracy that are in current circulation. For there is little point in mounting a discussion about the relationship between the oral and the written if the former is definitionally hobbled at the outset by phrases like 'non-cognitive' and 'communication skills' while the latter is hyped by grandiose intellectual and indeed moral claims of the kind that we quoted from Harvey Graff.

It is to the reciprocal vision so well enunciated by Gordon Wells that I believe we should hold: a vision of talk and text 'enrich[ing] each other through an exploitation of the intertextual relationships between them'; of 'participants mov[ing] back and forth between text and talk, using each mode to contextualise the other, and both modes as tools to make sense of the activity in which they are engaged'; of 'the interpenetration of talk, text, and action . . . [to give students] semiotic apprenticeship into the various ways of knowing'.[114]

Footnote: another way in?

For historical and political reasons touched on previously, recent UK education policy has served the cause of spoken language very badly. The problem, as I have analysed it, has been aggravated by the way ministers have tended to view spoken language as belonging to English/Language Arts and therefore in competition with literacy. The polarising of oracy and literacy, as we have seen, is unsound and unnecessary. But the territorial assumption is also open to question, for while no English/language arts programme is complete unless it gives proper attention to language in all its major forms, the same applies to the teaching of any language.

In England, a foreign language is statutory in Key Stages 2 and 3 – that is, for students aged 7–14. The requirement for younger students was initiated by the Labour government[115] and maintained in the 2011–13 national curriculum review of its coalition successor.[116] In Scotland, the Scottish Government accepted the recommendations of its Languages Working Group that schools should offer students an additional language from Primary 1 (Reception in England, Pre-Kindergarten in the USA) and a second additional language from Primary 5 (Y4/3rd grade), with the entitlement maintained until the end of S3 (Y9/8th grade).

Thus, after decades of being the laughing stock of Europe for the inability of most of its citizens to speak any language other than their own, the education systems of the UK are falling into international line, though not without difficulty, since the historic neglect of foreign languages in schools has produced a serious deficit in qualified language teachers. Moreover, OECD evidence shows that the time devoted to a foreign language in English state schools is as yet, at 4 per cent, much lower than the OECD average, and the expected allocation of 30 minutes a week in primary schools, or 2 per cent of curriculum time, is just too little to have a meaningful impact.[117]

Yet, in relation to our cause, there is one sense in which these developments are encouraging: nobody questions the centrality of speaking and listening to the learning of a second language, and the literature – governmental no less than non-governmental – has given considerable and enthusiastic attention to this aspect, and indeed to that 'knowledge about language' which was advocated in a succession of reports from the late 1960s onwards but fell victim to the curriculum and culture wars of the 1980s and 1990s.[118]

So perhaps foreign language teaching can serve as a Trojan horse for a heightened commitment to spoken language across the curriculum, while the analysis of language both spoken and written (or the KAL of Rosen, Bullock, Cox and Kingman), which is central to foreign language teaching, might be encouraged to apply in the teaching of English/language arts too. That this has not yet happened speaks to subject-departmentalised thinking in secondary schools and subject-compartmentalised thinking in education generally.

Though not everywhere. Elsewhere I have been critical of the Labour government's 2003 Primary National Strategy.[119] It too was weak on spoken language. However, it made partial amends in a document which was published in 2009, just before the 2010 general election and therefore, along with other policies both good and bad, was dismissed as a matter of electoral course by the incoming coalition government. The 2009 document envisaged, for the first time, a 'whole school language policy which brings together English, communication and [foreign] languages', and it explicitly re-introduced KAL while defining speaking and listening as part of both literacy and foreign language learning.[120] In these matters it drew on the 2009 Rose curriculum report.[121] The Cambridge Primary Review went even further in terms of scope and placed, within the domain of 'language, oracy and literacy', 'spoken language, reading, literature, wider aspects of language and communication, a modern foreign language, and ICT and other non-print media.'[122] In respect of KAL, the 2009 DCSF paper added:

> Whole-school approaches to the learning of language, both mother tongue (first language) and a new language, and the processes of teaching and learning, are vital to the coherence of children's experiences during their life in school. . . . Discussing language learning strategies and knowledge about language can result in an increase in the motivation to value language development. . . . Pupils will make more rapid progress in learning a new language if the linguistic concepts they are dealing with are already familiar to them from their own language. This highlights the desirability of making links between literacy-related work in English and foreign language learning. This has implications both for primary language learning and the learning of English for children with EAL.[123]

The 2010 government stifled such ideas at birth, replacing them with the segmented, exclusive and retrogressive framework for English in the 2014 national curriculum to which I have referred. They deserve to be revisited.

Notes

1 Wilkinson 1965; Wilkinson, Davies and Berrill 1990.
2 In July 2019, the MP membership tally of the All-Party Parliamentary Group on Oracy was: Conservative (the party of government) 3, Labour (the official

opposition) 13, Scottish National Party (which is not involved in English education) 1, Cross-bench 1, Liberal Democrat 0, Democratic Unionist Party 0; www.oracyappg.org.uk/about-us (accessed July 2019).

3 Mercer *et al.* 2020, 295.
4 Mercer *et al.* 2020, 295.
5 Alexander 2001, 566.
6 Mercer 2000, 16 (my italics).
7 Vygotsky reaches beyond the context-bound 'social' to the cultural and historical.
8 MacLure, Phillips and Wilkinson 1988.
9 DfEE 1999, 38.
10 Johnson, Hutton and Yard 1992, 5; Norman 1992; Keiner 1992.
11 Alexander 2014, 357–358.
12 DfE 2013b, 18–19.
13 DfEE/QCA 1999a, 1999b.
14 DfE 2013b, 11.
15 Robin Alexander, Neil Mercer and Jim Rose, sailing against a strong headwind.
16 The ministerial red pen is not a metaphor. As a member of the UK's Council for the Accreditation of Teacher Education (CATE) from 1989 to 1994, I was responsible for drafting requirements for the pre-service training of primary teachers for approval by education ministers in the then-Conservative government. The requirements included, among much else, knowledge of young children's development and learning. The ministerial official in attendance warned that if I did not delete this, the minister would do so, because the words 'children's development' smacked of that 'child-centred' progressivism which the government had vowed to destroy: 'We will take no lectures from those who have led the long march of mediocrity through our schools', proclaimed Prime Minister John Major in 1992. 'The progressives have had their say and . . . they've had their day.' (Quoted in full and contextualised in Alexander 1997, 194.) The requirements that survived the red pen were in DES 1993.
17 DfE 2013b, 11.
18 Edwards and Westgate 1994; Stubbs 1989.
19 DfEE/QCA 1999a, 51; DfEE/QCA 1999b, 47.
20 Barnes 1988; Cox 1991.
21 Oracy Cambridge webpage: www.hughes.cam.ac.uk/about-us/research-translation/oracy/ (accessed July 2019). The website cites Littleton and Mercer 2013 as its sole text. See also Mercer *et al.* 2020, 292–305.
22 Voice 21 home page: www.school21.org.uk/voice21 (accessed July 2019).
23 Oracy Cambridge homepage and masthead: https://oracycambridge.org (accessed July 2019).
24 Norman 1992, ix.
25 Mercer 2000, 16.
26 Mercer *et al.* 2020. This is the latest version at the time of going to press. School 21 (2019) has a slightly different sequence, as does Voice 21 (2019). The groundwork is discussed in Mercer, Warwick and Ahmed 2016.
27 Mercer *et al.* 2020, 295.
28 Alexander 2010b, 249.
29 Alexander 2010b, 250.
30 World Bank 2019 (my italics).
31 Bloom *et al.* 1956; Krathwohl, Bloom and Nasia 1956.
32 Alexander 2015c, 2015d.
33 Education Endowment Foundation 2018.
34 Education Endowment Foundation 2019.
35 DCSF 2008, 6.

36 DCSF 2008, 14.
37 DCSF 2008, 13.
38 ICAN/RCSLT 2018, 6.
39 ICAN/RCSLT 2018, 6.
40 ICAN/RCSLT 2018, 5.
41 Goody 1993.
42 Goody 1993, xv.
43 Graff 1991, 382.
44 https://en.unesco.org/gem-report/allreports (accessed July 2019).
45 OECD 1995.
46 Graff 1991, 83.
47 Graff 1991; Bantock 1966.
48 DES 1979; Alexander 2001, 350–355; Alexander and Willcocks 1995, 152–158.
49 I am aware that there is a burgeoning research literature on dialogue and digital literacy, for example, Asterhan 2015; Stahl 2015; Wegerif 2007, 2013; Mercer, Hennessy and Warwick 2017; Major *et al.* 2018; Wegerif and Major 2018; Major and Warwick 2020. However, the oracy/literacy dichotomy centres on text as traditionally framed, so that is my focus here.
50 Goody 1993, 263–264.
51 Tannen 1982, 2; Wells 1999, 146.
52 https://edition.cnn.com/2014/05/15/tech/mobile/guiness-record-fastest-text/index.html (accessed September 2019).
53 Chafe 1982, 36–37.
54 Carter 1997, 2004.
55 Carter 2004, 8–11.
56 DES 1975, 144.
57 Shakespeare, *Hamlet*, Act 1, scene 5.
58 Heath 1999, 111.
59 Labour leader Jeremy Corbyn: www.youtube.com/watch?v=cVENSWFptIM (viewed July 2019).
60 Davie 1982, quoted in Alexander 2008b, 164, as part of an account of Douglas Brown's teaching entitled 'Words and music.'
61 DfE 2013b, 18.
62 Bernstein 1971; Rosen 1972; Edwards 2010; Jones 2013.
63 Heath 1999, 368.
64 Edwards and Westgate 1994, 31.
65 Heath 1999, 375.
66 Myhill and Newman 2020, 363.
67 DES 1979, 82.
68 Scottish poet Douglas Dunn.
69 Alexander 2001, 'Lesson structure and form', 297–321.
70 Alexander and Willcocks 1995, 156.
71 DES 1979, 82.
72 DES 1979, 82.
73 Wells 1999, 146.
74 Wells 1999, 146–147.
75 Myhill and Newman 2020.
76 Graham and Perin 2007, 4 and 16.
77 Wilkinson, Murphy and Binici 2015, 37; Murphy *et al.* 2009.
78 Wilkinson *et al.* 2015, 46.
79 Resnick 2015, 441; Koedinger and Wiese 2015.
80 McKeown and Beck 2015, 59.
81 Nystrand and Gamoran 1997, 38–39.
82 Nystrand 2019, 89, 1986.

83 Dysthe 1996.
84 I have borrowed the title of Goody 1993.
85 Graff 1991, 5.
86 Crystal 2005, 266.
87 Goody 1993, 265–266; Crystal 2005, 222–253.
88 Alexander 2001, 523–524 and 564–569, 2008b, 81–91.
89 From the 1861 Newcastle Commission Report on elementary education, the 1993 Dearing Report on the National Curriculum and the 2007 Government White Paper *Excellence in Schools*. Quoted in Alexander 2010b, 175.
90 Ministère de l'éducation nationale (2010). See also Alexander 2009b.
91 DES 1979, 81–84.
92 Hargreaves and Galton 2002.
93 CBI 2006.
94 Alexander 2001, 339–355 and 563–569.
95 Mercer *et al.* 2020, 298.
96 Mercer *et al.* 2020, 298–302.
97 Wells 1999, 146–147.
98 Schwarz and Baker 2017, 206; Schwarz 2015.
99 Shi *et al.* 2019, 300.
100 Shi *et al.* 2019, 316.
101 VanDerHeide, Juzwik and Dunn 2016.
102 VanDerHeide *et al.* 2016, 290.
103 Rudduck 1976.
104 While most of these stretch even the metaphorical use of 'literacy' too far, news literacy makes sense, because it deals with the *reading* – interpretative rather than technical, but still reading – of words. For a useful text on media literacy, see Janke and Cooper 2017.
105 Kalantzis *et al.* 2016.
106 Newell *et al.* 2011, 276.
107 Reznitskaya and Wilkinson 2017, 137–146; Fisher 2003, 111–119. Both sets of criteria are for upper primary/elementary students.
108 Newell *et al.* (2011), 274–275.
109 VanDerHeide *et al.* 2016, 288.
110 Reznitskaya and Wilkinson 2017, 9.
111 Newell *et al.* 2011.
112 Newell *et al.* 2011, 277.
113 For example, Reznitskaya and her colleagues, again: Reznitskaya *et al.* 2001.
114 Wells 1999, 146–147. Beverly Derewianka offers an all-too-brief glimpse of a more flexible and reciprocal use of the spoken-written continuum in an article that conceives of communication as veering between the 'more spoken-like' and 'more written-like'. Derewianka 2018.
115 DCSF 2009a.
116 DfE 2013b, 226–230.
117 OECD 2014; Holmes and Myles 2019.
118 DCSF 2009b.
119 Alexander 2004.
120 DCSF 2009a.
121 DCSF 2009c.
122 Alexander 2010b, 268–271.
123 DCSF 2009a, 9.

6   Ingredient x

Once upon a time, before the arrival of liquid detergent and when television advertising was in its infancy, manufacturers of washing powders extolled the 'ingredient x' that enabled their products to achieve that dazzling whiteness that left their Stepford extras gasping with perfectly choreographed amazement.

We know why talk is essential to young children's cognitive development and learning. We have evidence that classroom talk that is configured reciprocally and dialogically is effective in relation to tested learning outcomes. But the research literature is less clear about which particular features of dialogic pedagogy exert the greatest leverage, or wherein lies dialogue's 'ingredient x'. We may push the metaphor so far and no further, because the nature of the washday 'ingredient x' was never divulged, and it may not even have existed. Here we must try to reveal all.

The parts and the whole

We start, however, with a caveat about the disaggregation that this quest seems to invite, assuming that it is possible. Take the 2014–17 EEF dialogic teaching project. Each of its two strands, pedagogical and professional, was designed holistically. So although it may have been statistically feasible to weigh the relative merits of, say, the teacher's 'questioning' moves and the 'extending' moves that then probe and build upon students' answers (see Chapter 7), such an exercise would have been logically untenable: for there can be no extending without prior questioning, and extending entails further questions. Each repertoire related to the others as a matter of logic, intent and practice. The same applied to the professional strand: while we exploited evidence showing that mentoring and training are effective tools of professional development, in our project these were interdependent, with mentors using the videos made by their teacher mentees as the primary focus of the mentoring sessions.

For the comprehensiveness of the project's conception of dialogic teaching was one of its defining features and strengths. In bearing simultaneously on talk's aspects and actors, we believed it was more likely to generate an interactive culture or stance that was *pervasively* dialogic than if we had tried to manipulate or train for, say, teacher questioning or feedback alone, or if we had concentrated only on small group or whole class discussion. What mattered, then, was the creation of a classroom ethos that became progressively and – we hoped instinctively – more dialogic in all its aspects.

Generic explanations

The project was comprehensive in another sense: it aimed to have application and purchase across the curriculum. That is why, in the trial, learning outcomes were assessed in three curriculum domains when in most EEF trials they are confined to one. This enabled EEF to venture, in its press release on the project evaluation report, its own ingredient x (the italics are mine):

> The consistent results *across subjects* suggest that the approach may improve children's overall thinking and learning skills rather than their subject knowledge alone. This is backed up by evidence summarised in the Sutton Trust/EEF Teaching and Learning Toolkit [constructed from findings from this and two other EEF projects, Philosophy for Children and Thinking, Doing, Talking Science] that advises that *metacognition approaches – strategies that encourage pupils to plan, monitor and evaluate their learning* – are a particularly effective way of improving results.[1]

Here EEF extrapolate a shared feature from three projects that used different talk-based strategies to advance the same principle: giving students a stake in the planning and evaluating of what they learn, a strategy that echoes the studies of talk and text by McKeown and Nystrand that we considered in the previous chapter. There can be, surely, no co-construction without co-ownership.

Lauren Resnick reviewed a much larger number of dialogic teaching studies before proposing three similarly generic explanations for the score gains achieved by the students involved.[2] First, there is what she calls the 'specific skills' explanation. Students in the projects reviewed by Resnick acquired 'knowledge or skills of performance that can be carried from one situation to another. . . . With repeated opportunities for reasoning through dialogue, students imitate and refine skills that then . . . become available to them in other domains.' This explanation, in fact, is close to that offered by EEF. Dialogic teaching, then, includes pedagogical features that combine to advance students' learning in a range of curricular contexts. Perhaps 'generic' or 'transferable' would be a more exact epithet for these capacities than 'specific'.

Second, Resnick proposes an 'I can learn' explanation, a variation on the 'Pygmalion in the classroom' proposition that students rate themselves as they are rated,[3] so that the heavily judgemental ambience of traditional classrooms causes some to spiral triumphantly up in their views of themselves as learners while others spiral irredeemably down, with learning outcomes following the same trajectories. Dialogic teaching, however, proceeds on the basis that *all* students are capable thinkers and reasoners, and that (Resnick's words, my italics):

> *Students' ability to reason is implicit* when teachers ask them to reflect on their own thinking, to explain what led them to a particular conclusion, to put another student's idea in their own words, or to agree or disagree with an idea that has been presented.[4]

She adds, citing Resnick, Michaels and O'Connor:

> Moreover, these kinds of conversation can change *teachers'* views of their students' abilities by giving teachers greater access to their students' thinking processes. It is not unusual for teachers who have begun to use dialogic instruction to express surprise at how 'smart' their students are.[5]

So, this argument goes, if we believe in our students, make this clear in our dealings with them, and invite them to engage in the kind of reasoning that in IRF/IRE is closed off by the third turn (F/E), they will believe in themselves.

Third, Resnick offers a 'culture of argumentation' explanation. This is about the power of the collective and what Mercer calls 'interthinking'.[6] It also provides a variant on Vygotsky's ZPD and 'what a child can do with help today, he/she can do alone tomorrow' (see page 13). Resnick writes (my italics and insertion):

> In a dialogic classroom, students engage [collectively] in a process of argumentation that has the potential to go beyond any *individual* student's power of reasoning. The students challenge one another, call for evidence, change their minds, and restate their claims, just as adults do . . . in the world outside school.[7]

I have added 'collectively' in brackets to accentuate the counterpoint to 'individual'. The unvoiced final clause here is 'though *inside* school this is precisely what students are not normally expected to do'. In Chapter 7, we shall see that 'collective' heads the list of core principles or criteria of dialogic teaching.

Resnick adds that what matters is the argumentation as such rather than adherence to the rules of argument observed, or at least claimed, by logicians, and that 'the focus is on reasoning and knowledge rather than its forms of expression.'[8] This, again, aligns with EEF's metacognition conclusion, quoted previously.

The synergy between these three explanations, EEF's comment about student ownership and metacognition and key aspects of this book's approach to dialogic teaching will become evident as the next two chapters unfold. Metacognitive transfer across the curriculum was presumed in the EEF project's rationale and design, the randomised control trial appeared to confirm it and in its press release EEF, as we have seen, promoted it. Resnick's 'specific skills'/transfer explanation gives added point to the scope and diversity of the 'learning talk' repertoire that will be explained in Chapter 7. This includes forms of student talk such as explaining, speculating, imagining, analysing, exploring, evaluating, justifying, questioning, discussing and arguing that are equally essential to literary, historical and scientific discussion and enquiry, while Galton's comparison of teachers and creative practitioners working with children shows how these forms are no less fundamental to artistic activity.[9] Similarly, Resnick's 'I can learn' underlines the importance of dialogic teaching's principle of supportiveness, while her 'culture of argumentation' endorses the principles of collectivity and reciprocity.

One further explanation suggests itself. Like EEF, Resnick properly concentrates on the transferability of dialogic habits of *student* talking and thinking across curriculum domains. But the 'culture of argumentation' embraces *teachers* no less than students, and 'I can learn' is most likely to convince the students when their teacher believes 'I can teach' (dialogically). After all, it takes two, at least, to dialogue. One reason why recitation persists is that it enables the teacher to retain control of the trajectories of both lesson content and student behaviour. Exposure to the consequences of publicly and perhaps incorrectly answering 'test' questions[10] is highly risky for students, and in the interest of maintaining their ascendancy, some teachers prefer to keep things that way. Hence the well-documented student counter-culture of classroom risk-avoidance[11] and the tactics that students adopt in response to what they perceive as the prevailing view of 'communicative competence' – by, for example, bidding to answer questions in a way that 'balances the risks of not being noticed against the risks of being ignored as too enthusiastic'.[12]

In contrast, dialogic teaching is predicated on ceding to students a significant degree of control of both content and behaviour, and it therefore transfers some of the risk of public exposure back to the teacher, and not all teachers are happy with that. At the same time, the dialogic teaching principles of collectivity, reciprocity and supportiveness (to be discussed in Chapter 7) aim in different ways to minimise students' sense of risk and their fear of its consequences, because only then will they talk as freely as true dialogue requires; while, through the various teacher talk repertoires, the teacher scaffolds exchanges that guide, prompt, reduce choice and expedite 'handover' of concepts and principles.[13]

Similarly, Galton's suggestive descriptions of creative practitioners working with children show – perhaps as much because they are not teachers as because they work in the creative domain – how they instinctively allow wait/thinking time and democratise control of exchanges: 'Creative practitioners seem more comfortable with silence . . . [and frequently] reverse roles so that the pupils and not the adult ask the questions.'[14] Compare this again with the EEF's deduction that the common feature in its trials of dialogic teaching, primary science and P4C was 'strategies that encourage pupils to plan, monitor and evaluate their learning.'

Resnick extrapolates one more important finding from the studies she reviews from the 2011 Pittsburgh conference: that most of them were able to achieve positive results, in terms of outcomes, retention and transfer, on the basis of relatively short but intensive spells of dialogue. That, too, chimes with the findings of our EEF project, in which an intervention of just 20 weeks accelerated attainment gains by two months; and with those for P4C, which concentrates broadly dialogic activities into one or two intensive sessions each week. We aim for a culture of argumentation, but can be reassured that a little dialogue appears to go a long way.

Specific explanations

In search of additional 'ingredients x', we turn next to two large-scale projects which have tried, empirically, to tease out the specific moves in dialogue that make the greatest difference. Earlier I warned of the dangers of attempting to disaggregate such moves in approaches that are conceived holistically as total pedagogies with interdependent elements. That warning should be kept in mind.

We start, inevitably, with the EEF project. As I have noted, the imposed methodology of an independently executed randomised control trial (RCT) concentrated on the impact of our dialogic teaching package *as a whole* on test score outcomes in English, mathematics and science. It did not look more discriminatingly at cause and effect. However, alongside the external RCT the project team undertook its own diagnostic study of classroom processes and teacher perceptions using interviews and coded lesson videos. The video analysis is particularly pertinent here because it compared lessons from matched intervention and control group classrooms and tracked changes in both groups over time, that is, at the start of the 20-week intervention to which just one of the groups was subject, and close to its end.

The video dataset included 134 lessons in the three subjects tested in the RCT: English, mathematics and science. A report from the project team and two papers by Jan Hardman describe the methodology, including the video coding frame, in full.[15] Here it suffices to note the headline findings.

Lessons in the intervention group – the group whose students made significant test score gains by the end of the programme – showed a marked and increasing divergence from those in the control group in respect of the following features. (Note that the video analysis dealt only with teacher-student interaction in whole class settings: the project itself, in line with the imperative of repertoire, encouraged a wider range of interactive possibilities.)

- *The balance of closed and open questions.* Intervention group teachers made greater use of open questions than their control group peers.

- *Teacher talk moves.* Intervention group teachers made significantly greater use, especially in mathematics and science lessons, of wait time, revoicing (the teacher verifies his/her understanding of what the student has said), rephrasing of student contributions, seeking evidence of the student's reasoning, challenging students' responses and inviting justification of them.
- *Balance of recitation and discussion/dialogue.* Changing this balance in favour of the latter, while not excluding the former, was one of the intervention's chief aims, and with the intervention group teachers it was achieved.
- *Balance of brief and extended student contributions.* Again, the ratio of brief to extended student contributions shifted markedly towards the latter in the intervention group but remained constant in the control group.
- *The repertoire of student talk.* Perhaps most strikingly, students in the intervention group became markedly more expansive in their contributions and exhibited much higher levels of explanation, analysis, argumentation, challenge and justification. Their talk, then, was clearly more dialogic than that of their control group peers.[16]

Taken together, these aspects of teacher and student talk can fairly be presumed to have contributed to the test score gains made by the intervention group students, and bearing in mind the concern I expressed earlier about disaggregating talk moves that are logically interdependent, the fact that our analysis was not able to differentiate the precise impact of the various dialogic features listed is not necessarily a failing.

However, one recent project has attempted to do just this. The 2015–17 ESRC-funded project 'Classroom dialogue: does it really make a difference for student learning?' was led by Christine Howe, Sara Hennessy and Neil Mercer. Bringing complex statistical techniques to bear on coded lesson videos from 78 classes in 48 schools featuring whole class teaching rather than group work, they concluded that the most productive teacher talk moves in respect of student outcomes as measured in the Year 6 SATs (the tests in English and mathematics taken by 11-year-olds in English primary schools) were:

- 'Elaboration invitations', defined as 'invites building on, elaboration, evaluation, clarification of own or another's contribution.'
- 'Elaboration' (i.e. students' response to the previous item), defined as 'builds on, elaborates, evaluates, clarifies own or other's contribution.'
- 'Querying', defined as the teacher's 'doubting, full/partial disagreement, challenging or rejecting a statement.'[17]

These are consistent with the following higher frequency teacher talk moves associated with greater test score gains in the EEF project:

- Revoicing (teacher verifies own understanding of a student's contribution, which requires a student response, e.g., 'So, are you saying . . .?', 'Then I guess you think . . .?').

- Rephrasing (teacher asks a student to repeat or reformulate own or another student's contribution, e.g. 'Can you say that again . . .?', 'In your own words, what did X say?').
- Evidence of reasoning (teacher stays with the same student, or asks another, and requests evidence of reasoning, e.g., 'Why do you think that . . .?', 'What is your evidence?').
- Challenge (teacher provides a challenge or counter example, e.g., 'Does it always work that way?', 'What if . . .?', 'Is that always true?').[18]

In our case, however, the range of higher-frequency teacher talk moves (and corresponding student talk moves) in the intervention group was bigger. Interestingly, science was the anomaly in both projects. In the Howe *et al.* ESRC project, the three moves listed previously were more productive for English and mathematics outcomes than for science; while in the EEF project, it seemed that in science lessons our teachers used more obviously dialogic moves from the outset. We can speculate that the particular character of scientific questioning and reasoning may have been a factor, or – in the case of the Howe *et al.* project – that because science is no longer included in the national tests at age 11, its teaching is lower stakes.

Purists and pragmatists

Another paper from the Howe/Hennessy/Mercer ESRC project[19] raises a rather different issue, and it too resonates with this book's approach. Howe's team used their video analysis to test what they claimed is an assumption by enthusiasts for dialogue that there is not much of it around, and that undiluted recitation remains the default. They showed that although recitation is indeed widespread, the classic IRF/IRE discourse structure is often mixed with moves that can be defined as dialogic.

For those of us who have taught, studied teaching and worked with teachers over many years, this is hardly a revelation. Very few teachers are methodological purists, and although in many classrooms recitation may be the centre of gravity, the dynamics of classroom talk may orbit fluidly and not always predictably around it. Our approach to dialogic teaching has always acknowledged the fact of, and need for, such practical eclecticism, and views it as a strength rather than a weakness – hence the primacy of the idea of *repertoire*. So, as will be seen in Chapter 7, our approach actually includes not only recitation but also the much derided rote, because for certain purposes these fit the bill (the repetition that is rote's signature, for example, aids memorisation), and they therefore have their place in the repertoire of teacher-led talk alongside the discussion and dialogue to which we wish to give greater prominence. Eschewing all educational dichotomies as I have insisted we must, we should also resist the polarising of recitation and dialogue. However, some advocates of dialogue, spurred by proselytising zeal, do just that, seeking an exclusivity in dialogue which is matched by their implacable opposition to recitation. Dialogue is thereby idealised, recitation parodied, and only the two are on offer. That is tough for teachers working in real-life classroom settings, for it may oversimplify the way they work, underestimate the quality of what they achieve, and set standards to which they are expected to aspire which are not so much unattainable as inappropriate.

The inclusiveness of this book's approach to dialogic teaching is, I believe, distinctive. Yet in some commentaries that inclusiveness, and the idea of a generous repertoire that straddles patterns of talk that are both more *and less* dialogic, is missed.[20] I go so far as to suggest that one reason why this book's predecessor proved so popular with teachers is that it spoke not to some unattainable dialogic ideal but to teaching as it is, to its often messy realities, to the tensions, compromises, frustrations and dilemmas that are intrinsic to the job.[21]

Principle, not recipe

Few people have put better than Martin Nystrand and Adam Gamoran the case for inclusivity, flexible repertoire and the need for teaching, however configured, to be driven by pedagogical principle rather than technical recipe (and conversely the need to understand that supposedly dialogic moves may not live up to their billing). They therefore deserve to be quoted at length. The italics are theirs.

> The results of our study suggest that authentic questions, discussion, small-group work, and interaction, though important, do not categorically produce learning; indeed we observed many classes where this was not the case. We also found that recitation is not categorically ineffective; rather, its effectiveness varies depending on whether and how teachers expand IRE sequences. The underlying epistemology of classroom interaction defines the bottom line for learning: what ultimately counts is *the extent to which instruction requires students to think, not just report someone else's thinking.* . . . Authentic questions, discussion and small group work have important instructional potential, but unless they are used in relation to serious instructional goals and, more important, unless they assign significant and serious epistemic roles to students that the students themselves can value, they may be little more than pleasant diversions.[22]

Or, as Michaels and O'Connor succinctly conclude from the evaluation of their Talk Science Project: 'The simple deployment of talk moves does not ensure coherence in classroom discussions or robust student learning.'[23]

Note that Nystrand's 'bottom line' (which he repeats in his 2019 autobiography)[24] is *not* an 'ingredient x' in the expected sense of one or more specific talk moves. Instead, it expresses the *quality and dynamics* of the interaction to be aimed for, allowing for the possibility that these can be approached by different routes.

If readers detect a certain ambivalence in the discussion so far, they are right, for the evidence seems to point simultaneously in two directions. On the one hand, we have the proposition, born of pragmatism, understanding of the dilemmas, tensions and compromises of teaching as it is lived, and an essentially holistic stance on dialogic pedagogy, that what makes the difference is the transformation of classroom culture and relationships. That transformation can be effected by various means, but its trajectory always needs to be towards student engagement, empowerment and metacognition, or ensuring that students have a significant stake in the manner of their learning and the way it is conceived and discussed. It is this that unites Barnes's and Mercer's 'exploratory talk'; Resnick's 'I can learn'; her 'culture of argumentation'; the metacognitive capacities fostered by the three EEF projects; Nystrand's 'bottom line' of getting students to think for themselves rather than report or repeat what others have thought, said and written; Galton's insight from creative practitioners on the democratisation of classroom discourse; the preoccupation of Matusov, Boyd and Markarian with dialogic stance; Wegerif's idea of 'dialogic space'; and, as the corollary of all these, 'I can teach' – the teacher's confidence to offer students much greater agency in their talking and learning than is traditionally allowed, without feeling threatened or de-skilled, and the added confidence that comes from seeing that for all parties this works.

All this supports the principles of teacher repertoire, agency, choice and judgement that are central to this book's version of dialogic teaching. Among the various models of dialogic teaching jostling for space in an increasingly crowded educational market, there is no 'best buy'.

The third turn and the unquestioned answer

On the other hand, the evidence also takes us to a more specific destination. From the Howe/Hennessy/Mercer ESRC study, we conclude that teacher talk moves that encourage students to elaborate their own and each other's ideas have particular potency, and this is confirmed by the video analysis in the EEF project, which showed the significantly higher incidence among intervention group teachers – those whose students made greater learning gains – of revoicing, rephrasing of student contributions, seeking evidence of the student's reasoning, challenging students' responses and inviting students to justify them; and of the consequential repertoire of talk displayed by the students: explanation, analysis, argumentation, challenge and justification. In a similar vein, Nystrand is right to warn against presuming too much of dialogue and too little of recitation, as do Boyd and Rubin,[25] but he also argues that transformative learning is most likely when teachers 'ask authentic questions *and follow up student responses*' (my italics).[26]

This second strand of evidence points unerringly to a particular moment in the typical exchange: the third turn, or, whether the exchange is teacher-student or student-student, what happens after a question has been posed and an answer has been given. In recitation, the third turn is mostly predictable: 'F' or 'E', feedback or evaluation, both usually of a minimal kind. So while among discourse analysts 'initiation' (I) and 'response' (R) are treated neutrally as to intent and character, 'F' and 'E' carry specifically judgemental baggage from the outset.

But does it have to be like that? Neutrality would be sustained if 'F' and 'E' were replaced by a question mark, and indeed that would signal that this is the critical moment of choice: the moment when an exchange can stop or continue, when it can open up the student's thinking or close it down, when feedback can be replaced by feed-forward: IR(?). This is in line with the conclusion of Nystrand and Gamoran that 'recitation is not categorically ineffective; rather, its effectiveness varies depending on whether and how teachers expand IRE sequences.'[27] This, again, supports our principle of repertoire and our warning about polarising recitation and dialogue.

From his classroom observations and recordings, Neil Mercer has extrapolated five recurrent teacher moves that have their counterparts in everyday conversation, seek to 'build the future on the foundations of the past' and begin to fill the third-turn space in 'IR?'. They are:

- *Recapitulation*: summarising and reviewing what has been said or done earlier;
- *Exhortation*: encouraging students to 'think' or 'remember' what has been said or done earlier;
- *Elicitation*: asking a question or questions intended to encourage students to reflect on what they have heard;
- *Repetition*: repeating a student's answer, either to affirm it or encourage alternatives;
- *Reformulation*: paraphrasing a student's response to make it more accessible to others or to improve upon it.[28]

I have re-ordered these (in Mercer's list exhortation comes last) so as to distinguish the two free-standing moves from those – repetition and reformulation – which are embedded in the three-part exchange structure as third-turn alternatives to F and E. (Elicitation can be either.) In fact, they may become so habitual that unless we are careful they may lose their power to stimulate and advance children's thinking. Thus, as Edwards and Mercer note, elicitations may be *cued* – that is, a question may incorporate a clue to its required answer – so heavily that answering questions degenerates into a mere word-completion ritual.[29] Repetition – like praise – may become so habitual, with every final word or phrase of the student repeated by the teacher, that it seems more like a verbal tic than a meaningful response. (Having become aware of this by viewing their lesson videos, teachers in the EEF project became perhaps overly self-conscious about it.) And reformulation may leave children wondering whether their answers are being celebrated, dismissed or charitably salvaged. In such circumstances, the paralinguistic is as eloquent as the linguistic.

No less important, of these five commonly observed moves, only elicitation and reformulation have potential to take a specific answer or statement forward, assuming that they are used deliberately and unambiguously. Yet on their own they hardly constitute a dialogic repertoire. It is not sufficient, then, to repeat or reformulate a pupil's contribution: what is said needs to be reflected upon, discussed, even argued about, and the dialogic element lies partly in getting pupils themselves to do this. Here the activities which accompany questioning in Palincsar and Brown's 'reciprocal teaching' – clarifying, summarising and predicting – may begin to break the question-answer-repetition mould of this barely extended variant of recitation.[30]

Sarah Michaels and Cathy O'Connor have invested particularly heavily in this moment. They agree that repetition on its own may achieve little and treat what they call 'revoicing' (cf. Mercer's 'reformulation') as a more productive alternative to the E (evaluation) move of IRE, because it 'contains a cue to the addressee to accept, reject, or clarify the speaker's interpretation of the addressee's prior utterance',[31] and it can 'create a sense of engagement, or helping the insecure or struggling student make their contribution in ways that can be heard and appreciated by others.'[32]

Of course, the cue needs to be acted on, and the insecure or indeed secure student needs to feel comfortable in taking up the teacher's invitation and then in challenging the revoicing if it is deemed inaccurate or inadequate. In the fascinating paper quoted in the previous paragraph, O'Connor and Michaels recount their painstaking efforts to build on their initial insights about the potential of revoicing and how, through various projects and iterations over many years, these yielded the nine 'talk moves' in their *Talk Science Primer*,[33] all of which elaborate the third turn rather than the first or second, and therefore these moves take as their starting point whatever the student has said and in different ways build on this to nudge the talking and thinking forward. These moves are comparable to, but go well beyond, the 'elaboration invitations' in the Howe, Hennessy and Mercer project.[34] They resonate, too, with the emphasis on *uptake* in the studies of Nystrand and his colleagues, uptake being either 'the incorporation of a previous answer into a subsequent question'[35] or 'when one conversant . . . asks someone else . . . about something the other person said.'[36] Nystrand stresses that 'to qualify as uptake, a question must incorporate a previous answer, not a previous question', because only then can it establish 'intertextual links between speakers . . . [and] promote coherence within the discourse.'[37]

The importance of the work of Michaels and O'Connor here is that it transforms descriptive categories into procedural and linguistic options that have been successfully trialled by teachers: 'say more', 'revoice', 'rephrase', 'add on', 'ask for evidence of reasoning', 'challenge' and so on.[38] Michaels and O'Connor argue that such moves enable the student

> to explicate his or her reasoning so the teacher gains a better sense of the student's understanding and all students can work with it. In the process of responding . . . the student also gains metacognitive and communicative skills that will support more robust reasoning in future turns.[39]

Which also takes us back to our claim that dialogic teaching empowers the teacher as well as the student, because by giving him or her access to the student's thinking it facilitates a precision in assessment for learning that the closed third turn denies. (Like philosophy for children, assessment for learning – AfL – is a field whose ideas display synergy with those that inform dialogic teaching.)[40]

Elsewhere, joining forces with Jie Park and Renee Affolter, Michaels and O'Connor justify their claim that the third turn is pivotal for classroom talk in general and dialogic teaching in particular. Once again, the relevance of their approach to the stance taken in this book is such that I need to quote them at length:

> Why not focus on the teacher's first turn, and the quality of teachers' questions in starting a conversational sequence? Or why not focus on the second turn, exploring in detail what a student says that was prompted by the first turn? Why not focus on an interactive episode as a whole, instead of an utterance? The reason is that the third turn has a special status. . . . The third turn in everyday conversation or the classroom looks both backwards and forward in a unique way. . . . The third turn is where a lot of interesting things happen, things that can position students very differently, with respect to the teacher, their peers, and the academic content under consideration.[41]

That properly cautious phrase 'can position' reminds us that nothing is inevitable. The intention of a cued elicitation, which mirrors the mouthing of the prompter in the theatre wings, is transparent enough: it tells the student exactly what to say. But Mercer's recapitulation/reformulation and Michaels and O'Connor's revoice/rephrase may serve contrasting purposes. In the spirit of dialogue, they may indeed 'help pupils listen carefully to one another . . . share, expand and clarify their thinking';[42] or, in the guise of helpful scaffolding, they may revoice/rephrase in order to keep the student's thinking in line with the teacher's and effect a 'cognitive take-over'.[43] The latter is the risk or tendency that, as we saw in Chapter 4, Segal and Lefstein call 'exuberant voiceless participation'.[44]

Yet provided that we remain alive to Austin's distinctions between an utterance's 'locutionary', 'illocutionary' and 'perlocutionary' force – or the difference between the face meaning, actual intention and consequences of what we say to students[45] – there is indeed an inexorable logic in all this, over and above what the research evidence suggests. For it is the third turn that makes talk dialogic rather than monologic, or fails to do so. A dyadic question and answer (IR) sequence is *dua*logic (two persons) but not *dia*logic, because control of its trajectory rests squarely with the questioner (I). The same applies in the triadic IRF/IRE sequence, because although in commenting on an answer a questioner may stand on the brink of dialogue, the questioner's comment is a unilateral judgement (F/E), and it reinforces rather than diminishes his or her control, so again the talk remains monologic. And it does so epistemically as well as pedagogically. That is to say, the handling of the third turn signals not only whose voices matter but also the extent to which the knowledge with which teachers and students deal is immutable or negotiable, closed or open, singular in its meaning or capable of different interpretations, to be transmitted and dutifully replayed or open to scrutiny and exploration.

This, too, is the double pedagogical force of Bakhtin's celebrated maxim that 'if an answer does not give rise to a new question from itself, it falls out of the dialogue',[46] for it intimates the dialogue of ideas as well as persons. If there is no uptake or extending move, if an answer does not give rise to a new question, then not only is the sequence's forward learning momentum halted, but the thinking, understanding and misunderstanding embedded in the student's answer, and the teacher's opportunity to probe these to everyone's advantage, will also evaporate. Talk is transitory. Talk that matters is more likely to make its mark if it evokes some kind of response than if it passes unchecked; and student talk really does matter.

Perhaps, therefore, in thinking about how our classroom exchanges with students might be improved, we should attend not only to the unanswered question – a familiar enough focus of concern – but also to the *unquestioned answer*.

Whose question?

But there's a sting in the tail: who controls the third turn, and who gets to ask those 'new questions' that, in order to keep the dialogue alive, every answer should prompt?

In teacher-led discussion, whether whole class or small group, that privilege falls to the teacher. James Dillon reports an exercise in which he observed 721 students engaging in discussion in 27 classrooms and heard questions from just eight of them. That's eight out of 721:

> Questions accounted for over 60 per cent of the teachers' talk and for less than one per cent of the students' talk . . . 80 questions per hour from each teacher and two questions per hour from all the students combined . . . not a single question from 713 adolescents nearing graduation from secondary school.[47]

The massive asymmetry of classroom discourse has been recognised as a near-constant since long before 1963, when 'Between the end of the Chatterley ban/And the Beatles' first LP' life was 'never better' for British poet Philip Larkin, but US academic Ned Flanders preferred his self-denying 'law of two thirds': two thirds of classroom time is devoted to talk, two thirds of this talking time is occupied by the teacher and two thirds of teacher talk is direct instruction.[48] This asymmetry was one of the spurs to dialogic teaching, and it is useful to juxtapose Flanders and Dillon because, having formulated his 'law', Flanders continued to treat IRF/IRE as the default for his classroom observation instruments, paradoxically encouraging future researchers to give far more attention to the talk of the teacher than to that of the student, even as they cited his critique of this imbalance in what they were observing. Dillon, in contrast, was so determined to break the mould of asymmetric discourse that he inverted the usual convention of starting with teacher talk moves and began one of his books with student questions, arguing that it is they that are most likely to unlock learning.[49]

Yet Dillon also showed how the teaching culture into which students and teachers have been socialised combines with its unequal power relations to make it hard for even the best-intentioned teachers to generate a significant shift in the frequency and character of student questions as long as they themselves make the initiating moves. So perhaps the most direct way to signal and invite this shift is for the teacher to withdraw so that students have no option but to ask and answer the questions themselves. That, of course, is the essential dynamic of small group discussion, and it is one good reason why, alongside the well-managed third turn in teacher-student exchanges, small group discussion is essential to the repertoire of dialogic teaching.[50] But if Dillon is right, students and teachers need not only to agree to norms or ground rules for discussion in the way that most dialogists advise, but also to ensure that these apply to all parties – for ground rules are more typically confined to how *students* should behave – and that it is the teacher's task, following Dillon again, to 'provide for student questions, make room for them, invite them in, wait patiently for them, welcome the question [and] sustain the asking.'[51]

Conclusion and a meta-analytic footnote

Back, then, to 'ingredient x'. In seeking to understand what it is about dialogic teaching that makes a difference, we arrive at both holistic and atomistic explanations. On the one hand, the sum of dialogue's parts yields a classroom culture, a pattern of relationships and a pedagogical and epistemic stance that together foreground and explicitly signal the empowerment of the student as speaker, thinker, reasoner, learner and evaluator. Such empowerment may by attained by various patterns of organisation, most obviously though not inevitably, and certainly not exclusively, by small group discussion, because when managed well, this turns students from answerers into questioners. It was this transformation that enabled Nystrand's students to use peer discussion so strikingly to improve the quality of their writing.[52] (See Chapter 5.)

On the other hand, studies that have attempted to isolate the points of maximum leverage in student-*teacher* talk converge on the third turn and the various moves through which, at that critical moment, teachers aim more directly to steer the empowerment to which I have referred. The two categories of explanation are complementary, so while it is clear that we should be aiming for nothing less than the comprehensively dialogic classroom, there is considerable practical value in knowing where, in the way we handle the classroom talk from which so much else flows, we and our students might concentrate our efforts: overall dialogic stance and classroom culture, students as questioners, student-student small group discussion, opening up the relationship between talking, reading and writing, enhanced teacher-student exchanges focusing closely on the third turn . . . and more.

There is one piece missing from this explanatory jigsaw: evidence from studies that lie outside the domain of dialogic pedagogy. For to confine our quest for explanations of the power of dialogue to the dialogic literature is to risk missing something important. An obvious port of call is John Hattie's synthesis of 800 meta-analyses of research on the relationship between specific teaching approaches and student learning outcomes.[53]

Hattie's study is as controversial as it is vast, for its judgements of efficacy are based on effect sizes and the research paradigms that produce them, and a great deal of research offering different but equally valuable insight into teaching is thereby ruled out; and his decision to set the bar at an effect size of 0.40 across 800 meta-analyses and over 50,000 individual studies of different kinds, topics and scales may also be regarded as problematic. Further, his synthesis covers relatively few randomised control trials, and, for these, the Education Endowment Foundation (EEF) treats as statistically significant effect sizes lower than 0.40, as one of its senior staff argues:

> Don't take the magnitude of effect sizes at face value. Huge effect sizes (more than +1.00) are most likely the results of poor experiments, but a small size (+0.10) from a large, well-run trial might still be educationally important. Compare like with like.[54]

Hattie's conclusions are mostly congruent with our own, though on the basis of the studies he reviews he is cautious about small group learning and downright sceptical about the teacher as facilitator. However, he elaborates neither strategy in terms that the advocates of small group discussion or P4C, as discussed here, would recognise, equating both with lack of teacher guidance. His preference, again on the basis of the studies reviewed, is for teachers taking a proactive and active role, and he is intensely critical of the general disdain for direct instruction, on the grounds that more often than not it is based on a chalk-and-talk caricature of what actually takes place when the teacher consciously guides the student's learning. Direct instruction, as Hattie defines it, is not a parody of recitation but an approach where:

> The teacher decides the learning intentions and success criteria, makes them transparent to the students, demonstrates them by modelling [and] evaluates if they understand.[55]

But while Hattie finds high effect sizes for specific strategies that are part of dialogic teaching as discussed here – reciprocal teaching, feedback, metacognition, self-questioning – it is his overall conclusion that speaks most directly to our approach. Uncannily echoing our preoccupation with the third turn, and indeed with transfer, he says:

> The art of teaching, and its major successes, relate to 'what happens next' – the manner in which the teacher reacts to how the student interprets, accommodates, rejects, and/or reinvents the content and skills, how the student relates and applies the content to other tasks.[56]

Then, providing a strikingly dialogic corrective to the top-down view of feedback as embodied in classic IRF, Hattie says (his italics):

> It was only when I discovered that feedback was most powerful when it is from the *student to the teacher* that I started to understand it better. When teachers seek . . . feedback from students as to what students know, what they understand, where they make errors, when they have misconceptions, when they are not engaged – then teaching and learning can be synchronised and powerful. Feedback to teachers makes learning visible.[57]

This is of a piece with Dillon's insistence on the need for students to ask their own questions and with our earlier discussion of voice (Chapter 4). Reciprocal teaching finally escapes from the bonds or habits of recitation, actual or disguised, when it entails reciprocal questioning and feedback as well as, or as part of, the extending moves in the third turn. Hattie doesn't go quite that far, but he justly celebrates, under the banner of 'visible teaching – visible learning', those moments when 'teachers see learning through the eyes of the student and . . . students see themselves as their own teachers'.[58]

Squaring the circle between direct instruction and students as their own teachers, Hattie would probably argue, is not as problematic as it may seem, for he reconceptualises direct instruction as necessarily reciprocal, and this quality immediately distances it from recitation. Hattie's meta-analytic syntheses certainly reinforce several 'ingredient x' specifics that we have discussed here, but equally they are in line with our belief in the importance of a *stance* that is identifiably dialogic and pervades the entire enterprise in which teachers and students are jointly engaged.

Notes

1 https://educationendowmentfoundation.org.uk/news/eef-publishes-four-new-independent-evaluations/, 7 July 2017 (accessed May 2018).
2 Resnick 2015, 444–447.
3 Rosenthal and Jacobson 1968.
4 Resnick 2015, 446.
5 Resnick 2015, 446; Resnick *et al.* 2010.
6 Mercer 2000.
7 Resnick 2015, 446.
8 Resnick 2015, 447.
9 Galton 2008.
10 Nystrand *et al.* 1997.
11 Doyle 1983; Pollard 1985; Galton 2008.
12 Edwards 1992, 235.
13 Bruner 1978, 1983, 2006.
14 Galton 2008, 38.
15 Alexander *et al.* 2017; Hardman 2019, 2020.
16 Alexander *et al.* 2017, 8–9; see also Hardman 2019, 2020.
17 Howe *et al.* 2019, 15.
18 Alexander *et al.* 2017, 11.
19 Vrikki *et al.* 2018.
20 One of the more seriously inaccurate accounts is in Schwarz and Baker (2017), an important book to which I refer at several points in the present publication but whose lengthy critique of my approach to dialogic teaching (pp. 48–52) is based on a single early reference (2005) and manages to get pretty well everything wrong. This includes claiming that the approach was unsuccessful, despite evidence to the contrary that was available even in 2005, let alone in 2017.
21 I first explored the notion of teaching as intrinsically dilemma-bound in a video-based enquiry with a group of teachers in the mid-1980s (Alexander 1988, reprinted in Alexander *et al.* 1995). With John Willcocks and Nick Nelson, I revisited the idea in a mid-1990s study of educational change and professional response (Alexander *et al.* 1996), returning to it yet again in a commentary for Lefstein and Snell 2014 (pp. 72–74) entitled 'Triumphs and dilemmas of dialogue'.
22 Nystrand and Gamoran 1997, 72.
23 Michaels and O'Connor 2015, 358.
24 Nystrand 2019, 91–92.
25 Boyd and Rubin 2006.
26 Nystrand 2019, 107.
27 Nystrand and Gamoran 1997, 72.
28 Mercer 2000, 52–56.
29 Edwards and Mercer 1987, 142–146.
30 Palincsar and Brown 1984; Brown and Palincsar 1989.
31 O'Connor and Michaels 2018.
32 O'Connor and Michaels 2018.
33 Michaels and O'Connor 2012.
34 Howe *et al.* 2019.
35 Nystrand and Gamoran 1997, 37–38.
36 Nystrand *et al.* 2003, 145.
37 Nystrand *et al.* 2003, 146.
38 Michaels and O'Connor 2012, 11.
39 Michaels and O'Connor 2015, 348.
40 Black *et al.* 2003.

41 Park *et al.* 2017, 18.
42 Michaels and O'Connor 2012, 11.
43 Edwards and Westgate 1994, 144.
44 Segal and Lefstein 2015, 1.
45 Austin 1962.
46 Bakhtin 1986, 168.
47 Dillon 1988, 9.
48 Cited and discussed in Dunkin and Biddle 1974, 54–57. The facetious Philip Larkin reference is to his poem 'Annus Mirabilis'. 'Chatterley' is just too English to be explained.
49 Dillon 1988, 6–41.
50 Barnes and Todd 1977, 1995.
51 Dillon 1988, 24.
52 Nystrand 2019, 89, 1986.
53 Hattie 2009.
54 Haslam 2018. For the EEF effect size/months' progress conversion table, see: https://educationendowmentfoundation.org.uk/evidence-summaries/about-the-toolkits/attainment/ (accessed July 2019). Comparing like with like, in the case of EEF trials, must include methodological anomalies such as: the absence of pre-test; missing data; the insistence that even if they withdraw from a project before it starts and are in no way involved in it, schools that provisionally agree to take part must be included in the analysis; and a professional development programme that in our case was confined by the terms of the grant to a much shorter period than the research evidence on effective professional development advises. EEF admits that all of these are likely to cause effects to be underestimated (Jay *et al.* 2017).
55 Hattie 2009, 206.
56 Hattie 2009, 2.
57 Hattie 2009, 173.
58 Hattie 2009, 238.

7   Frameworks and fundamentals

So far . . .

At this point, the book changes direction and – as the numbers and bullet points signal – style, so before we proceed a brief recapitulation may be helpful.

Chapter 1 summarised the case for dialogic teaching and described the journey that started in the mid-1980s and led, with diversions and interruptions, to this book. The chapter also argued that the recent brutalising of public and political discourse, and a spreading disdain for truth and well-founded argument, have injected added urgency into efforts to realise the spoken word's educative power.

Chapter 2 reviewed in greater detail evidence on the vital role of talk in children's thinking, learning and social development, and the consequent need for teachers at every level of education to strive to enrich its quality. Yet the well-documented persistence of recitation, overt or disguised, reminded us that this need is still not as willingly or effectively addressed as it should be, while the chapter's cautionary tale of recent curricular and pedagogical initiatives reminded us that language in education, and talk in particular, have always carried a political charge.

Chapter 3 investigated responses to this evidence, many of which aim to unite the cognitive, social and pedagogical under the umbrella of 'dialogue'. However, the term's use across languages, cultures and academic disciplines generates considerable variation in how it is defined and conceptualised, while the contingent term 'argumentation' is equally polysemous. So we categorised the various shades of definition of both of these terms before proceeding via the idea of dialogic stance to a comparison of some of the many versions of dialogic pedagogy now on offer. Their extent of common ground may well be more limited than has been claimed, and there is certainly dissonance between those approaches which are essentially about pedagogical technique in pursuit of any ends and those which – in the Bakhtinian spirit that hovers over all of this book's discussion – seek simultaneously to foster the dialogue of persons, ways of knowing and ways of being, and hence see dialogue as an end in itself.

Chapter 4 considered dialogue in other words and guises, for teaching branded as 'dialogic' neither has a monopoly of effective classroom talk nor says all that should be said about it. *Voice* raises important questions about the control and ownership of talk and the ideas it expresses, and larger questions about student rights and needs, and these challenge the too-easy assumption that dialogue of itself promotes equality. Then, though conceived independently of dialogic pedagogy, we saw how *philosophy for children* develops and exploits talk of a recognisably dialogic kind, and does so within a 'community of enquiry' that takes an avowedly equitable and indeed democratic stance on student voice. It also happens to have been positively evaluated by the Education Endowment Foundation alongside our own approach to dialogic teaching. We then returned to *argument* and *argumentation*, which, when conceived as particular kinds of talk (and writing), have been viewed by some scholars as aspects of dialogue or contingent on it, and recently have been boosted by the high profile given to 'argument literacy' in the US Common Core Standards. In contrast, the UK's official curriculum equivalents take a more restrictedly technical approach to language and, dare we say, a less democratic one.

Chapter 5 continued the examination of dialogue 'in other words' by investigating what among teachers is perhaps the most familiar of its contingent terms: *oracy*. In recent usage, as opposed to the way it was first conceived by Andrew Wilkinson and then applied in the National Oracy Project, the term has been somewhat diminished by branding that aligns it with the reductionist 'skills' movement. Elsewhere, it has been more appropriately coined in order to focus attention on the needs of children and students with language and communication difficulties and to guide therapeutic interventions. So the term is highly problematic. There are also important questions about its relationship to literacy. Here we encountered the 'grand dichotomy' which too often positions the spoken and the written in an unequal or oppositional relationship, and, within formal education, relegates talk to a supporting role. The dichotomy is equally unsatisfactory linguistically, for even though there are clear and obvious differences between speech and writing, these are more validly viewed as overlapping registers. On that basis we argued for, but did not find much evidence of, pedagogies that set the oral and the written in a genuinely reciprocal and dialectical relationship.

Chapter 6 ventured towards synthesis by seeking evidence of 'ingredient x', or the particular property or properties of dialogic pedagogy that exert the greatest leverage on students' thinking, learning and understanding. We initially identified generic outcomes of a clearly enabling kind: cross-curriculum transfer; metacognitive capacities; teachers' more positive views of students and students' more positive views of themselves; and the growing confidence by all parties that comes from acquiring ownership of what is said. Thus far, 'ingredient x' comprised what are probably the minimal requirements for a mutually respectful, lively and productive classroom culture. But we then found, from two recent large-scale projects, evidence of a more specific kind that those talk moves which encourage students to elaborate their ideas have particular potency, and that in all exchanges a great deal hangs on the way the third turn is managed: it may open cognitive doors or, as in classic IRE/IRF, it may close them, and this evidence empirically supports Bakhtin's dialogic maxim about the need for answers always to give rise to new questions.

We then stepped back from evidence generated by the dialogic community itself and found in Hattie's synthesis of 800 research meta-analyses across the entire field of educational research reassuring confirmation that we were on the right track; but also suggestions that the dialogic ideal of reciprocity may need to be taken further than some dialogists realise.

The framework

Although the framework that follows is more extensive than its predecessors, including the one used in the 2014–17 EEF project,[1] it has the provenance of continuity, evolution and application in a variety of educational settings going back to its first iteration in 2002.[2]

The framework's centrepiece is a set of eight dialogic teaching repertoires that aim to help the teacher to engage with essential aspects of classroom culture and organisation, appropriate forms of student and teacher talk, the moves with which these are typically associated, and further moves in the key areas of questioning, extending, discussion and argumentation.

Although we have made much of professional agency, its exercise requires judgement, and judgement entails knowledge, critique and reflection. So using the framework can be neither random nor merely pragmatic, and an explicit educational stance is required, together with justifications and principles, in order to give the framework purpose and coherence in use, and to ensure that what is practised in the name of dialogic teaching is both dialogic in the way we have defined that word and educationally defensible.

Then, in the chapter following this one, we suggest ways that the framework and the book as a whole might be used to support professional development, planning and review in the practice of dialogic teaching.

The framework is in nine sections, three of them explanatory and the remaining six constitutive.

- Purpose
- Distinctive features
- Differences between this and earlier versions
- Definitions
- Stance
- Justifications
- Principles
- Repertoires
- Indicators

Purpose

The framework's purpose is to identify and explain the nature, dimensions and elements of this book's approach to dialogic teaching as it might be applied. The framework is both descriptive and prescriptive. It is conceived as a comprehensive pedagogy rather than a strategy for managing specific talk situations such as group work.

Distinctive features

The framework has six segments:

1   *Definitions.* These cover both dialogue as such and dialogic teaching, for the two are not synonymous.
2   *Stance.* This expresses the rationale for the approach as a whole.
3   *Justifications.* These summarise the main educational arguments for talk of the kind proposed.
4   *Principles.* These guide the application of the repertoires and provide criteria whereby the overall dialogic quality of the resulting teaching can be judged.
5   *Repertoires.* Teachers draw on these according to circumstance and need, ideally reconciling professional agency with dialogic principle. The repertoires include *settings* for dialogic teaching, some of its *forms*, and some of its salient *transactions* and *moves*.
6   *Indicators.* Replacing the 61-item list in earlier versions, this now proposes just 15 broad indicators of dialogic teaching.

Commentators have responded to previous versions in different ways. Some have concentrated on the principles and bypassed the rest, including the all-important ideas of repertoire and agency. Others, conversely, have dwelled exclusively on the repertoires and indicators and have therefore concluded that the approach is essentially pragmatic and technicist.[3]

What seems to cause difficulty to some commentators is the idea that repertoire and agency can co-exist with principle and stance. This juxtaposition may well provoke tensions – which, as any teacher striving to reconcile circumstances with ideals will affirm, is hardly novel – but it is surely possible to exercise choice in a principled way, and indeed to presume otherwise is somewhat insulting to those many teachers who achieve this synthesis.[4] Equally, there will be other teachers who prefer to pick and choose, perhaps adopting or adapting those ideas that appeal to them. Criticism of these teachers, too, is not so much presumptuous as unrealistic, for domesticating novel ideas and practices, rather than implementing them precisely as they stand, is what thinking professionals generally do. In any case, practice is always 'theory-soaked', and every teacher operates on the basis of – at the very least – a relational and epistemic stance of some kind, even though it may not be explicit.

Differences between this and previous versions

I ought to have kept a copy of the first (2004) edition of *Towards Dialogic Teaching*, but, having revised it, I didn't. However, the first North Yorkshire evaluation report (2003) and a 2005 conference keynote[5] retained the dialogic teaching framework more or less as it was initially adumbrated in 2002. It included, alongside justifications and principles, just three repertoires: 'organising interaction', 'teaching talk' and 'learning talk'. Over the next decade, these were refined and expanded so that in the version trialled in the 2014–17 EEF project the initial repertoire trio was supplemented by three more: 'everyday talk', 'questioning' and 'extending'.[6] In the present (2020) version, there are eight repertoires, and the treatment of discussion, deliberation and argumentation is more explicit. The rationale for the framework as a whole, and for each of its parts, is also more fully explained, and the repertoires that focus on talk moves are more detailed than they were. I have also revised and reduced the indicators: in previous versions these were somewhat repetitious, and the elaboration of the repertoires has made many of them redundant.

Despite these changes, I hope that those who found earlier versions useful will feel that their spirit, if not their format, has been retained, and that this version adds value. Now to the framework itself.

1   Definitions

Dialogue is defined here as the oral exchange and deliberative handling of information, ideas and opinions.

Dialogic teaching is a pedagogy of the spoken word that harnesses the power of dialogue, thus defined, to stimulate and extend students' thinking, learning, knowing and understanding, and to enable them to discuss, reason and argue. It unites the oral, cognitive, social, epistemic and cultural, and therefore manifests frames of mind and value as well as ways of speaking and listening.

2   Stance

Frames of mind and value take us from definition to stance, or to the point where dialogic teaching becomes a promising candidate for the list of problematic 'keywords' that Raymond Williams might have investigated, had he been alive today and had his celebrated 1970s exercise ventured rather further into the educational sphere than it did.[7]

The problem arises partly because our lexical definitions of dialogue and dialogic teaching are multifaceted, and partly because each of the facets in question is in itself less than straightforward, while some are contentious.

The statement that best encapsulates our stance first appeared as one of the 12 core aims for public education on which the late Michael Armstrong and I worked during 2008[8] and which were proposed in the final report of the 2016–10 Cambridge Primary Review. There, alongside aims concerning the development of the individual and the individual's relationship to others and the wider world, we proposed four that unpacked 'learning, knowing and doing' in the more immediate context of the classroom.[9] The last of these, uniting the others, was 'enacting dialogue', and it is quoted here in full. In recognition of the wider sectoral reach of this book, I have replaced 'child'/'children' in the original by 'student/students'.

Enacting dialogue

To help students grasp that learning is an interactive process and that understanding builds through joint activity between teacher and student and among students in collaboration, and thereby to develop students' increasing sense of responsibility for what and how they learn.

To help students recognise that knowledge is not only transmitted but also negotiated and re-created; and that each of us in the end makes our own sense out of the meeting of knowledge both personal and collective.

To advance a pedagogy in which dialogue is central: between self and others, between personal and collective knowledge, between present and past, between different ways of making sense.[10]

In Chapter 3 we identified eight dimensions or foci of a pedagogical stance: developmental, relational, procedural, ratiocinative, epistemic, cultural, ethical and ontological. It will be seen that 'enacting dialogue' includes all of these:

- Teaching and learning as uniting the cognitive and social (developmental, relational, cultural, procedural);
- Education as progress towards self-direction and the acceptance of accountability (developmental, relational, ethical, cultural);
- Understanding as the product of encounters between different ways of arguing, knowing and making sense (ratiocinative, epistemological, cultural, procedural);
- Education as a growing consciousness of where, in relation to other people, other minds, other places and other times, we stand (developmental, relational, cultural, ontological).

If the ghosts of Vygotsky, Dewey and Bakhtin can be glimpsed here, I raise no objection and hope they don't either. Whether the stance amounts to a philosophy, or perhaps an ideology, is for others to decide. At the end of his exhaustive and perhaps exhausting exercise in defining 'ideology' for his *Keywords*, Raymond Williams caustically commented: 'In popular argument . . . sensible people rely on *experience*, or have a *philosophy*; silly people rely on *ideology*.'[11] As a teacher used to write alongside statements in my student essays that were questionable but not entirely beyond redemption: 'H'm . . .'.

3 Justifications

A dialogic stance such as that presented above embodies, in itself, justifications for the practice undertaken in its name. However, teachers reflecting on how talk is handled in their classrooms may find more focused justifications useful, and those contemplating a dialogic turn will wish to convince themselves of its value. They may also find themselves having to defend their preoccupation with talk to sceptical parents, governors, inspectors and even colleagues. For such encounters, this book's previous chapters should be helpful. However, it may also be useful to have the following eight portmanteau justifications to hand.

- *Talk for thinking.* Talking and thinking are intimately related. Language builds connections in the brain; during the early and pre-adolescent years, pre-eminently so. As we talk and exchange thoughts with others, so do we learn to think for ourselves.
- *Talk for learning.* Learning is a social process, and talk helps to scaffold thinking from the given to the new. Within classrooms, talk also engages students' attention and motivation, increases their time on task and produces observable and – where appropriate measures exist – measurable learning gains.
- *Talk for mastery.* Through talk, students deepen their understanding within each curriculum domain, subject or area of learning, acquiring familiarity with its register, taking ownership of its language and concepts, and achieving epistemic fluency and mastery.
- *Talk for communicating.* We use language of all kinds to exchange and negotiate meaning and engage in everyday transactions; but it is principally through spoken language that we do so.
- *Talk for relating.* Talk builds and consolidates social relationships and gives us the confidence and competence to handle them. Reading and writing are largely solitary (though they do not need to be) and, in some circumstances, competitive too. Talk by its nature is interactive and ideally collaborative and inclusive. 'Ideally', because at one end of the argument continuum it may also be confrontational.
- *Talk for acculturation.* Talk expresses and helps us to engage with what we have in common with others in our community and culture. It locates the individual within society, and society within the individual.
- *Talk for democratic engagement.* Talk is vital for civic participation and engagement. Democracies, and institutions at every level within them, need people who can argue, challenge, question, present cases and evaluate them; and who can test the argument and rhetoric of others.
- *Talk for teaching.* Well-structured talk gives teachers access to students' thinking and thereby helps them to diagnose needs, devise learning tasks, probe understanding, assess progress, provide meaningful feedback, and support students through the challenges they encounter; and hence teach more effectively.

4   *Principles*

What *kind* of talk, then? The following six principles (five in earlier versions) are intended both to guide the planning and conduct of classroom talk and to serve as criteria for judging how far it can fairly be called 'dialogic'. In a sense, therefore, the principles operationally or behaviourally gloss the definition, stance and justifications above.

- *Collective*. The classroom is a site of joint learning and enquiry, and, whether in groups or as a class, students and teachers are willing and able to address learning tasks together.
- *Supportive*. Students feel able to express ideas freely, without risk of embarrassment over contributions that are hesitant or tentative, or that might be judged 'wrong', and they help each other to reach common understandings.
- *Reciprocal*. Participants listen to each other, share ideas, ask questions and consider alternative viewpoints; and teachers ensure that they have ample opportunities to do so.
- *Deliberative*. Participants discuss and seek to resolve different points of view, they present and evaluate arguments and they work towards reasoned positions and outcomes.
- *Cumulative*. Participants build on their own and each other's contributions and chain them into coherent lines of thinking and understanding.
- *Purposeful*. Classroom talk, though sometimes open-ended, is nevertheless structured with specific learning goals in view.

These six principles subdivide. Collectivity, supportiveness and reciprocity characterise the classroom culture within which dialogue is most likely to prosper, its learning potential has the best chance of being realised, and students will be most at ease in venturing and discussing ideas. Of these three, collectivity and reciprocity set parameters for dialogue as behaviour, but supportiveness is its affective essential, a *sine qua non* for talk that has the freedom that dialogue implies and which liberates but also protects the student's voice in the various senses explored in Chapter 4. Meanwhile, reciprocity and deliberation bridge talk's context and content, for they reflect and steer the relationship of ideas as well as people. Cumulation attends more specifically to the epistemic content and trajectory of talk, transforming it from conversation into a dialogue of meaning as well as moves.

As the final principle – purposefulness – reminds us, classroom discussion, though valuable and even enjoyable in itself, differs from everyday social discussion in that it is a means to an educational end. It must therefore square the circle of a Bakhtinian commitment to dialogue as theoretically unending with a time-limited commitment to the student's understanding and mastery of specific ideas. Similarly, attention to the principles of cumulation and deliberation, which underpin enquiry and knowledge growth in academic communities as well as classrooms, ensures that discussion is genuinely dialectical yet builds on what has gone before, advances understanding and is not merely circular. Deliberation also reflects this book's concern with the need to build students' argumentation capacities for use both in the class-room and in those public, institutional and political spheres where argument is too often debased or traduced.

Cumulation, we have found, is the most difficult of the principles to enact. Collectivity, reciprocity and supportiveness require us to modify classroom organisation and relationships, and most teachers in our various develop-ment projects were able to make these adjustments. But cumulation makes demands, simultaneously, on the teacher's professional skill, subject knowl-edge and insight into the capacities and understanding of each of his/her students. Except in a context where teachers take a strictly relativist view of knowledge, cumulation requires the teacher to match discourse to learner while respecting the form and modes of enquiry and validation of the subject being taught, seeking then to scaffold understanding between the student's and the culture's ways of making sense.

The essential tool here, as we noted towards the end of Chapter 6, is a degree of reciprocity that includes not only the exchange of ideas but mutuality in feed-back and questioning too. Compounding the challenge, cumulation also tests the teacher's ability to receive and review what has been said and to judge what to offer by way of an individually tailored response which will take learners' thinking forward, all in the space of a few seconds, hundreds of times each day.[12]

Incidentally, to avoid confusion and as an example of the definitional mine-field that is dialogic teaching, we note that Mercer and Littleton give 'cumula-tive' and 'cumulation' different meanings from mine. They characterise talk as 'cumulative' when 'speakers build positively *but uncritically* on what oth-ers have said'.[13] While excluding critical interventions may meet our second criterion (supportiveness), this may discourage argumentation and propel discussion towards premature or unfounded consensus, thereby foreclosing cumulation of the more exacting kind referred to in the previous list. Within the dialogic teaching framework outlined here, our definition of cumulation is closer to 'accountable talk' as defined by Resnick, Michaels and O'Connor:[14] 'Speakers make an effort to get their facts right and make explicit their evidence behind their claims or explanations. They challenge each other when evidence is lacking or unavailable.'[15] Mercer and Littleton classify this kind of talk as 'exploratory', which suggests that their use of the term 'cumulative' deals more with the social relations of talk than with its substance and trajectory.

This may be simply a problem of dictionary definitions: lexically, 'cumula-tion' means not only accretion but also growth and gain, whereas 'accumu-lation' signals mere increase. Perhaps, then, confusion would be avoided if Mercer and Littleton were to characterise the expanding but uncritical talk they have in mind as 'accumulative'. We return to this matter when explain-ing repertoires 7 and 8, Discussion and Argumentation.

The six principles are not confined to any one preferred pattern of organ-isation, and our interest in building a comprehensive pedagogical repertoire contrasts with, say, Mercer's initial preoccupation, following Barnes and Todd,[16] with the particular benefits of small group discussion,[17] which in the present model is just one of the several patterns of interactive organisation that dialogue can enrich, albeit an important one that should be fully exploited. As we work through the repertoires, this will become clearer.

5 Repertoires

Why repertoire?

There are four main arguments for making the idea of repertoire central to our approach.

First, teaching is more complex than any single 'best practice' formula can possibly accommodate. The notion of 'best practice' is in any case deeply flawed. Who decides what is 'best'? On what warrant or evidence? Is my 'best practice' also best for you and everyone else? Is it even 'best' for all the circumstances that I myself am likely to encounter? Is 'best practice' ever anything more than an attempt to corner the market or impose on the unwary?[18] The repertoires acknowledge and speak to this complexity, but in a way that tries to bring to it a degree of order and principle so that it becomes possible to talk about the decisions and dilemmas of teaching on the basis of a shared language.

Second, across classrooms, and even cultures, teachers and teaching may have much in common; and in the *Culture and Pedagogy* research, the task of determining and defining such invariants was an essential preliminary to analysing classroom data from the very diverse contexts and settings that we encountered.[19] At the same time, each classroom's dynamics, and each of its encounters between teachers and students, is unique. Teaching therefore requires the exercise of a succession of *choices* and *judgements*. Some of these may be considered and planned; many others must be instantaneous. In both cases, but especially the latter, our ability to make the right choice and the right decision is greatly enhanced if we not only have a good range of options at our fingertips but have also internalised these to the extent that we don't need to think too long or hard about them before acting. The dialogic teaching repertoires are an attempt to set out some of these options in relation to the handling of classroom talk.

Third, if teaching is about judgement and choice, and every setting and encounter is to an extent unique, then it is the teacher, and only the teacher, who can decide what to do and how to act. The other side of the repertoire coin, therefore, is *agency*. But dialogic teaching, as we have made clear, aims to liberate the voice and thinking of the student, so in the dialogic classroom agency is indivisible, and the imperative of acquiring and internalising options applies to the student too. For that reason, our framework includes repertoires of both teacher and student talk. Indeed, it is towards the expansion and application of the student's repertoires for talking, thinking and reasoning that our efforts are chiefly directed.

Fourth, repertoire is a corrective to the dichotomising tendency that has long been endemic in education.[20] Here are some familiar examples, all made adversarial rather than merely binary by the use of vs (versus): student-centred vs teacher-centred (or subject-centred); informal vs formal; progressive vs traditional; process vs product; knowledge vs skills; whole class teaching vs group work; instruction vs discovery; ability vs effort; basics vs breadth; learning vs teaching; and, of course, recitation vs dialogue. There are many others.

Not one of the dichotomies exemplified here is tenable, and some are meaningless. Those that do mean something treat as incompatible what are in fact complementary. We can and should develop students' knowledge *and* skill, and indeed – as discussed in Chapter 5 – most if not all skills acquired through education depend upon knowledge. The sensible teacher mixes whole class teaching with group work and indeed other patterns of organisation. Teaching is of itself the aspiration and, hopefully, the achievement of bringing about learning. A curriculum can and should combine 'basics' with breadth, and indeed school inspection evidence shows that the 'basics' are most successfully taught as part of a broad and rich curriculum.[21] And, in the present context, recitation and dialogue may be very different kinds of classroom talk, but a genuinely dialogic view of dialogic teaching – that is, one that encourages dialogue about its own assumptions – allows for the possibility that recitation may have a place too.

Dichotomies, then, force us to take sides and reduce our options, and while their linguistic or logical frailties can readily be exposed, sense isn't what they are primarily about. In claiming, 'We teach children, not subjects' – an evident nonsense because teachers do both – users of this phrase may be less interested in semantics than in demonstrating that they are on the right side, and in this respect, 'We teach children, not subjects' functions more as a shibboleth in its original, Biblical sense: a password that when uttered correctly and with conviction secures safe (cultural) passage.[22] Yet:

> Naive dichotomous representations of complex realities persist in part because there is unfilled conceptual and political space in which they can flourish. People polarise either when it serves their personal or collective interests to deny the possibility of a middle ground, or when they know no other way.[23]

And, with today's polarised and polarising public discourse in mind:

> In a context where political rhetoric is bounded by the atavism of us and them, the free and the oppressed, the chosen and the damned, to corral educational ideas and practices into the warring camps of 'traditional' and 'progressive' appeals not just to lazy minds but also to more alert calculations about how the world is best represented for the purposes of selling newspapers and winning elections.[24]

Repertoire provides the 'both . . . and' corrective to 'either . . . or',[25] while agency frees us of the obligation to join this camp, that camp or indeed any camp, including those branding themselves as 'best practice'. It thus illustrates an ontological stance as well as a pedagogical one.

Talk in its pedagogical context

Although much of the literature examines talk in isolation, if we wish to translate the evidence into viable practice it is essential to understand how talk relates to other aspects of teaching and to the classroom setting and culture.

The 'irreducible' proposition about teaching that we encountered in Chapter 3 –

> *Teaching, in any setting, is the act of using method x to enable students to learn y.*

– has a corollary:

> *Teaching has structure and form; it is situated in, and governed by, space, time and patterns of student organisation; and it is undertaken for a purpose.*

For the *Culture and Pedagogy* data analysis, these linked propositions were translated into a model containing (i) three broad analytical categories: the context or *frame* within which the act of teaching is set, the *act* itself and its *form*; and (ii) a set of elements within each such category. Thus, *task, activity, interaction* and *assessment*, the core acts of teaching, are framed by *space, student organisation, time* and *curriculum*, and by *routine, rules and ritual*. They are given form, and are bounded temporally and conceptually, by the *lesson* or teaching session.[26] (See Figure 7.1.)

Here, *interaction* is our main interest, so most of the following repertoires are in effect its sub-categories. Repertoires 1 and 2, however, both enable and reflect the interaction's character.

Frame	Form	Act
Space		Task
Student organisation		Activity
Time	Lesson	
Curriculum		Interaction
Routine, rule and ritual		Assessment

Figure 7.1 A generic framework for investigating teaching

Note: Alexander 2001, 325

What do the repertoires comprise?

For the purposes of systematic analysis of classroom discourse, one of the best-known frameworks is that developed during the 1970s by Sinclair and Coulthard. In application, it revealed the ubiquity of IRF/IRE and prompted its further study.[27] Modelling their framework on Halliday's grammatical hierarchy (sentence, clause, group, word, morpheme),[28] Sinclair and Coulthard proposed five spoken discourse 'ranks': lesson, transaction, exchange, move and act. *Acts*, which are irreducible, include, among others, 'elicitations', 'directives' and 'informatives'. They combine to form *moves* such as, in IRE, questions, responses and evaluations. Taken together in their turn, a related sequence of moves forms an *exchange*, one such, again, being the IRE: question + response + evaluation. A sequence of linked exchanges, for example when one IRE leads to another, forms a *transaction*. We might wish to interpose a further rank between transaction and lesson, the *episode*.

In the comparative analysis of lesson discourse in the *Culture and Pedagogy* data, we undertook structural analysis at the level of the lesson and discourse analysis from the levels of episode and transaction down to act, working from both video and transcript.[29] Our task here, however, is somewhat different: we aim to identify the main *kinds* of talk (for the moment I use a neutral and non-technical collective noun) that together offer teachers a valid and workable basis for thinking about their practice, not only in private study or collective discussion away from the classroom but also 'thinking in action' – while they are actually teaching and interacting.[30] In the latter context, up against the constraints of time, attention and purpose, and mindful of 10, 20, 30 or 40 pairs of eyes and ears of varying degrees of alertness and goodwill, it is just about possible to think in action about transactions, exchanges and moves as they gallop inexorably by, but probably not about acts. Further, I am impressed by the argument of Michaels and O'Connor that, for teachers themselves, the *move* is probably the level that most repays attention,[31] especially as it chimes with the 'ingredient x' evidence discussed in the latter part of Chapter 6.

Consequently, the repertoires are framed somewhat eclectically and selectively. They include broad forms and functions of talk that extend across exchanges and transactions, for example, discussion and argumentation; enabling patterns of classroom organisation such as whole class teaching and group work; norms for talk which are as much about the student's attitude and relationship to others as talk itself; and specific moves such as questioning and extending. The complete scheme is summarised in Appendix 1 (pages 200–03). It will be seen that the repertoires fall into three groups:

- Culture and organisation (repertoires 1 and 2)
- Patterns of exchange (repertoires 3 and 4)
- From transaction to move (repertoires 5, 6, 7 and 8).

Being the engine of dialogic teaching, the moves are described in greater detail than the exchanges and transactions that they create.

Repertoire 1: Interactive Culture

Productive classroom talk requires a shared understanding of the way talk should be managed. Mostly this is tacit, but in some classrooms explicit 'ground rules' are prominently displayed. For example: 'We listen carefully . . . We look at the speaker . . . We respect others' ideas . . . We talk one at a time . . . We don't interrupt . . . We don't hog the conversation . . . We give others time to think'[32] (though with older students displaying such rules would almost certainly be viewed as demeaning). In a dialogic classroom, needless to say, ground rules should be observed by all parties, not just the students. Ideally, too, ground rules should arise from discussion. Researchers agree that lists of ground rules should be kept short: between three and five (Michaels and O'Connor) or four or five to begin with (Reznitskaya and Wilkinson).[33]

Norms for the management of talk form part of the wider framework of routines, rules and rituals that shape and maintain the culture of the classroom.[34] A routine is a procedure which through habit and use becomes unvarying. However, 'routine' also shades into the weak sense of 'rule' as a routine to which is added an expectation that the unvarying procedure in question is required rather than merely habitual; while, in its strong sense, a rule is an explicit direction, requirement or regulation which must be obeyed and whose transgression may well invoke sanctions. 'Ritual' stands slightly apart from the routine-rule continuum when it signifies a prescribed and established ceremony, though here again the word has both a strong and a weak sense. There is the world of difference between the grand ritual events of church, temple, state and indeed school and what people choose to call their 'daily rituals', which may be little more than routines or habits.

In the management of talk, then, what we aim for are procedures that may well start as explicit norms but progressively, and we hope quickly, become routinised through reinforcement and use. Discourse norms or ground rules, then, are not procedural add-ons but an essential part of what Michaels and O'Connor call the 'culture of productive talk.'[35] They are necessary, Osborne argues, because researchers agree that students do not instinctively know how to work together and therefore need to be taught.[36] However, we shall see later that the work of Douglas Barnes and Frankie Todd suggests that students might be given a little more credit in this matter.

In the *Culture and Pedagogy* classroom data we identified five broad categories of rule and routine, or aspects of classroom life in relation to which rules and routines were evident in our five countries: *temporal, procedural, behavioural, interactive, linguistic* and *curricular*. Of these, behavioural and interactive aspects of classroom life were by far the most prominent focus for explicit rules and embedded routines, and most of these governed turn-taking,[37] or the way in which 'transitions [are] managed from one speaker or topic to the next . . . turns at speaking are bid for, claimed, taken and conceded.'[38]

In the literature on dialogic teaching, ground rules are a common response to the view that classroom discussion is most likely to be effective if it is managed in a way that eliminates the gamesmanship of bidding and equalises students' opportunities to speak. That takes us back to the problematic issue of 'voice' discussed in Chapter 4. There, it will be recalled, we placed talk in the context of *rights:* the right of every student to speak and be heard and, indeed, to remain silent; the right of teachers as well as students to enter controversial territory without fear of complaint or sanction; and the obligation of all participants to recognise that talk is easier for some students than others and to develop appropriate sensitivity.

If after due consideration some readers feel that the phrase 'ground rules', as used by other writers on dialogic teaching, is too suggestive of imposition rather than consent, control rather than facilitation, or uniformity rather than diversity, then 'discourse norms' may be preferable though less tidy, and voice should be regarded as the proper point of entry. Mercer himself notes that the term 'ground rules' has been imported from competitive field sports,[39] so even though he goes on to commend it for non-competitive discussion, that may be a good reason why we should *not* do so. (If one student is verbally off-side do the others have a free kick?) Voice, in contrast, approaches the management of talk from the standpoints of equity, rights and needs, and of academic freedom rather than regulation and arbitration.

Either way, discourse norms may be categorised. Rezniskaya and Wilkinson differentiate 'social' and 'cognitive' norms,[40] though since dialogists argue that dialogue *unites* the social and cognitive, it may be safer to consider alternatives. I prefer a tripartite distinction that covers both the relational and epistemic aspects of classroom discourse:

- *Communicative norms* concern the transactional character of discourse. For example: 'we listen carefully to each other', 'we make eye-contact with the person who is speaking or whom we are speaking to', 'we don't interrupt or talk over someone else', 'we don't dominate the discussion', 'we encourage others to speak', 'we give each other time to think'.
- *Deliberative norms* govern the handling of discussion, deliberation and argumentation. Here we might find: 'we state our position as clearly as possible', 'we try to distinguish between fact and opinion', 'we give reasons or evidence for what we claim', 'we are prepared to challenge what has been said, but also to say why', 'we state our position but are also prepared to modify it in the light of others' questions and comments'.
- *Epistemic norms* relate to the specific content of the discussion, so they may vary between curriculum domains and perhaps between lessons

within a domain too. I refer here to norms for managing domain-specific discussion rather than the specialist vocabularies of school subjects, though because speech genres are about ways of thinking and modes of meaning as well as forms of talk, boundaries are fluid.[41] If initiation into – say – scientific, historical or mathematical thinking is a process of paradigmatic socialisation and a conscious move away from 'common sense' explanations, it dictates specialist reasoning norms as well as specialist vocabularies. Referring back to the discussion of voice in Chapter 4, these norms will address the handling of sensitive or controversial language and ideas in domains such as literature, history and citizenship.

This section is limited to encouragement to note the communicative/deliberative/epistemic distinction and consider framing talk norms in terms of classroom culture and participant voice rather than regulation. That is because it is for teachers and students to create and agree upon the repertoire in question and the norms that will govern the conduct of collective discussion, whether in small groups or with the class as a whole. Within subjects, especially in secondary and higher education where epistemic framing is more pronounced, teachers will wish to talk about domain-specific deliberative and epistemic norms within their subject groups or departments as well as with their students. With younger students, a single, undifferentiated list of 'norms for speaking and listening' may be deemed more appropriate.

Repertoire 2: Interactive Settings

The talk for which we aim can be facilitated or inhibited by the way interaction is organised (*relations*); by the way, physically, that students are *grouped*; by the handling of classroom *space* and layout; and by the way *time* is apportioned.

Relations

- *Whole class*
- *Group (teacher-led)*
- *Group (student-led)*
- *Individual (teacher and student)*
- *Individual (student pairs)*

The three main *relational* options to consider are whole class, small group and individual, and these yield five possibilities for organising the interaction itself: whole class teaching, teacher-led group work, student-led group work, student-student one-to-one (paired talk) and teacher-student one-to-one. Just as we need to deploy a range of teacher talk in order to encourage a range of student talk, so we need to facilitate both kinds of talk by varying the way interaction is organised. So, for example, a small group discussion led by the students themselves produces different patterns of talk, and different ideas, from one led by their teacher.

Grouping

- *Size*
- *Student membership: attainment/friendship/gender/other*
- *Function: individual/co-operative/collaborative*

In many classrooms, small groups typically have four or six students – not for educational reasons but because this is what space and furniture allow (two or three tables, with two students at each, pushed together). But this number also happens to work well for productive discussion if other conditions are met. Galton and Williamson differentiate 'seating groups', in which each student has a separate task; 'working groups', in which all group members undertake the same task but work independently; 'co-operative groups', in which members undertake separate but related tasks; and 'collaborative' groups, in which all members work together on a single task.[42] As to the composition of groups, the familiar alternatives are random (students choose) and engineered (teachers choose), and in the latter case, the usual options are prior attainment (comparable or mixed) and gender (single or mixed). By way of guidance on the various permutations, we quote the comprehensive survey of research on classroom grouping undertaken for the Cambridge Primary Review by Peter Blatchford and his colleagues:

> If group work is to be effective, pupils must be able to work in a socially inclusive manner . . . and not be dominated by same-gender and friendship. . . . In order for pupils to be . . . less dependent on teachers in their learning, the physical (seating and furniture layout), interactional (group composition and size) and curriculum contexts must be co-ordinated.[43]

Space

- *Rows*
- *Cabaret*
- *Horseshoe*

With layout, there are again three basic options: tables arranged separately in rows, tables arranged side by side in a squared-off horseshoe, with the teacher on the open fourth side, or tables pushed together to seat small groups in what conference organisers fancifully call 'cabaret style'. Each strongly signals a particular pattern of talk and who controls it: teacher-controlled recitation, instruction or exposition (rows), student-student small group discussion (cabaret), whole class collective interaction (horseshoe). We have found that the horseshoe arrangement is the most flexible, for with minimal physical adjustment it allows whole class direct instruction, whole class collective discussion and paired talk, while by the simple and speedy expedient of switching chairs to the inside of the horseshoe it also facilitates small group discussion.

There are two problems with the small group or 'cabaret' layout that remains the default in many British primary classrooms. First, although it signals collaboration and discussion, students mostly work individually and therefore may distract each other while doing so. Second, whole class discussion requires necks to be craned or chairs to be reversed.

Time

- *Lesson length*
- *Balance of talk-based and text-based tasks and activities*
- *Range and balance of different talk forms*
- *Pace*

The final member of this organisational trio is *time*, starting with lesson length, moving on to the proportion of time within lessons spent on talk-based and text-based activities (reading and writing) and to the relationship between them; then on to the balance of different kinds of talk and, finally, the *pace* that governs how much is accomplished within a specified period of time. Here, the conventional Ofsted notion of pace – 'covering' content, doing things quickly (what does 'covering' mean when speed is its main criterion?) – comes up against the imperative of giving pupils time to think and understand. A lesson pursued at a cracking pace may satisfy inspectors, but in terms of students' learning it may be less effective, even counterproductive. Here it is useful to distinguish between '*organizational* and *interactive pace* . . . the speed at which lesson preparations, introductions, transitions and conclusions are handled . . . the pace of teacher-pupil exchanges' and '*cognitive* and *learning pace* . . . the speed at which conceptual ground is covered, the ratio of new material to old and of task demand to task outcome . . . how fast pupils actually learn.'[44] The latter is what really matters: time spent on securing understanding is surely time well spent, regardless of an external observer's arbitrary judgement about pace.

Being forms of organisation rather than kinds of talk, the elements in this repertoire in effect mark one axis of a grid, while the various kinds of talk outlined in repertoires 3–8 occupy the other axis. The resulting (virtual) grid immediately and vastly expands the possibilities captured by the framework and reminds us that while group discussion, whole class teaching and paired talk offer distinct social, communicative and affective payoffs, the cognitive leverage they exert depends more on the character and quality of the talk being pursued than on their organisation as such, even though each organisational form entails opportunities and constraints that are different from the others. That is what some 1990s enthusiasts for 'interactive whole class teaching' failed to understand.[45]

Repertoire 3: Learning Talk

We move now from dialogic teaching's cultural, normative and organisational framing to the character of the talk it embodies. Just as Dillon challenges conventional pedagogical wisdom when he starts with student questions,[46] so we use the student's 'learning talk' as our springboard. For even when the teacher opens an exchange, in dialogic teaching it is to the quality of the student's response that this first move should be directed.

Just as there are many kinds of thinking and learning, so there are many kinds of learning talk. Students need not only to answer the teacher's questions – a form of talk in which schooling probably gives them more practice than they need – but also to ask questions of their own, to explain and expand their ideas and explore the ideas of others. For the latter, they must learn to listen and respond, respect others' viewpoints and their right to put their case, and think carefully about what is said, in the way encouraged by repertoire 1 and anticipated in our consideration of voice in Chapter 4.

Then, framing the various talk moves are the different *registers* of subjects and situations – scientific, mathematical, formal, informal, technical, digital, vernacular and so on – and the *codes* of language in daily use. Chatting with friends or family entails less formal patterns of talk than are used, say, in job interviews or presenting a case at a meeting; and although children learn without adult intervention to code-switch and code-slide between standard and non-standard forms, and between these and the argot of playground, friendship group or gang, the idea of register should nevertheless be overtly explored. For education is in part about the skill and language of transition between contexts, situations, subjects, tasks and problems, or knowing both what to say and how and when to say it.

With the early years in mind, Halliday identifies seven functions of young children's spoken language:

- *Instrumental*: to express wants and needs
- *Regulatory*: to control
- *Interactional*: to communicate and relate
- *Personal*: to express feelings
- *Heuristic*: to find answers
- *Imaginative*: to tell and respond to stories
- *Representational*: to convey information.[47]

The first four express physical and emotional needs; the remaining three help the child make sense of the world. The latter also have affinities, though not direct correspondence, with Barnes's distinction between *presentational* and *exploratory* talk:

> In presentational talk the speaker's attention is primarily focused on adjusting the language, content and manner to the needs of an audience,

and in exploratory talk the speaker is more concerned with sorting out his or her own thoughts. . . . Exploratory talk is hesitant and incomplete because it enables the speaker to try out ideas, to hear how they sound, to see what others make of them.[48]

This distinction reminds us of the salience of 'tenor', or how talk relates to its participants.[49] Both presentational and exploratory talk address an audience, as most talk does, but they do so in different ways. One of the characteristics of IRE is that it does not readily accommodate thoughts other than the finished and polished, whereas if talk is genuinely for learning as well as presenting or repeating, then hesitancy, false starts and changes of direction are unavoidable and perhaps essential.

The list that follows aims to: (i) provide a degree of continuity from Halliday's list of language functions in early childhood, bearing in mind that readers of this book work with children and students of different ages; (ii) include a range of learning talk that leans less towards the fulfilment of basic needs and more towards the educational tasks of learning and making sense; (iii) reflect Barnes's exploratory/presentational distinction because this captures learning as process as well as outcome, and it encourages us to think about the stance of the listener as well as the speaker.

- *Transactional*: manage encounters and situations
- *Expository*: narrate, expound and explain
- *Interrogatory*: ask questions of different kinds and in diverse contexts
- *Exploratory*: venture, explore and probe ideas
- *Deliberative*: reason and argue
- *Imaginative*: contemplate and articulate what might be
- *Expressive*: put thoughts into words, nuance ideas, articulate feelings and responses
- *Evaluative*: deliver opinions, form and articulate judgements.

With the exception of interrogatory talk, in which function and form combine in the move and act of the question, each of these kinds of learning talk focuses more on function than form. They can therefore be elaborated by reference to some of their constituent moves or acts, and this process is initiated in the following (readers are invited to pick up the baton). A test of whether we have made this shift is to try turning each of the verb stems below into the third person singular of its present tense: 'She asks', 'He instructs', 'She explains', 'He argues', 'She speculates' and so on. This works in most cases, though not all.

- *Transactional*

    ask, answer, instruct, inform, explain, discuss

- *Expository*

  tell, narrate, explain, describe, expound, expand

- *Interrogatory*

  bid, ask, enquire, answer

- *Exploratory*

  suggest, venture, speculate, soliloquise, hypothesise, probe, clarify

- *Deliberative*

  reason, ask, argue, question, hypothesise, challenge, defend, justify, analyse, synthesise, persuade, decide

- *Imaginative*

  speculate, visualise, soliloquise, tell, describe, envisage, create

- *Expressive*

  narrate, speculate, qualify, argue, insist, wonder, exclaim

- *Evaluative*

  opine, estimate, assert, argue, judge, justify

A note on 'expressive'. Most talk combines the linguistic and paralinguistic, and even a deadpan face conveys meaning over and above that of the accompanying words on their own: irony, perhaps, or fear of creating alarm. But while intonation, facial expression and gesture moderate all of the previous forms of talk, *expressive* talk is particularly dependent on the way these elements combine. Expressiveness lies in delivery as much as words, and an expressive statement or question flatly delivered may convey meaning some way from what is intended:

Macduff: Your royal father's murder'd.
Malcolm: Oh, by whom?[50]

Of the eight forms, expressive talk is therefore the least amenable to efforts to exemplify it as specific verbs.

Repertoire 4: Teaching Talk

It is a basic tenet of dialogic teaching that while children need to talk in order to learn and understand, and schools must therefore develop their capacity to do so, it is usually the *teacher's* talk that triggers and shapes this process. Teachers, therefore, also need to have a diverse talk repertoire rather than be confined to instruction, exposition and a limited range of questioning moves. If the scope of teaching talk is restricted, those kinds of learning talk that are contingent on what the teacher says or asks will also be restricted; but if the teacher's vocabulary and exchange repertoire are rich, and the teacher values and nurtures reciprocity, then the student's talk will blossom.

Some of the generic categories of talk for learning in repertoire 3 have their counterparts as talk for teaching, but by no means all. Classroom studies show that teaching talk is more likely to be transactional, expository, interrogatory and evaluative than exploratory, deliberative, imaginative and expressive,[51] so if the teacher's utterances cue those of the student, as frequently they do, then it is to moves that encourage the last four that we might particularly look.

The 'teaching talk' list that follows reflects both what may be readily observed in the world's classrooms (first group) and what, to be consistent with the stance we have adopted and the justifications we claim, we would like to see more of (second group).

- *Rote*: memorising facts, formulae, routines or texts through constant repetition.
- *Recitation*: using short teacher question/student answer sequences to recall what has previously been encountered, or to test what is presumed or required to be already known.
- *Instruction*: telling students what to do and/or how to do it.[52]
- *Exposition*: imparting information, explaining ideas or procedures, narrating.

- *Discussion*: exchanging ideas and information, uncovering and juxtaposing viewpoints.
- *Deliberation*: weighing the merits of ideas, opinions or evidence.
- *Argumentation*: making or testing a case by reference to reasons or evidence.
- *Dialogue*: working towards common understanding through structured questioning, probed and elaborated responses and an interactive dynamic that strives to be collective, reciprocal and supportive as well as cumulative, deliberative and purposeful.

Scanning the list, readers may be perplexed: why, given all that has been said about the limitations of recitation/IRE, is it there at all? And as for rote. . . .

Recitation is there in part precisely because it is ubiquitous and, in the teacher's overall repertoire, has its place; partly because we have consistently warned against those untenable dichotomies that bedevil educational and pedagogical discourse, in this case 'recitation vs dialogue'; and partly because, as Nystrand and Gamoran found, 'Recitation is not categorically ineffective; rather, its effectiveness depends on how teachers expand IRE sequences.'[53] Therefore:

> There is a danger . . . that we consign all but [discussion, deliberation, argumentation and dialogue] to the despised archive of 'traditional'

methods. In fact, exposition, recitation and even rote have a place in teaching, for facts need to be imparted, information needs to be memorised, and explanations need to be provided, and even the deeply unfashionable rote has a place (memorising tables, rules, spellings and so on). However, the joint solving of problems through discussion, and the achievement of common understanding through dialogue, are undeniably more demanding of teacher skill than imparting information or testing recall through rote or recitation.[54]

And:

> Dialogue . . . is not so much a discrete category as a characteristic which several kinds of discourse may share. Clearly rote does not scaffold and basic recitation may offer limited opportunities, but a well-judged explanation . . . may scaffold students' learning and understanding no less effectively than carefully-judged questioning and follow-up.[55]

Dialogic teaching, therefore, encompasses the full range of teaching talk listed previously but privileges the last four – discussion, deliberation, argumentation and dialogue – and especially talk of whatever kind is able to achieve the spectrum of student learning talk proposed in repertoire 3. For this reason, repertoires 5 and 6 will now concentrate on the questioning and extending moves that are dialogue's transactional foundation, while the composite repertoires 7 and 8 pay closer attention to discussion and argumentation as ways of talking and reasoning that have their own added imperatives.

Repertoire 5: Questioning

We come next to two critically important talk moves: the *questions* with which much classroom talk is initiated and the moves for *extending* or *elaborating* which, in a dialogic classroom, aim to do something productive with what students say, whether in response to a question or some other stimulus.

Even allowing for progress since Flanders proposed his 'rule of two thirds', classrooms remain places where it is the teacher who asks most of the questions, so a dialogically informed questioning repertoire must allow for the possibility that students too will have questions to ask and will be encouraged and if necessary trained to do so.

Considering the extent to which students' lives in classrooms are steered and circumscribed by questions, the literature is surprisingly thin on taxonomies of the kind that teachers would find helpful when thinking about the questions they ask. Even the work of Dillon, who is pre-eminent in this field, deals more with the dynamics and management of questions than their content.

The late Ted Wragg, who directed two major empirical studies of teaching during the 1980s (the Teacher Education Project and the Leverhulme

Primary Project), noted that most analyses progress no further than minimal categories of question *scope* (narrow-broad), *form* (open-closed) and *function* (observation-recall-thought), possibly because when he undertook his research these marked the boundary of the questioning repertoire in the teaching that he observed.[56] He then sought to remedy the deficiency by differentiating questions in the 'cognitive' domain (recall, deduction, justification, problem-solving, evaluation) and in the 'speculative, affective and management' domains (inviting speculation, encouraging expression of feelings, directing attention and asserting control). Of the questions recorded by his research team, 67 per cent invited recall or simple deduction, fewer than 20 per cent required complex responses and 13 per cent were concerned with speculation, feelings or management. The tendency to ask only simple questions was less true of arts than science teachers.[57]

Repertoire 5 starts with options for managing students' participation and responses, together with Rowe's well-known idea of 'wait time',[58] which I prefer to call 'thinking time', since thinking is what we have paused for and expect. (Scheffler quotes a Chicago teacher who had no truck with either waiting or thinking and barked, 'Don't stop to think, tell me what you know!' To avoid being accused of maligning Chicago teachers, I should add that the quote is dated 1892.)[59]

Then comes Martin Nystrand's classic distinction between 'test' and 'authentic' questions. This sets the scene for a more detailed categorisation of question purposes and structures which is intended to apply to *all* questions, regardless of whether it is the teacher or student who poses them.

- *The management of questions*
  - *Manage* the classroom processes and procedures of which questioning is a part: 'May I remind you of how we have agreed to handle discussion . . . ?'
  - *Response cue – bidding*: the question is open to anyone to answer, and students typically bid by raising hands, or adopt well-tried strategies to avoid being singled out: 'Who can tell me what . . . ?'
  - *Response cue – nomination*: the question is posed with a particular student, and that student's perceived capacities, in view. 'Donald: how would you define "truth"?'
  - *Thinking time (aka 'wait time')*: signals that a question requires thought and, indeed, is worth thinking about. Concomitant to authentic questions.
  - *Participation cue – rotation*: the teacher ensures that as many students as possible get to answer questions in the course of a lesson.
  - *Participation cue – extension*: the teacher uses extending moves (see *The purposes of questions* later and repertoire 6) to probe, discuss and build upon students' answers, thereby reducing the number of students in a given lesson who get to answer questions.

- *The character of questions* (from Martin Nystrand)

  - *Test questions:* these allow only one answer, and they check recall rather than encourage reasoning.
  - *Authentic questions:* these allow various answers, including those that have not been anticipated; they 'convey the teacher's interest in the student's opinions and thoughts.'[60]

- *The purposes of questions*

  Initiate

  - *Recall/review* what has been previously discussed or learned: 'What did we learn about x in yesterday's lesson?'
  - *Elicit facts or information:* 'What . . . ?' 'Who . . . ?' 'Where . . . ?' 'How . . . ?'
  - *Elicit reasons:* 'Why . . . ?'
  - *Elicit observation or opinion:* 'What do you think about x . . . ?'
  - *Elicit deduction:* 'Can you work out how many . . . ?'
  - *Invite reflection or speculation:* 'What would happen if . . . ?' 'Why do you think that y . . . ?'
  - *Invite affective or empathetic response:* 'How do you feel about x . . . ?' 'How would you feel if . . . ?' 'How do you think that y felt when . . . ?'

  Probe

  - *Probe or test* the thinking behind a response: 'Why do you say that . . . ?' 'How do you/we know that . . . ?' 'Will you explain that . . . ?' 'Are you sure . . . ?' 'Any other suggestions . . . ?'
  - *Clarify* the thinking behind a response or the way it has been expressed: 'Do you mean . . . ?' 'Can you put it another way . . . ?'
  - *Invite evaluation:* 'What do you think about x . . . ?' 'Is y right?' 'Do you agree? Why?'

  Expand

  - *Expand* the initial exchange: 'Can you give me another example . . . ?' 'Is there an alternative explanation . . . ?'
  - *Sustain or develop* a line of thinking through connected questions. 'How do you think . . . ?' 'But what if . . . ?' 'Who agrees with x on this . . . ?' 'What happens/happened/might happen next . . . ?'

- *The structure of questions*

  - *Open:* allows various responses.
  - *Closed:* requires a particular response ('1066'/'King Harold') or response category ('Yes'/'No'/'I don't know').

- *Leading*: inadmissible in a court of law, but – especially as 'cued elicitations'[61] – common in classrooms.
- *Narrow*: brief, direct and context specific; usually requires an equally specific response.
- *Discursive*: broad, perhaps even rambling, may combine several questions in one; requires a generalised and perhaps extended response.

The questioning purposes above are in three by no means watertight groups. *Initiating* questions do just that. *Probe* questions investigate responses made. *Expand* questions build on them. Both replace the F/E in IRF/IRE by a third turn that goes somewhere. Repertoire 6, later, treats the second and third categories more systematically.

The response and participation cues (bidding/nomination and rotation/extension) require explanation, for they arose from the *Culture and Pedagogy* project. Having been socialised (in the UK) into patterns of questioning that tended to invite bidding ('Now who can tell me . . . ? Yes, Diane . . .') and the gamesmanship, attention-seeking, attention-avoidance and embarrassment that may attend it (for unless the question is so simple that it is not worth asking, some students certainly won't know the answer), I was struck by the way that in some other cultural contexts questions were as likely to be constructed with particular students, and the perceived capacities of those students, in mind. This practice seemed both more efficient and more equitable. In fact, there is a choice here: a broad question to the class as a whole is one way to draw people and ideas together at the beginning or end of a lesson, while more focused and targeted questions suit the lesson's middle, when the hard thinking is being done or hoped for.

Equally, from the same project, we recorded a fairly sharp distinction between those teachers who believed that the way to maximise student participation and attention was, within a given lesson, to ask as many questions of as many students as possible (rotation) and those who believed in the value of extended exchanges with a few (extension).

In pursuit of the latter, as I noted in a commentary on a lesson featured by Adam Lefstein and Julia Snell,[62] to reinforce the idea of collective engagement through speaking, listening and thinking in combination teachers may draw on three procedures. First, they may ask a few children to articulate their thinking while others listen. The principle here is that 'the child who . . . works through a problem, aloud and at length, is less an individual being tested and compared with others than their representative.'[63] Second, they may opt for extended exchanges with a few children rather than brief exchanges with many, on the provable grounds that in their learning outcomes such exchanges are more productive. Third, instead of insisting that in a given lesson all children must speak, however briefly, dialogic teachers may use the day or week as their unit, ensuring that over a longer period every child has an opportunity for the probing exchanges for which the research evidence calls. However – a crucial proviso – those who do not speak *must* listen and think. Fully engaged listening is as critical to the repertoire of learning talk as those vocalised elements like questioning, explaining, arguing and justifying.

In accordance with the idea of repertoire, rotation and extension are presented here as alternative strategies for teachers to use as appropriate. As with bidding/nomination, it is not proposed that one should be completely abandoned in favour of the other.

Repertoire 6: Extending

In its quest for the 'ingredient x' of dialogic teaching, Chapter 6 nominated the third turn in the typical three-part teaching exchange as 'the moment when an exchange can stop or continue, when it can open up the student's thinking or close it down, when feedback can be replaced by feed-forward.' The third turn is also the moment on which, as we saw, different kinds of research evidence on the measurable effectiveness of dialogic teaching converge. Whether they use the ESRC project's 'elaboration' and 'querying',[64] or our EEF project's 'revoice', 'rephrase' and 'challenge',[65] or Mercer's 'recapitulation' and 'reformulation',[66] or Palincsar and Brown's 'clarify', 'summarise', 'predict',[67] researchers agree on the need to seize that moment and respond to what students say with moves that prompt reasoning and sustain the dialogue.

This is not to deny the importance of feedback. Rather, we should ensure that it delivers something other than categorical judgement with no right of reply or room for discussion, or than praise that encourages – 'Wow!' 'Fantastic!' 'Brilliant!' 'Nice job,' 'Way to go'[68] – but because it neither discriminates nor informs soon becomes merely phatic. And in considering feedback as such – for to many teachers this is still what the third turn is about – we should heed Hattie's view that for teaching to be genuinely reciprocal, feedback should come from students as well, so that teachers are able to work on the student's thinking while it is 'live' rather than only on the outcome of that thinking in the form of a 'correct' or 'incorrect' answer.[69]

In respect of feedback, too, there are questions of voice and equity (see Chapter 4). If student voice is unevenly elicited, heard or valued, teacher feedback may lack the evidence it requires and hence risk compounding the inequity to the detriment of the student's learning as well as his or her self-esteem. In any event, even the most scrupulously fair-minded teacher knows that it is hard for feedback not to be tinged by views of, or assumptions about, the individual student, or the group to which that student belongs, which go beyond what he or she has just said.

Confirming this risk, Sortkaer's study of feedback to 15-year-olds in schools in Denmark, Finland, Iceland, Norway and Sweden, all of them cultures in which equality and social justice are supposedly prized, showed nevertheless that feedback is differentially given and perceived. Students from high socioeconomic status (SES) families were more likely than those from low-SES families to receive 'facilitative' feedback which, rather than merely telling them how they had done and what to do next (which Sortkaer called 'directive' feedback), encouraged that self-regulation that supports the development of metacognition and independent learning and which is one of the contenders for dialogic teaching's 'ingredient x'. Feedback, Sortkaer concluded, may exacerbate inequality by its nature rather than its incidence, for both student groups received comparable amounts of 'directive' feedback. Regrettably, though the study hints at causes that align with Bernstein's work on class and codes,[70] it did not collect SES data on the teachers to set alongside that on the students.[71]

Those thoughts, and our earlier discussion about voice and equity, might inform the way we now think about the third turn.

Of the six repertoires in the version of the dialogic teaching framework used in the 2014–17 EEF project and trial, one drew heavily on the work of Sarah Michaels and Cathy O'Connor. As we saw in Chapter 6 – to which readers should refer to find out more – their preoccupation with 'academically productive talk' over many years led them to the formulation of 'strategic talk moves designed to open up the conversation and support student participation, explication and reasoning'[72] and to the view that using these within the third turn would give them maximum leverage.

Their own evaluation of teachers' use of their talk moves in everyday settings was painstaking and positive,[73] and because their moves were so well-founded and clearly articulated, and their overall approach aligned so readily with our own, we requested and received permission to incorporate the moves into the version of the dialogic teaching framework used in the EEF project. Teachers were as positive about the value of the moves in the UK as the US, so Michaels and O'Connor have kindly extended their permission from the EEF project to this book.

Actually, the Michaels and O'Connor framework has not one repertoire but two: the 'talk moves' and 'talk formats' (whole class, small group and pair).[74] 'Talk format' is comparable to the 'relations' part of our Organisational Frames (repertoire 2), though we subdivide 'small group' and 'pair', while the moves themselves are in line with our insistence that doing something with what the student says is the *sine qua non* of dialogic teaching. The only change we made was to rename the moves 'extending' rather than the multi-purpose 'talk', because that was how, in the EEF project and here, we wished them to be particularly understood.

This repertoire is the logical complement and sequel to questioning (repertoire 5), and it offers as prompts utterances that are at once memorable and epistemically positioned and through which teachers may take student responses and contributions and build them into discussion chains, thereby modelling as well as advancing the principle of cumulation outlined earlier. However, practically suggestive though these moves are, Michaels and O'Connor echo Martin Nystrand in warning that 'the simple deployment of talk moves does not ensure coherence in classroom discussion or robust student learning.'[75]

The four goals towards which the nine moves are grouped later in this chapter arose from the concern of Michaels, O'Connor and their colleagues that teachers need to have reasons for choosing and using the moves, and that their deployment can never be merely mechanical (in the way that IRE so often is). They say (their italics):

> First, in order to have an academically productive discussion, one must be able *to get students to say something, to make a contribution that can be heard and understood*. . . . Second, one must be able to *get students to orient to one another and truly listen*. . . . Third . . . discussion must reach beyond superficiality and . . . *[get] students to dig more deeply into their own reasoning.* Fourth, the ultimate goal is to *get students working with the reasoning of other[s].*[76]

These four goals structure their framework:

- *Goal: Individual students share, expand and clarify their own thinking.*

  1 *Time to think*: partner talk; writing as think time; wait time.
  2 *Say more*: 'Can you say more about that?' 'What do you mean by that?' 'Can you give an example?'
  3 *So, are you saying . . . ?*: 'So, let me see if I've got what you're saying. Are you saying . . . ?' (Always leave space for the original student to agree or disagree and say more.)

- *Goal: Students listen carefully to one another.*

  4 *Rephrase or repeat*: 'Who can repeat what A just said, or put it into their own words?' (After a partner talk) 'What did your partner say?'

- *Goal: Students deepen their reasoning.*

  5 *Ask for evidence or reasoning*: 'Why do you think that?' 'What's your evidence?' 'How did you arrive at that conclusion?' 'Is there anything in the text that made you think that?'
  6 *Challenge, or seek counter example*: 'Does it always work that way?' 'How does that idea square with B's example?' 'What if it had been a copper cube instead?'

- *Goal: Students think with others.*

  7 *Agree/disagree and why?* 'Do you agree/disagree? (And why?)' 'Are you saying the same thing as C or something different, and if it's different, how is it different?' 'What do people think about what D said?' 'Does anyone want to respond to that idea?'

8   *Add on*: 'Who can add on to the idea that E is building?' 'Can anyone take that suggestion and push it a little further?'
9   *Explain what someone else means*: 'Who can explain what F means when she says that?' 'Who thinks they could explain in their words why G came up with that answer?' 'Why do you think he said that?'[77]

Repertoires 7 and 8: Discussing, Deliberating, Arguing

In Chapter 3, our quest for definitional clarity led us to differentiate *discussion* (exchanging information and ideas), *deliberation* (weighing the merits of an idea, or considering a question or problem, in the hope of reaching an agreed opinion or decision) and *argumentation* (making or testing a case by reference to sound reasons and/or defensible evidence that are able to withstand challenge). Argumentation itself could be *deliberative* or *disputatious*, depending on whether the intention was to agree, persuade or defeat, and the dispute might be ritualised as in a formal debate or legal encounter, or it might abandon norms and constraints and descend (or maybe ascend) into a quarrel.

Thus defined, and with conversation added for good measure, the terms occupy overlapping segments of a continuum: conversation – discussion – deliberation – argumentation. Yet in the present context each might also be thought sufficiently distinctive to warrant separate repertoires. After all, a freewheeling discussion with no purpose other than the airing of views is qualitatively different from the disciplined process of making a case or proposing a hypothesis, testing it against evidence and deciding on its merits. In fact, I propose just two repertoires at this point, and therefore need to explain why. I shall do so by reference to four approaches to classroom talk with which readers will by now be familiar.

Douglas Barnes and Frankie Todd treat discussion as their preferred alternative to recitation because it embodies their view that learning is ideally collaborative rather than transmissive and dialogic rather than monologic. To that end, they identify four nodal discussion moves: *initiating, eliciting, extending* and *qualifying*. These four moves, Barnes and Todd say, are

> mutually supportive. By taking the trouble to elicit an opinion from someone else, or by utilising what has been said by extending it further, the group members ascribe meaningfulness to one another's attempts to make sense of the world.[78]

So far, so consensual. Yet Barnes and Todd also allow for differences of opinion and thereby nudge discussion a little way along our continuum towards argumentation. However, the critical point about disagreement, they say, is that 'provided it is understood as a qualification and not a dismissal [it] plays a crucial part in advances in understanding.'[79] This, then, is argument in its deliberative rather than disputatious sense, and as thus elaborated it appears to subsume both deliberation and argumentation within discussion.

Next, however, it is discussion that looks to be the redundant term, in as far as the relevant index entry in Neil Mercer's 2000 book reads: 'Discussion: *see* argument'.[80] Obeying that instruction, we find that the index entry for 'argument' differentiates its 'cumulative', 'disputational' and 'exploratory' forms.[81] However, when we track these entries back into the text, we are offered 'a comparison of three models' not of argument but of 'discussion' – 'cumulative talk' (that is, lexically, *ac*cumulative talk), 'disputational talk' and 'exploratory talk' – with a firm steer towards the last of these.[82] So discussion it is, after all.

Meanwhile, although Mercer offers a helpful distinction between argument 'as a persuasive monologue, as a competitive dispute and as a reasonable dialogue',[83] he brackets all three, competitive dispute included, within the quest for consensus, which again curtails argument's scope some distance from the continuum's end. Argument, surely, is not obliged or invariably destined to end in agreement; and it may well prove inconclusive. Indeed, just as Karl Popper shows us the essentially provisional nature of the scientific claim that to some appears evidentially incontestable, so Bakhtin alerts us to the necessary impermanence of the ostensibly clinching argument.[84] If that takes us uncomfortably into the zone of post-modernist or post-truth relativism and Trumpian 'alternative facts', we can at least help students to understand that, in life as in the classroom, many arguments will and should remain open.

But, while definitely not irrelevant, this is to digress from the immediate concern. Noting the evident terminological confusion here over 'argument' and 'discussion', and my warning against presuming that every argument must end in consensus and closure, we can see that Mercer's 'disputational talk' is comparable to my 'disputatious argument' in as far as it is characterised by 'an unwillingness to take on another's point of view, and the consistent reassertion of one's own' and is competitive rather than co-operative.[85] Mercer contrasts this with 'cumulative talk', which at first sight resembles my dialogic principle 5, 'cumulation' – 'participants build on their own and each other's contributions and chain them into coherent lines of thinking and understanding' (my definition) – except in one vital respect: Mercer means talk that amasses words but not necessarily substance – that is *ac*cumulative talk – whereas here 'cumulation' injects critical edge into the discussion in order that it goes somewhere. This problem was discussed earlier.

In any event, Mercer's 'exploratory talk' comes close to my earlier definition of 'deliberation' and to Walton's account of 'deliberation dialogue'. This starts with a dilemma or practical choice and works collaboratively towards deciding the best course of action.[86]

In contrast to Barnes and Todd (who subsume deliberation and argument within discussion) and Mercer (who says a great deal about argument but veers between making it separate from and synonymous with discussion and ends up with something closer to deliberation), Reznitskaya and Wilkinson foreground argument for its own sake. They do so because their goal is not so much the generic one of talking to learn (though they are interested in that too) but the specific one of advancing 'argument literacy' in accordance with the US 2010 Common Core State Standards (see Chapter 4). There, like other 'literacies', 'argument literacy' is deemed to be something no student or citizen should be without; and students should learn to 'think critically and deeply, assess the validity of their own thinking, and anticipate counterclaims in opposition to their own assertions'.[87]

Reznitskaya and Wilkinson offer their own, slightly less astringent, definition of argument literacy as 'the ability to comprehend, formulate and evaluate arguments through speaking, listening, reading and writing'.[88] Its principal tool is what they call, adopting Walton's term[89] but not his precise meaning, 'inquiry dialogue', which they define as

> A type of talk in which participants work to collectively formulate the most reasonable judgements about complex questions . . . collaborate with each other and . . . engage in rigorous argumentation.[90]

Their inquiry dialogue is close to my earlier definition of deliberation ('Participants discuss and seek to resolve different points of view, they present and evaluate arguments, and they work towards reasoned positions and outcomes'), and their argumentation appears to be embedded within inquiry dialogue/deliberation rather than separate from it. Yet – and here perhaps is why these terms turn out to be so problematic – argumentation has distinct logical imperatives as well as a generic discursive or dialogic form, and these imperatives distinguish it from other kinds of discussion. Further, they also translate it into sequential moves. Argumentation, then, has forward momentum. It leads somewhere, or at least hopes to. Discussion may or may not, and that is sometimes its value, because, being more openly framed, it permits the tangential, speculative, creative and imaginative. In that sense, Mercer's non-cumulative 'cumulative talk' is not necessarily to be avoided.

Reznitskaya and Wilkinson identify four criteria (in italics below) and 11 'practices' to steer and facilitate argumentation as it progresses from a 'big question' through 'inquiry dialogue' to an outcome:

- *Diversity of perspectives*: centring on contestable questions; sharing responsibilities; discussing alternatives
- *Clarity*: clarifying meaning; connecting ideas; labelling reasoning processes and parts of an argument; tracking the line of enquiry
- *Acceptability of reasons and evidence*: evaluating facts; evaluating values
- *Logical validity*: articulating reasons; evaluating inferences.[91]

In turn, these may be compared with the three features or tests of 'accountable talk' proposed by our fourth group of witnesses, Resnick, Michaels and O'Connor. Such talk is:

- *'Accountable to the learning community* . . . talk that attends seriously to and builds on the ideas of others.
- *Accountable to standards of reasoning* . . . talk that emphasizes logical connections and the drawing of reasonable conclusions.
- *Accountable to knowledge* . . . talk that is based on facts, written texts or publicly accessible information that all . . . can access.'[92]

Yet 'accountable talk' is packaged here not as argument but as 'productive *discussion*' that 'support[s] reasoning and deepen[s] student understanding of complex material'[93] and, indeed, as conditions for *all* talk, in a range of pedagogical and curricular settings, that aspires to be 'academically productive'. It is linked, as on the basis of authorship one might expect, to the 'talk moves' of Michaels and O'Connor on which our repertoire 6 is based, and in terms of our discussion of stance in Chapter 3, it neatly and explicitly combines the relational (condition 1 above), the ratiocinative (condition 2) and epistemic (condition 3) in its quest for talk that is not only productive but also has regard for truth. To these, in a further explication of accountable talk, Michaels, O'Connor and Resnick add the ethical and cultural, arguing the relationship between dialogue, deliberative pedagogy and deliberative democracy.[94]

So, armed with teaching and learning talk repertoires that explicitly highlight discussion, deliberation and argumentation (repertoires 3 and 4), and repertoires that operationalise these through moves that question and extend and hence open up reasoning, evidence and engagement with the ideas of others (repertoires 5 and 6), and mindful of the fact that repertoires 3–6 may be deployed in whole class, small group (teacher-led or student-led) or one-to-one (teacher-student or student-student) organisational settings (repertoire 2), do we actually need any more repertoires to cover the broad range of options and needs in dialogic teaching?

I believe that we do, for while repertoires 3–6 include many of the transactional prerequisites and opportunities for discussion, and although the questioning and extending moves in repertoires 5 and 6 are clearly deliberative in character and trajectory, these preceding repertoires do not capture all of discussion's properties, especially discussion which students undertake without the teacher. Nor, at the other end of the continuum, do repertoires 3–6 encompass all the logical and sequential saliencies of deliberation and argumentation as these have emerged from our attempt here and in Chapter 4 to define them.

So I choose to call these final two repertoires *discussing* and *arguing*. This differentiates discussion (which can take many forms and pursue different purposes) from argumentation (which follows a particular trajectory and incorporates generally agreed elements). Deliberation, it seems to me, can move in either direction on our continuum: towards the relative openness of discussion or towards the discipline and momentum of argumentation. Momentum, in any case, is signalled by the last three dialogic teaching principles enunciated earlier in this chapter: deliberative, cumulative and purposeful, so in this book's model it is a condition of dialogic teaching itself.

Repertoire 7: Discussing

Notwithstanding my conclusion that we need additional repertoires for discussion and argumentation, discussion is essentially synoptic. So in the following, instead of proposing specific exchange patterns and moves, I point mainly to relevant aspects of other repertoires.

From Repertoire 1, Discourse Norms and the Culture of Talk

The further away from recitation and exposition we move, the more important it becomes for participants to discuss and agree upon discourse norms. In recitation and exposition, these are embodied in the exchange structure itself. Being highly variable in the forms it takes, discussion of itself has no embedded norms, so participants need to create them.

Examples are given under repertoire 1, earlier, and the tripartite distinction there between *communicative*, *deliberative* and *epistemic* norms reminds us that discussion must be about something: confining norms to communicative matters is a start but is also insufficient to inject rigour into the way that discussion handles ideas.

Here, as under repertoire 1, the norms are for teacher and students to determine, so discussion's first item is discussion itself.

From Repertoire 2, Organisational Frames

- *Relations.* Discussion may be undertaken by the class as a whole, by groups or by student pairs. Group discussion may be teacher-led or student-led. The former is in effect scaled-down whole class teaching. The latter transfers the burden of responsibility for managing the discussion onto the students themselves.
- *Grouping.* Discussion *per se* is generally 'collaborative' as defined in repertoire 2, but groups may subdivide into, say, pairs, to undertake contributory 'co-operative' spoken or written tasks.[95]
- *Space.* As explained under repertoire 2, the horseshoe layout works best for whole class discussion, and it delivers the appropriate relational signals, while cabaret or modified horseshoe facilitate small group discussion. The principle here is that layout should be congruent with, and supportive of, the kind of talk intended.

- *Time*. It is possible to sustain a whole class discussion for a complete lesson, but student-led small group discussions are better conceived as lesson segments, perhaps combined with text-based tasks and opportunities for plenary feedback.

From Repertoire 3, Learning Talk

One of the benefits of discussion is that it allows almost the full range of desirable learning talk to be exploited, especially:

- *Interrogatory*: ask, answer
- *Exploratory*: suggest, speculate, hypothesise, probe, clarify
- *Deliberative*: reason, ask, argue, question, hypothesise, challenge, defend, justify, analyse, synthesise, persuade, decide
- *Imaginative*: speculate, visualise, describe, envisage
- *Expressive*: speculate, qualify, argue
- *Evaluative*: estimate, assert, argue, justify.

From Repertoire 4, Teaching Talk

Three of the listed kinds of teaching talk are obviously pertinent, and – no surprises here – they are:

- Discussion
- Deliberation
- Argumentation.

From Repertoire 5, Questioning

The relevant parts of this repertoire are

Questioning purposes

- *Initiate*: recall, elicit, invite
- *Probe*: probe, clarify
- *Expand*: expand, sustain/develop

Questioning structure

- *Open*
- *Narrow*
- *Discursive*

In the context of discussion, however, the really fundamental question about questions is who asks them. In teacher-led discussion, whether whole class or small group, it is all too easy to regress to quasi-recitation simply because students have been socialised into assuming that if the teacher is present, he or she will take the lead. Dillon tells us that the remedy is simple:

> The single most effective act [teachers] can take . . . is *to stop asking questions*. We make room for student questions by stopping our own questioning at selected points . . . or by asking fewer questions overall.[96]

However, Dillon warns that the power of the inherited classroom culture is such that merely creating space will not release a flood of student questions, and there will be all kinds of reasons why many students will not wish to take the opportunity they have been given. (And, reader, think of those lectures you have attended where 'Any questions?' at the end is met by tense silence, yours included, and by the greatest possible care not to imply, by accidental eye-contact or hand movement, that one has a question to ask.) Dillon therefore proposes that questioning be taught, perhaps starting in the least exposed way with inviting students to pose and pool *written* questions. In fact, the exercise of question-generation is one that many teachers use, though as with answers in IRE, so with questions: students may strategically search for questions which they think the teacher will like to hear, anticipating the usual signals: 'That's an excellent question, X!' or 'Well ye-es . . . but could you think of a different question?'

But another route is via student-led small group discussion. Once the teacher withdraws, students will have little alternative but to ask questions of each other, provided that they have learned that discussion is more than a competitive parade of personal opinions. Here the guidance offered by Barnes and Todd and by Mercer and his colleagues is particularly helpful.[97]

From Repertoire 6: Extending

If students have become familiar with the moves used by teachers to probe and build on students' responses, they will begin to adopt them in their own discussion. Indeed, Barnes and Todd recorded students using some of these unprompted.[98] Some of the moves in repertoire 6 clearly have the teacher in mind as initiator, notably those that are directed at the class or group as a whole, but others are equally appropriate for students to ask. For example:

* Say more
* Ask for evidence of reasoning
* Challenge or seek counter example
* Agree/disagree and why.

From Repertoire 8: Arguing

Not all the moves in repertoire 8, which follows this, are unique to argumentation. Several apply equally and generically to discussion. For example:

- Clarify meaning
- Connect ideas
- Track the line of enquiry
- Evaluate fact
- Articulate reasons.

Conditions for teacher-led discussion

Here we can do no better than refer back to the four requirements that inspired the talk move header goals of Michaels and O'Connor (see repertoire 6, earlier).

Conditions for student-led discussion

The first decision in the planning of classroom discussion is who leads it. Whole class or small group discussion led by the teacher can readily be framed by repertoires 5 (questioning) and 6 (extending), and it therefore requires no further comment here. Small group discussion led by the students themselves is another. Yet, as noted earlier, Barnes and Todd found 13-year-old students using extending moves in small group discussion unprompted by the teacher:

- *Initiate*. Participants introduce a new perspective or idea: 'I think that . . .' 'I don't think that . . .' 'What do you think about x?' (see repertoire 5, questioning: initiate).
- *Elicit*. The discussion is sustained, once it has been initiated, by

  - Requests to someone to continue what they are saying
  - Requests to expand a previous statement
  - Requests for support for the speaker's opinion
  - Request for information (see also repertoire 5, questioning: initiate and probe).

- *Extend*. The group collectively works on each other's ideas to take them further (see repertoires 5 and 6).
- *Qualify*. In the course of extending ideas, they are collectively modified (see repertoires 6 and 8).[99]

This should be underlined. These moves, in naturalistic settings, were initiated and deployed by students, not teachers. However, while Barnes and Todd found secondary school students deploying some of the key moves in discussion without being prompted to do so by the teacher, Neil Mercer's research with younger students caused him to warn that 'simply putting children into groups and leaving them to solve problems by themselves is not enough to ensure that they will use co-operation and dialogue to good effect.'[100] On the basis of their extensive work on student-led small group discussion in primary schools, Mercer and Dawes propose three conditions:

- *Teachers should model they ways they expect students to talk and behave*: 'If, in group discussions, pupils are expected to treat tentative ideas with respect, to ensure that different points of view are heard and to elaborate ideas so that everyone understands them, the teacher must do likewise when talking with the class.'[101]
- '*Teachers should establish an appropriate set of ground rules for talk in class* . . . different ground rules will . . . operate in . . . different settings [i.e. depending on whether discussion is teacher-led or student-led] but if the potential value of dialogue in teaching and learning is to be realised, *all* the talk . . . must be underpinned by . . . common principles and . . . rules.'[102]
- *Group activities should be so designed that they* '*elicit debate and joint reasoning*. . . . Good activities are those which require a careful reasoned consideration of different ways of solving problems, or the evaluation of different possible explanations.'[103] In other words, the tasks on which students work in small groups should be of a kind that demand discussion rather than merely benefit from it.

Popular though it is among dialogists, I have already signalled my reservations about the term 'ground rules' and what it might imply, especially in relation to older students, so 'teachers should establish' might be replaced by 'teachers and students should discuss and agree upon'. But subject to the determining of discourse norms being viewed as a way of modelling the desired climate for discussion rather than as extraneous to it (see repertoire 1), the procedural conditions proposed by Mercer and Dawes make evident sense.

Repertoire 8: Arguing

Here, as with the 'extending' moves in repertoire 6, I am deeply indebted to colleagues who have done much of the heavy lifting – in this case Alina Reznitskaya and Ian Wilkinson. They have kindly given me permission to use, slightly adapted, their Argumentation Rating Tool (ART)[104] as the basis for this repertoire's moves. I also draw on Walton's work on the dialogues of argumentation.

The features or imperatives of argument identified by Reznitskaya and Wilkinson are 'position', 'reasons', 'evidence', 'challenges to evidence' and 'responses to challenge'.[105] These resemble an attenuated version of Toulmin's *claim, ground, warrant, backing, qualifier* and *rebuttal* discussed in Chapter 4. Their possibilities as moves can be clarified by placing a verb before each noun:

- State position (claim)
- Present reasons or evidence (ground)

- Connect reasons or evidence to a claim (warrant/backing)
- Challenge the reasons or evidence (qualifier)
- Respond to challenge (rebuttal).

Walton, as we saw in Chapter 4, presents forms of argumentation as, in action, types of dialogue, and follows these through to a further discourse level, that of speech act. For example:

> Is this so? (Ask)
> It is so. (Assert)
> On what basis? (Challenge)
> Because x, y and z and therefore. . . . (Argue)
> I agree. (Concede)
> I don't agree. (Retract)[106]

Such acts can play themselves on and on indefinitely as successive claims and reasons are presented, challenged, probed, discarded or accepted, so Walton frames such variation within a broad argumentation framework that has just three stages:

- Opening stage: a question is raised, a problem is posed, a claim is made or a premise is presented.
- Argumentation stage: through a series of moves and counter-moves, participants put forward reasons and/or evidence to support, challenge or refute premises, hypotheses or claims, to solve the stated problem or address the identified question.
- Closing stage: the argumentation is weighed, and the best-supported solution or reasonable answer is accepted.[107]

I note elsewhere that the 'reasonable answer' may not be a solution, 'best-supported' or otherwise, and we should anticipate that some arguments will end reasonably but inconclusively. After all, the unspoken Bakhtinian rider to 'best-supported' is 'in these circumstances, with the evidence or arguments we have been able to assemble, but we could go on . . .'.

Reznitskaya and Wilkinson's four criteria and 11 'practices' for steering and facilitating argumentation through Walton's three stages are presented below. Their status as moves is emphasised by changing participles into active verbs. So, in (1), the authors' 'identifying' becomes 'identify'. Thus:

- *Foster and explore different perspectives.*

  1 *Identify contestable questions, claims or problems*: 'Today our big question is . . .'
  2 *Share responsibilities*: 'Discuss this in pairs for a few minutes . . .' 'Would you like to nominate someone else to tackle this?'

3 *Discuss alternatives*: 'Which part do you disagree with?' 'Is this the only explanation?' 'Can anyone offer a different example?' 'How about this possibility . . . ?'

- *Be clear in the language and structure of arguments.*

4 *Clarify meaning*: 'Is this what you mean?' 'So are you saying that . . . ?' 'Would this be the same as . . . ?'
5 *Connect ideas*: 'How does this relate to what A has said?' 'B, how do you want to respond to C?' 'What does this mean for our big question?'
6 *Label reasoning processes and/or parts of an argument*: 'is this a reason for or against . . . ?' 'A, are you questioning B's assumption?' 'Is this a different point, or just another way of saying x?' 'Should we put C's suggestion in this column or the other one?'
7 *Track the line of enquiry*: 'Let's recap on where we have got to.' 'Can we list all the reasons we have heard so far?' 'Which of them seem most convincing at this stage?' 'Can we eliminate any of them?'

- *Use reasons and evidence that are well examined, well sustained and accurate.*

8 *Evaluate facts*: 'How do we know this?' 'Where does this information come from?' 'Is it a good source?' 'Is this always true, in every case?' 'Considering what's at stake, is this evidence good enough?'
9 *Evaluate values*: 'Who says so?' 'Can we trust what they say?' 'Can both of these things be true at the same time?' 'How important is this compared to the other things we have talked about?' 'Is this fact or opinion?'

- *Be logical in the way positions and reasons are connected.*

10 *Articulate reasons*: 'What is your reason for saying that?' 'Can you explain why you disagree?' 'What counts as evidence for that position?'
11 *Evaluate inferences*: 'Does this follow from what A has said?' 'Are we jumping to conclusions here?' 'Are you assuming that . . . ?' 'Is that reason enough to accept your conclusion?' 'Is that generalisation safe?'

Even though each of the 11 argumentation 'practices' is framed as a directive, their illustrations as acts are all questions. The emphasis, then, is on the 'ask' and 'challenge' stages of Walton's scheme, which puts the onus on the respondent to 'assert', 'argue', 'concede' or 'retract'. At face value, many of them are in fact 'extending' moves of the kind exemplified from Michaels and O'Connor in repertoire 6. However, it is the structure within which Reznitskaya and Wilkinson have placed their questions that turns an extending question into an argumentation move. That structure, and the italicised criteria and practices, should be kept firmly in mind as teachers (or students) work to initiate and maintain the forward momentum of the argument.

Indicators

This, then, is our dialogic teaching framework. For easy reference, its themes and headings are listed in Appendix 1.

We end this chapter with an answer to the expected question: 'Yes, but how do we know dialogic teaching when we see it?' In dialogic class-rooms – subject to diligence about the dangers of over-simplification – we witness:

- Respect for the situation, needs and rights of every student, especially those from communities whose voices are not treated equitably or who for social or clinical reasons find it difficult to express themselves in front of others.
- Agreed and respected norms for speaking, listening and discussion.
- A preparedness both to attend to talk for its own sake and to re-think its relationship with reading and writing.
- A broad and flexible repertoire of teaching strategies, modes of interaction and forms of both student and teacher talk.
- Interactions which encourage students to think and to think in different ways.
- Questions which invite more than simple recall and are posed by students as well as teachers.
- Answers which are justified, followed up and built upon rather than merely received.
- Feedback which takes thinking forward and is offered by students as well as teachers.
- Extending moves which probe and collaboratively expand student contributions.
- Exchanges which chain together into coherent and deepening lines of enquiry.
- Discussion in which ideas are freely shared, heard and explored.
- Argumentation which tests and builds evidence and cases.
- Patterns of organisation which, in the handling of classroom layout, student grouping, time, pace and the balance of whole class, group and individual interactions, are conducive to the above.
- A classroom culture in which the dynamics of talk are collective, reciprocal and supportive, and its content and trajectory are deliberative, cumulative and purposeful.
- A recognisably dialogic stance on learning, knowledge and human relationships as well as on interaction more narrowly defined.

If there is a 'bottom line' test of the dialogic quality of a typical classroom exchange, we cannot do much better than quote Martin Nystrand and Mikhail Bakhtin:

- What ultimately counts is the extent to which teaching requires students to think, not just repeat someone else's thinking.[108]
- If an answer does not give rise to a new question from itself, it falls out of the dialogue.[109]

Notes

1 Cambridge Primary Review Trust / University of York 2015.
2 In the North Yorkshire Talk for Learning Project (2002–7), in which the author worked with 42 schools in the north of England (Alexander 2003, 2005a). A similar project in London, the Barking and Dagenham Teaching Through Dialogue Initiative, ran with nine schools from 2003–6 (Alexander 2005b).
3 See Chapter 6, footnote 20, referring to Baker and Schwarz 2017, 13–14 and 48–55.
4 Accounts that show a good grasp of the approach, and of the dilemmas and compromises intrinsic to all teaching, include Lefstein and Snell 2014; Jones, Simpson and Thwaite 2018; Kim and Wilkinson 2019.
5 Alexander 2003; the 2005 conference keynote ('Culture, Dialogue and Learning: notes on an emerging pedagogy', for the International Association for Cognitive Education and Psychology, University of Durham), was later revised as chapter 5 of Alexander 2008b.
6 As described in Alexander 2018, 564–570.
7 Williams 1988. He included 'educated' but not 'education'. That has been remedied by the *Keywords for Today* project, in which a group of academics from the universities of Cambridge and Pittsburgh have revised and extended Williams's list (MacCabe *et al.* 2018, 102–105).
8 Alexander 2016; Armstrong 2019.
9 For the full list, with commentary and an account of how after extensive public consultation, the aims were arrived at, see Alexander 2010b, 174–202. On using the aims within schools, see Armstrong 2019. The 12 headings are: *The Individual*: Wellbeing; Engagement; Empowerment; Autonomy. *Self, Others and the Wider World*: Respect and Reciprocity; Interdependence and Sustainability; Local, National and Global Citizenship; Culture and Community. *Learning, Knowing and Doing*: Exploring, Knowing, Understanding and Making Sense; Fostering Skill; Exciting the Imagination; Enacting Dialogue.
10 Alexander 2010b, 199.
11 Williams 1988, 157 (his italics).
12 Cazden 2005.
13 Mercer and Littleton 2007, 51 (my italics).
14 Michaels *et al.* 2008; Resnick *et al.* 2010.
15 Michaels *et al.* 2008, 283.
16 Barnes and Todd 1977, 1995.
17 Mercer and Littleton 2007.
18 See the chapter 'Politics of good practice' in Alexander 1997, 267–287; also Lefstein and Snell 2014, 4–6. In 2019, Voice 21, architect of the view of oracy about which I expressed certain reservations in Chapter 5, published what it claimed was 'the UK's first cross-phase, robust and realistic framework to guide best practice in oracy education' (Voice 21, 2019).

19 Alexander 2001, 320–325.
20 See the chapter 'Beyond dichotomous pedagogies' in Alexander 2008b, 72–91.
21 The HMI and Ofsted school inspection and survey evidence on the positive relationship between curriculum breadth and standards in the 'basics' is discussed in Alexander 2010b, 243.
22 Bible, Judges 12:6, and Milton, *Samson Agonistes*, lines 287–289. There is an extended discussion of slogans and shibboleths in education in Alexander 1988, and of educational slogans in Scheffler 1971.
23 Alexander 2008b, 75.
24 Alexander 2008b, 73.
25 Cazden 2001, 56.
26 The model is applied in Alexander 2001, 265–528.
27 Sinclair and Coulthard 1975; Mehan 1979.
28 Halliday 1961.
29 Alexander 2001, 427–528.
30 The phrase is Donald Schön's (Schön 1983).
31 Michaels and O'Connor 2015.
32 For examples of ground rules for classroom talk, see Mercer 2000; Dawes *et al.* 2004; Michaels and O'Connor 2012; Reznitskaya and Wilkinson 2017.
33 Michaels and O'Connor 2012, 6; Reznitskaya and Wilkinson 2017, 52.
34 'The other 3Rs: routine, rule and ritual' in Alexander 2001, 380–390.
35 Michaels and O'Connor 2012, 6.
36 Osborne 2015, 407.
37 Alexander 2001, 383–384.
38 Edwards and Westgate 1994, 115.
39 Mercer 2000, 28.
40 Reznitskaya and Wilkinson 2017, 52–53.
41 Barnes and Sheeran 1992.
42 Galton and Williamson 1992.
43 Blatchford *et al.* 2010, 564.
44 Alexander 2001, 424.
45 'Interactive whole class teaching: the 1990s totem of educational effectiveness', in Alexander 2008b, 31–41.
46 Dillon 1988.
47 Halliday 1975.
48 Barnes 2008, 5.
49 Halliday 1989.
50 Shakespeare, *Macbeth*, Act 2, Scene 3.
51 Alexander 2001, 526–527. In this international study, we observed six recurrent patterns of teaching talk across classrooms in the five cultures: rote, recitation, instruction, exposition, discussion and dialogue. The last two were less frequently observed than the first four.
52 Note that 'instruction' is used here in its narrower British English sense, as meaning the specific kind of teaching I have indicated, rather than in the broader American sense of teaching in general. Bruner's *Toward a Theory of Instruction* is about children's growth, development and education, not telling them what to do. Likewise but confusingly, the European Association for Research in Learning and Instruction (EARLI) has opted for American rather than British English. In anticipation of Brexit?
53 Nystrand and Gamoran 1997, 72.
54 Alexander 2001, 527.
55 Alexander 2001, 527.
56 Wragg 1993, 137–152, 1991, 103.
57 Wragg 1991, 105–119.

58 Rowe 1986.
59 Scheffler 1971, 40. He quotes Joseph Rice's 1892 report on American public schools.
60 Nystrand 1997, 7.
61 Edwards and Mercer 1987, 142–146. The 'cue' may be in the question wording (as in a leading question), by sounding the initial letter of the answer, by miming or by other thespian gestures.
62 Alexander in Lefstein and Snell 2014, 74.
63 Alexander 2001, 454.
64 Howe *et al.* 2019.
65 Alexander *et al.* 2017; Hardman 2019.
66 Mercer 2000, 52–56.
67 Palincsar and Brown 1984.
68 From the poster '101 ways to praise a child', viewed in many Michigan elementary school classrooms during the *Culture and Pedagogy* fieldwork. Alexander 2008b, 74.
69 Hattie 2009, 173–178.
70 Bernstein 1971, 1975.
71 Sortkaer 2019.
72 Michaels and O'Connor 2012, 7.
73 Michaels and O'Connor 2015; O'Connor and Michaels 2018; O'Connor *et al.* 2018.
74 Michaels and O'Connor 2012, 7–20.
75 Michaels and O'Connor 2015, 358.
76 O'Connor and Michaels 2018; See also Chapin, O'Connor and Anderson 2009.
77 Michaels and O'Connor 2012, 11. Reprinted in this slightly modified form with the authors' kind permission. For fuller discussions of the moves, their genealogy and use, see: Michaels and O'Connor 2015, 2017; O'Connor *et al.* 2017; O'Connor and Michaels 2018.
78 Barnes and Todd 1995, 38.
79 Barnes and Todd 1995, 38.
80 Mercer 2000, 204.
81 Mercer 2000, 203.
82 Mercer 2000, 104. My italics.
83 Mercer 2000, 104.
84 Popper 1963; Bakhtin 1981.
85 Mercer 2000, 97.
86 Walton 2013, 9–10 and 191.
87 National Governors Association Center for Best Practice, quoted in Reznitskaya and Wilkinson 2017, x.
88 Reznitskaya and Wilkinson 2017, 7–8.
89 Walton 2013, 69.
90 Reznitskaya and Wilkinson 2017, 37.
91 Reznitskaya and Wilkinson 2017, 196.
92 Resnick *et al.* 2010; Michaels *et al.* 2008. For historical background to the concept of Accountable Talk, see O'Connor, Michaels and Chapin 2015, 112.
93 Michaels and O'Connor 2012, 1. My italics.
94 Michaels *et al.* 2008.
95 Galton and Williamson 1992.
96 Dillon 1988, 25.
97 Barnes and Todd 1995; Mercer 2000; Mercer and Littleton 2007; Dawes *et al.* 2004; Mercer and Dawes 2008.
98 Barnes and Todd 1995, 27–28.
99 Adapted from Barnes and Todd 1995, 28–38.

100 Mercer and Dawes 2008, 69.
101 Mercer and Dawes 2008, 70.
102 Mercer and Dawes 2008, 70.
103 Mercer and Dawes 2008, 70.
104 Reznitskaya and Wilkinson 2017, 183–200.
105 Reznitskaya and Wilkinson 2017, 21.
106 Adapted from Walton 2013, 8.
107 Adapted from Walton 2013, 233.
108 Adapted from Nystrand *et al.* 1997, 72.
109 Bakhtin 1986, 168.

8 Professional development

A strategy (for those who seek one)

There are many ways that talk for learning and teaching can be informed, expanded and enhanced by the ideas explored in the preceding seven chapters. Indeed, to be true to the dialogic imperative, as well as to the principle of professional agency, such variety might be deemed obligatory.

Context matters too. Although the author's ideas about dialogic teaching have tended to be associated with the education of pre-secondary children, they have also been taken up in secondary and higher education, and even in non-educational settings. They have been used in many countries and education systems other than the UK and on every continent apart from Antarctica,[1] and by trainee teachers, teachers in mid-career and those with years of experience behind them, not to mention educational researchers and administrators. Combining these dimensions of sectoral, geographical, cultural, developmental and occupational diversity would yield an astoundingly complex matrix and stifle the phrase 'one size fits all' before anyone dares to utter it.

Yet while many readers will choose to go their own way with what this book provides, reading it (and reading into it) how and what they wish, others will welcome guidance on how they might progress from exploration to action. Among the latter, this chapter has in mind two particular constituencies: trainee teachers and teacher educators; and serving teachers who work in schools or – if they are in secondary or higher education – in subject departments, where a decision has been made to make classroom talk the focus for collective exploration as part of a professional development or school improvement plan. The strategy outlined later in this chapter is predicated on this commitment to collective activity and therefore to treating the practical application of this book's ideas as a matter of enacting dialogue not only in the classroom but also in the way, outside the classroom, teachers and others engage with them.

The strategy is loosely based on that devised for the 2014–17 EEF project. This had two strands: pedagogical and professional. The pedagogical strand was essentially an earlier version of the framework elaborated in Chapter 7, that is to say, an account of dialogic teaching as a pedagogy of permissive repertoires through which, steered by ethical, epistemic and procedural values and principles, teachers seek to energise their own and their students' talk. The professional strand, fully revised and considerably expanded in this chapter, combined seven elements in all:

- Induction and training
- Mentoring
- Video and audio recording
- Cycles of planning, target-setting and review
- Whole school buy-in
- Materials and professional study
- Monitoring and support from the project team.

Induction and training

The induction and training were project-specific, so they do not readily translate. However, induction into and thorough familiarisation with a professional programme's ideas are always essential, so this element has been reconfigured as the orientation units detailed later in this chapter. If anything can be counted essential in a permissive framework, these certainly are.

Mentoring

Mentoring is an established and well-regarded adjunct to professional learning and development in a wide range of occupations, including teaching. In the EEF project, each school was asked to appoint one of its teachers as mentor. These were experienced teachers, though not necessarily members of the school's senior management team. Indeed, a hierarchical and hence implicitly inspectorial approach to mentoring was discouraged, and schools were asked instead to foster a relationship of peers embarking on a shared journey in which professional learning is mutual and discussion is open, advisory and non-judgemental. Such a relationship is particularly important in the arena of classroom talk, which is at the heart of every teacher's professional activity yet also raises questions which are as much personal as professional, and which need to be handled with sensitivity to the feelings of those involved. Further, those appointed as project mentors started by not necessarily knowing any more about dialogic teaching than their mentees, so the journey metaphor was doubly apposite.

It was and is the task of the mentor to:

- Be thoroughly familiar with the programme's ideas and materials.
- Establish and nurture the relationship of peer discussion and support referred to earlier in a manner that itself illustrates the principles of dialogic teaching: collective, reciprocal, supportive, deliberative, cumulative, purposeful.

- Steer his/her mentees through the programme.
- Help mentees to plan their work in each cycle, then monitor progress and initiate its joint review.
- Record the planning decisions taken, targets set and conclusions agreed.
- Ensure that the specified video/audio recordings are made, indexed and retained.

In relation to each of the programme's cycles, mentors worked with their teacher mentees to foreground within the planned lessons those aspects of teacher and/or student talk on which they were invited to focus. At the end of each cycle they jointly reviewed video examples of the resulting practice in accordance with protocols provided in a linked review booklet, noting strengths and areas for further development. Typically, this meeting then moved from review to planning for the next cycle.

Many schools routinely use mentoring for professional support, and in the UK it has been widely adopted in universities. My own university distinguishes between 'induction mentoring' for new members of staff, 'peer mentoring' and 'developmental mentoring'. The last two are apposite here, and among the university's conditions for the mentor-mentee relationship are the following:

> Peer mentoring should . . . be about progress and development, and be equally supportive of each partner. . . . Developmental mentoring is about the synergy that two (or more) people can create between them to generate solutions, strategies and action plans, to build on success. . . . [A good mentor is] interested in helping others to succeed, even if they may surpass you in achievement . . . capable of active listening – not interrupting, picking up important cues . . . able to reflect back the relevant issues and check understanding . . . able to question someone sensitively but empoweringly.[2]

A final, practical point. Recording 'planning decisions taken, targets set and conclusions reached' is the mentor's responsibility, and it is an extremely important one. In the EEF project, mentors were given a planning/review booklet – available in print and electronically – in which, in response to a succession of specific prompts, these matters were duly noted.[3] In a randomised control trial, such uniformity was necessary in order to secure the required degree of treatment consistency across schools in the intervention group. In the present case, it would probably be regarded as an impertinence, and the looser format of a planning/review journal will suffice.

Video and audio recording

Video and audio are not only ideal for capturing classroom interaction as both sound and behaviour, for talk is what is signalled by body language and gesture as well what we say and hear. They are also powerful tools for professional self-evaluation and development and provide a vivid shared focus for mentoring discussions. (Too often, mentoring happens away from the action and therefore may slip into something closer to counselling. That is not its function here.) In the EEF project, video was used during the induction and training, but its principal purpose was to provide the material which, within each cycle, teachers and mentors would view and discuss. Recordings fixed teachers' entering pedagogy as baselines for tracking and assessing their progress; and when subjected to close analysis they enabled teacher and mentor to identify particular aspects of classroom talk on which it might be beneficial and, in some instances, essential to work.

As one who had used video and audio recording since the 1980s both for studying talk and supporting professional development, I had noticed teachers' tendency when viewing classroom video clips to concentrate more frequently on the actors' observable behaviours than on the words uttered or meanings exchanged, and to criticise rather than analyse: 'I wouldn't have done that . . .' 'Look at those three children at the back . . .' 'Hasn't the teacher noticed?'

In order to alert participants to this tendency as well as to counter it, the induction/training sessions worked in turn on three versions of the same lesson extract. First an audio recording directed attention to the form and meaning of talk, and to these alone. With an audio recording, listening is one's only option. Then a transcript allowed more detailed study in which specific speech exchanges, moves or acts could be tracked and revisited as many times as necessary, and participants could speculate on effective and alternative moves, for example: 'What, precisely, prompted the student to say that?' 'Could the teacher's question have been differently phrased?' 'Did that extend the student's contribution or close it down?' 'Is that student saying what she thinks or what she believes the teacher wants to hear? . . . How do we know?' 'What kind and level of understanding (or misunderstanding) of the problem does that student's contribution reveal?' Finally, the video clip of the same episode enabled participants to observe the interplay of talk's linguistic and paralinguistic features and place within its full pedagogical context the talk heard, read and now viewed. The same exercise is proposed as orientation unit 4 later in this chapter. The project teachers were impressed and sometimes startled by what this highly disciplined process revealed about the possible discrepancy between what in teaching is conventionally held to matter and what ought perhaps to matter more. Especially, using audio trains one to *listen*.

For the technically minded, we mention that in the EEF project each intervention school was provided with one Panasonic HC-W570EB-K Full HD Camcorder with Twin Camera (which allows wide angle classroom shots to be combined with close-ups), one Olympus VN-732PC 4Gb Digital Voice recorder, one Hama Star 61 Tripod, 1 Transcend 64 Gb Premium SDXC Class 10 Memory card, a camera case and batteries.

The brands (probably out of date by the time this book is published) are of course less important than the quality, and it is impossible to over-emphasise the importance of a responsive microphone, either integral to the camera or free-standing, so that what is said can be clearly heard when replayed. In earlier projects, I combined three kinds of microphone: camera, radio (usually worn by the teacher) and an omnidirectional pressure-zone or conference microphone of the kind that can be placed in the middle of a discussion group. In the EEF project, the digital audio-recorder provided a viable substitute for the latter, though these days all the equipment listed is well within the budget of most schools and should be regarded as essential by any institution engaged in teacher training, so users need not, and should not, rely on camera microphones alone.

If the teacher uses video unassisted, he or she will need to experiment with camera positioning and consider its impact on the account of teaching created. In any event, a tripod is essential. A camera at the back of the room, with students' heads in the foreground and the teacher in the distance, signals something rather different from a teacher's-eye view of students' faces. The preferred project compromise was to place the camera on its tripod at the side and use wide-angle to capture both teacher and students in profile, yet also try different camera positions for each cycle. If someone else is available to make the recording, the task, obviously, is easier, and the camera can be moved within lessons as well as between them.

Lighting is important too. To avoid glare and images of participants in silhouette only, the camera should not be placed facing a window, and in dark classrooms or during winter at high latitudes it is helpful to supplement daylight by switching on the classroom lights.

Having good equipment for playback and review is equally essential. In some of the pilot schools, we found teachers and mentors crouched over laptops barely able to hear what was being emitted from their machine's tiny and tinny loudspeaker. For viewing, videos can be uploaded to and played through the institution's large-screen system. If only a laptop is available, then it should be used with powered external speakers. Again, teachers and mentors *must* be able to hear the recorded exchanges. There is no point in going to the trouble of recording otherwise.

Within most of the development cycles (later), participants will need two recordings for each cycle, one at its start and the other made towards the end so as to allow an assessment of changes achieved. Given the luxury of unlimited time, each lesson would then be viewed and discussed in its entirety because beginnings and endings are in their way no less important than middles, and every lesson follows a trajectory of successive causes and consequences. But time is not unlimited, so with one exception (cycle 4), it will be necessary for teachers to nominate short episodes from each lesson that they consider typical or noteworthy, and for the mentoring sessions to work on these.

With progression as well as time also in mind, the entering or baseline video in a given cycle will usually be the one made at the end of the previous cycle. Thus, over the entire programme, the minimum number of lessons recorded in the classroom of each participating teacher will be nine: two for cycle 1 and one each for cycles 2–8.

The question of what makes a viable episode for the purposes of analysis is discussed and extensively illustrated in *Culture and Pedagogy*.[4] There it is noted that episodes should be:

> of a length which allows them to be . . . understood as coherent acts of teaching, not merely as disembedded instances of pedagogical talk. . . . The distinctive features . . . begin to make sense only when one sees where a particular exchange . . . comes from and leads to. To analyse the structure of such discourse without attending to its meaning is . . . a pointless exercise.[5]

For study purposes, transcripts of analytically viable episodes may be accessed using the links in Appendix 2, pages 208–9.

Finally, readers will be aware that in many countries photographing and video recording children and students are subject to legal constraints and to strict protocols for permission and use. These, of course, must be scrupulously observed. Even when permission is not required, it should as a matter of courtesy be sought. In cases where permission is granted for most students in a class but not all, the camera must be positioned accordingly.

Cycles of planning, target-setting, teaching and review

In the EEF project, the programme comprised two days of induction and training, 11 planning/review/refocussing cycles, and two further days for debriefing, one at the project's mid-point and the other at its end. Each cycle lasted for two weeks except for the one-week cycles that opened and closed the programme, which was spread across two school terms and occupied 20 weeks. Each cycle began with planning and target-setting and ended with review, and the video/audio recordings contributed to one or both of these.

What was being planned for each cycle was not a deviation from the intended curriculum but a sharper and more self-conscious focus on the part within it that oral pedagogy might play. In this respect, the intervention was curricular as well as pedagogical. It required teachers to audit and map the talk in their classrooms, single out those aspects on which, within their planned lessons and the required focus of each of the intervention's cycles, they should work, and then do so in a systematic way. Baseline sessions initiated this process, but development came from repeating the planning/review sequence rather than waiting until the end of the programme to assess progress.

The piloted version of the programme had been relatively flexible, presenting in some detail the properties of dialogic teaching to be aimed for while leaving teachers and mentors free to devise their own routes to these. This produced excessive qualitative variation between teachers – some simply re-interpreted dialogic teaching as what they were already doing – and, critically, some sacrifice of epistemic cumulation to genial but circular discussion, so for the trial the loose framework of the pilot was replaced by a programme in which the focus and tasks for each cycle were more precisely specified.

At the same time, there needed to be room for variation in each teacher's circumstances, capacities and needs, so a distinction was made between the programme's 'directed' and 'responsive' foci. The *directed focus* was what we asked all schools to follow during the cycle in question in order to ensure consistency and progression. The *responsive focus* encompassed those aspects of classroom talk to which individual teachers and mentors decided they would like in addition to attend. The shift from the latitude that teachers were given in the pilot to the more closely prescribed framework of the trial was of such an order of magnitude that we feared that teachers might find it excessive. It was with some relief, therefore, that when we raised the matter at the mid-programme plenary, teachers and mentors agreed that they not only found the framework helpful rather than overly prescriptive but that anything less would have left some of them floundering. Yet they also welcomed the deviation that the responsive focus allowed.

In what follows, the structure of the programme is retained in its essentials, and it is entirely permissive. However, in place of the preliminary induction and training, there are seven orientation sessions. These take exploration of the idea and nature of dialogic teaching considerably further than the intensive but brief project training sessions allowed, and each of them entails the reading and discussion of designated previous chapters or parts of chapters. Then come eight planning/review cycles: again, each goes into greater depth than its project equivalent. The cycles are punctuated by two sessions that review progress and consider next steps.

It is suggested that for serving teachers (as opposed to pre-service trainees), the programme might last a full academic year rather than the 20 weeks (21 including induction and training) into which it had to be compressed in the EEF project. If the orientation sessions are scheduled weekly and three weeks are allowed for each cycle – as the EEF project teachers said they would have preferred – this is entirely feasible. In a teacher training context, a more radical and compressed adaptation of the programme is called for because so much else has to be accommodated within the same period of time.

Whole school buy-in

Individual development and innovation are most successful when they are supported by the school's leadership and embedded in its everyday professional discourse. Although the trial was confined to teachers and students in one school year, schools were encouraged to take ownership of both the pedagogy and the development strategy and to explore their application across the school.

Materials and professional study

It is axiomatic that teachers learn from examining the practice of both themselves and others, and that effective professional development requires understanding of the ideas and evidence on which the objectives of the development are based. To this end, all participants in the EEF project were provided with a suite of print materials and online access to these and other material. Central to these was the 68-page handbook.[6]

This book provides the equivalent resource, indeed a rather more extensive one. Specific readings are nominated for each of the development programme's units and cycles, and additional material, print and online, is suggested in the appendix.

Monitoring and support

During the EEF project, every intervention school was visited at least once by a member or members of the project team. Progress was reviewed, video clips were discussed, planning/review records were examined and problems needing resolution were identified and, ideally, resolved. In the context of a research project, such external monitoring was necessary, but in adapting the ideas contained in this chapter to suit their particular circumstances, schools and departments might consider this neither necessary nor appropriate. On the other hand, they may wish to find other ways to satisfy themselves that all is proceeding more or less to plan and that – for it does happen – the relationship between mentor and mentees is as insightful yet supportive and unthreatening as it needs to be. Thus, small schools within a cluster or trust might exchange staff in order to add this element of objective oversight. Larger schools might do so by crossing departmental boundaries.

The programme

The programme, with its structure and content revised in line with the new version of the dialogic teaching framework, comprises seven orientation units, eight planning/review cycles, and two stock-taking plenaries:

Orientation 1:	Planning the programme
Orientation 2:	Dialogic teaching – concept and stance
Orientation 3:	Dialogic teaching – framework and repertoires
Orientation 4:	Listening, reading, looking
Orientation 5:	Speaking, reading, writing
Orientation 6:	Dialogue and curriculum
Orientation 7:	Practicalities
Plenary 1:	Taking stock
Cycle 1:	Interactive culture
Cycle 2:	Interactive settings

Cycle 3:   Talk for learning
Cycle 4:   Talk for teaching
Cycle 5:   Questioning
Cycle 6:   Extending
Cycle 7:   Discussing
Cycle 8:   Arguing

Plenary 2:   Review and next steps

Orientation units

The orientation units are conceived as meetings attended by teachers and mentors participating in the programme. At each session, a designated topic or topics will be discussed and, at some sessions, decisions will need to be made. The discussion will be grounded in the specified readings from this book. It is suggested that most meetings will last for no less than one hour. They could be timetabled weekly during the first part of the academic year, or they could be intensively combined within, say, two in-service days.

The orientation units are proposed as the essential first part of the professional development programme. However, they may also be treated as a stand-alone sequence. For each unit, one of its participants will need to act as chair.

Orientation 1: Planning the Programme

• *Preliminary reading: Chapters 7 and 8.*

The meeting will consider, check and/or agree:

• That all participants understand what the framework and programme entail.
• Whether to implement the programme as specified or to adapt it, in which case in what way(s).
• Dates and times of orientation sessions 2–6 and plenaries 1 and 2.
• Length of cycles.
• The appointment of a mentor or mentors. In primary schools, this might be one teacher for KS1 colleagues, another for KS2; in secondary schools and universities, the mentor would probably be from the same department or discipline.
• Equipment available for recording and playback, paying particular attention to the imperative of audibility, and whether any additional equipment is needed.
• How the programme should be presented to students, parents and others, and the matter of permissions and protocols.

* * *

Orientation 2: Dialogic Teaching – Concept and Stance

- *Preliminary reading: Chapters 1–4.*

Discussion possibilities:

- Do we understand and accept the case for attending closely to the quality of classroom talk? (Chapter 1)
- Would an audit of talk in our school or department reveal a predominance of recitation, or is there greater variety? If the latter, how would we characterise the range? (Chapter 1)
- Do we understand the difference between dialogic teaching and oracy/speaking and listening as conventionally defined? (Chapter 2)
- Are we also clear about the distinction and relationship between dialogue and argumentation? (Chapter 3)
- What do we think about the idea that argument and argumentation should be prominent features of classroom talk? (Chapter 4)
- If we already undertake work in contingent areas like philosophy for children, how might one add value to the other? (Chapter 4)
- How can we maximise student voice in the senses discussed in Chapter 4? What about the right to remain silent as well as the right to speak and be heard? How do we align a heightened emphasis on classroom talk with the situation of children with speech, language and communication needs (SLCN)? (Chapter 4)

* * *

Orientation 3: Dialogic Teaching – Framework and Repertoires

- *Preliminary reading: Chapters 7 and 6.*

This session continues the exploration, by reference to this book's relevant chapters, of what dialogic teaching is about, reviewing the framework and drawing attention to which of its aspects are, according to the evidence, particularly important for the quality of learning.

- How do we respond to the overarching dialogic stance proposed? (Pages 128–9)
- Do we wish to add to, comment on or prioritise the justifications offered? (Page 130)
- Do we understand the meaning and significance of the six dialogic teaching principles and how we might regard them as ultimate tests of the quality of talk we achieve? Do we see any of them as problematic? (Pages 131–3)
- Then consider and discuss each of the repertoires in turn. (Pages 133–64)

- How do our current practices measure up to those aspects of classroom talk that, according to the research evidence, really make a difference to students' motivation, engagement and learning? What, if anything, needs to change? (Chapter 6)

* * *

Orientation 4: Listening, Reading, Looking

- *Preparatory task: obtain a short, videotaped lesson extract containing whole class teacher-student interaction (5–7 minutes maximum). Have it (a) transferred to audiotape, (b) transcribed. The transcription should be anonymised and can use the most basic transcription conventions: T for teacher, S for student, SS for more than one student speaking at once and '(inaudible)' as required.*

Introduction. Explain the nature and importance of this exercise by reference to the previous paragraphs on video and audio recording. The session chair should not distribute the transcripts until after the audio recording has been discussed. Sufficient context about the extract should be provided – subject, lesson aims, age of students – for the material to be meaningful.

Listen to the extract. After listening, consider:

- What is the teacher trying to do?
- What range of *teaching talk* (repertoire 4, pages 144–6) does the teacher use?
- What range of student *learning talk* (repertoire 3, pages 142–4) can be heard?

Distribute the transcripts. Listen to the extract again, this time following it as transcribed. It is now possible to go through it in stages. Here is one useful line of discussion:

- Locate and track a line of enquiry that is sustained over several exchanges from the teacher's initial question through students' various contributions to a conclusion, showing what leads to what.
- Track another that doesn't lead so far.
- Identify moments where a different question might have yielded a more productive response, or where a student's contribution has either been effectively extended and built on, or not.
- In the latter case, how might the teacher's moves have been better framed?

Now add vision, and this third time look as well as listen. Examples of issues to discuss:

- What can you deduce from the episode's paralinguistic elements – body language, gesture, expression, behaviour – that is not evident from just listening to or reading the extract? How does the paralinguistic moderate the linguistic?

- Having considered these three versions or layers of the same teaching episode three times, do you judge it differently from when you first listened to it? In what way? What has made the difference?

* * *

Orientation 5: Speaking, Reading, Writing

- *Preliminary reading: Chapter 5.*

This session focuses on the relationship between the oral and the written.

- (England) How can we redress the historic imbalance in status, quality and time between the written and the oral in our teaching?
- (Other countries) What is the balance between the written and the oral in our schools? Does it need to change?
- How can we most productively explore the relationships between them?
- (UK) How do we respond to the claim that the concept of oracy has been somewhat diminished since the days of the National Oracy Project?
- What are the implications of the chapter's arguments for the way we teach the designated first language (e.g. English in England)?
- And for the way we teach foreign languages?
- Is argument literacy, giving particular attention to building students' capacities to make and test cases, a useful way forward?

* * *

Orientation 6: Dialogue and Curriculum

- *Preliminary reading: Chapter 3 (epistemic stance), pages 38–43; Chapter 4 (the disciplinary dimension of argumentation), pages 65–72; Chapter 7 (repertoires 5 and 6), pages 146–53.*

This session has in mind, particularly though not exclusively, subject specialists in secondary schools and universities and curriculum leaders in primary schools.

(a) Primary schools

- How can we ensure that talk is prioritised across the entire curriculum, regardless of national curriculum policy?
- How can subject leaders help class teachers improve the quality of classroom talk in those subjects in which they are not specialists?

(b) Subject departments in secondary schools and higher education

- In respect of our particular subject(s) or domain(s), might we wish to qualify the epistemic stance proposed in Chapter 3?
- How far do different disciplines call for different kinds of talk? Is this solely a matter of vocabulary? How do our own discipline's modes of enquiry and tests of authenticity, proof or truth translate into distinctive patterns of classroom talk?
- Does such disciplinary distinctiveness call for particular emphasis on some repertoires, or aspects of those repertoires, rather than others?

* * *

Orientation 7: Practicalities

- *Preliminary reading: this chapter.*

This is the final planning session before the start of the classroom-based part of the programme. It invites participants to check that everything is ready. We suggest that the first part of the meeting focuses on the listed checks for all teachers and mentors involved, and that in the second part mentors and mentees get together in their separate groups to ensure that they are ready for cycle 1 (final question below).

- Have all participants thoroughly familiarised themselves with the book's arguments and evidence, and with the repertoires in Chapter 7 towards which the programme will now be directed?
- Have mentors been appointed?
- Do mentors fully understand their role?
- Planning decisions and review observations for each cycle will need to be recorded. How will this be done?
- Is the full complement of equipment available?
- Has it been checked and tested to ensure that everything is working?
- Are we confident that the playback sound quality is loud and clear?
- Have we established the best camera position(s)?
- Are we clear about the structure and process of each cycle?
- Are we ready for cycle 1?

* * *

Development units

The ten development units include eight planning/teaching/review cycles on which teachers and their mentors work together, and two plenary discussions that bring together all the teachers involved in the programme, perhaps with school leaders too, to share experiences, review progress and determine next steps.

Each cycle is essentially an exercise in action research:

- *Plan and set targets*: teachers and mentors jointly determine what will happen during the cycle and what changes and outcomes teachers hope to achieve in the character and quality of classroom talk.
- *Implement/experiment*: teachers teach the planned lessons.
- *Collect data/observe*: teachers and mentors view video footage of selected lesson episodes or lessons.
- *Review and interpret* with reference to the dialogic teaching framework in Chapter 7: teachers and mentors review and discuss what happened during the cycle as a whole and/or the selected episodes or lessons.
- *Refocus* in preparation for the next cycle.[7]

It is important to stress that the focus here is not on the *content* of lessons (which remains the responsibility of the teachers) but the kinds of talk through which that content might best be illuminated and pedagogically translated.

Each cycle is headed by aims and one or more 'signposts'. These are relevant sections of this book, including the appropriate repertoire or repertoires in Chapter 7, and are intended to provide, alongside the video clips chosen by teachers and mentors, the main points of reference for teacher-mentor analysis, review and refocussing.

* * *

Cycle 1: Interactive Culture

This cycle aims for a classroom culture that is conducive to talk freely ventured and respectfully handled, and it collectively identifies norms for talk (aka 'ground rules') by which all parties aim or hope to abide.

Signposts

Chapter 7, repertoire 1, interactive culture; principles; indicators.
Chapter 4, section on 'Voice.'

Plan/collect data

- *Teacher or mentor*. Make entering video of a lesson in which there is a great deal of talk.
- *Teacher*. Allocate lesson time early in the cycle to 'talk about talk' and think about how this might best be handled.

Implement/experiment

- *Teacher and students.* Introduce students to the enhanced focus on talk over the coming year (or however long the programme will take) and discuss ways that everyone can be encouraged to speak and feel comfortable doing so, especially those who are reticent or experience difficulties. Also discuss the importance of listening and turn-taking. Secure collective agreement for conscious effort in these matters from now on. Get students to suggest norms for speaking and listening that all will now try to observe. Firm up as written list which is either displayed or circulated.

Collect data

- *Teacher or mentor.* Towards the end of the cycle, make second video.

Review/refocus

- *Teacher and mentor together.* Take a short but typical episode from each recording. Play, review and assess progress. Identify how this initial exercise can be consolidated so that explicit norms become unspoken habits. Consider any special attention/provision needed for students with language or communication difficulties, and those for whom the language of teaching is not their first language. Discuss how teaching can become even more deeply sensitised to student voice in the various senses in Chapter 4.
- *Teacher.* Revisit the norms with students, review progress and discuss what more needs to be done. With older students, consider grouping the norms as in repertoire 1 (communicative, deliberative, epistemic) though not necessarily using these terms.

* * *

Cycle 2: Interactive Settings

This cycle reminds us that talk cannot be considered or fostered in isolation from the wider pedagogical context, and it helps us to turn to best oral advantage classroom layout, time, student grouping and the balance of whole class, group and individual interaction.

Signposts

Chapter 7, repertoire 2, interactive settings.
Chapter 7, 'Talk in its pedagogical context'.

Plan/review data

- *Teacher and mentor.* Discuss how the four organisational elements in repertoire 2 – relations, grouping, space, time – are currently deployed and how they might be adjusted with the improvement of talk in mind. Be prepared to re-use the second video from cycle 1 as entering data for this cycle.

Implement/experiment

- *Teacher.* This is very much an experimental cycle, and there are various options here. For example, try re-arranging the furniture so as to maximise opportunities for whole class, group and individual interaction. Or for group work (to be revisited in cycle 7), consider changing group composition for a trial period or for specific tasks. Or in respect of time, in a lesson with a substantial writing task try breaking it down into shorter writing episodes interspersed with discussion on ideas so far generated. Try just a few – the process can be continued throughout the programme.

Collect data

- *Teacher or mentor.* Video a lesson in which the changes have been made.

Review/refocus

- *Teacher and mentor.* Compare episodes from the two videos and, on the basis of this comparison and the teacher's own assessment, discuss the impact of the changes made. Consider how they might be consolidated, further developed (or even reversed).

* * *

Cycle 3: Talk for Learning

This cycle concentrates on mapping and seeking to expand the kinds of student talk that we wish to encourage and develop, in accordance with the principle that it is to the quality of the student's talk, and hence his or her thinking, that all our efforts should be directed.

Signposts

Chapter 7, repertoire 3, learning talk; repertoire 4, teaching talk; indicators.
Chapter 2, Talk for learning.
Chapter 6, Ingredient X.

Review data/plan

- *Teacher.* Take a typical episode or episodes from the video at the end of cycle 2, chosen to capture a range of student talk. Jointly categorise the kinds of learning talk exemplified by reference to repertoire 3.

- *Teacher and mentor.* Check for agreement on how each is categorised. Estimate (a) their relative frequency and (b) forms of talk that are important yet conspicuous by their absence. Then plan a lesson or lessons which prioritise some of the latter, considering by reference to repertoire 4 what kinds of teaching talk are most likely to generate the talk that has been targeted.

Implement/experiment

- *Teacher.* Teach the lessons in question, keeping the targeted forms of talk in mind.

Collect data

- *Teacher or mentor.* Make new video recording.

Review/refocus

- *Teacher and mentor.* Compare episodes, review progress and discuss ways that the repertoire of learning talk can be further expanded.

* * *

Cycle 4: Talk for Teaching

This cycle, the mirror or obverse of cycle 3, maps the range and relative preponderance of the various kinds of talk used by the teacher, considers the 'fit' between teaching talk and pedagogical aim, and how the full repertoire can be developed and appropriately exploited. It also draws attention to the power of the paralinguistic.

Signposts

Chapter 7, repertoire 4, teaching talk; indicators.
Chapters 2, 3 and 6.

Review data/plan

- *Teacher.* View again the video from the end of cycle 3, this time taking in the entire lesson (this is a rare instance when a short episode will not be adequate to the cycle's purpose). Categorise the kinds of teaching talk exemplified in the lesson as a whole by reference to repertoire 4.
- *Teacher and mentor.* Check that both parties agree on the categorisation, and estimate (a) their relative frequency and (b) forms of talk that are important yet conspicuous by their small showing or absence. Also note how the incidence of the different kinds of teaching talk relate to the lesson's stages.

- *Teacher and mentor.* Plan a lesson or lessons which prioritise the latter, considering by reference to repertoire 3 what kinds of teaching talk are most likely to generate the talk that has been targeted.

Implement/experiment

- *Teacher.* Teach the lessons in question, keeping the targeted forms of teaching talk in mind.

Collect data

- *Teacher or mentor.* Towards the end of the cycle, make new lesson video recording.

Review/refocus

- *Teacher.* Again, view entire lesson in order to compare the scope, frequency and use of the different kinds of teaching talk.
- *Teacher and mentor.* Track the kinds of learning talk (repertoire 3) thereby yielded. Select and compare a salient episode or episodes, review progress and discuss ways that the repertoire of teaching talk can be further expanded.

* * *

Plenary 1: Taking Stock

Dismount from the cycles.

- *Teacher and mentor.* (a) Check: check that video recordings are correctly stored and labelled and that salient episodes are indexed for later use. (b) Record: ensure that planning decisions and review judgements and recommendations from cycles 1–4 have been logged in the programme journal. (c) Flag: identify, in advance of the plenary, one or two examples of interesting practice – either to talk about or to show as a video or audio clip – plus any problems or questions. (d) Review: refer to the dialogic teaching principles and indicators to assess progress and areas for further development.
- *All teachers and mentors.* Come together to share successes (and perhaps clips), review progress, resolve any problems arising and prepare for the next stage, noting that cycles 5–8 move from broad spectrums of talk and classroom organisation to specific exchange patterns and moves.

* * *

Cycle 5: Questioning

Remount.

This cycle homes in on the ubiquitous practice of questioning. It again invites mapping of the teacher's existing repertoire and consideration of how this might be broadened. It also investigates where different kinds of question lead, and it explores how the skills of questioning can be developed for students as well as teachers.

Signposts

Chapter 7, repertoire 5, questioning.
Chapter 6, 'Specific explanations', 'Principle not recipe', 'The third turn and the unquestioned answer' and 'Whose question?'

Review data/plan

- *Teacher*. Select two episodes from the video at the end of cycle 4. One should exemplify questioning by the teacher, the other – if examples can be found – questioning by students.
- *Teacher and mentor*. Discuss repertoire 5. Categorise the questions in the two episodes by reference to the repertoire's questioning forms and moves. In relation to *teacher questions*, create a rough profile covering matters such as: thinking time and the balance of bidding/nomination and rotation/extension; the balance of test and authentic questions; and the various purposes of questions. In relation to *student questions*, again classify the different types. In each case, are there certain kinds of question that clearly predominate?
- *Teacher and mentor*. Plan a lesson or lessons for which (a) a broader range of teacher questions has been identified in advance (though obviously it will probably not be followed to the letter) and (b) which sets up an exercise in which students are invited to brainstorm about, and record, all the questions they think should be asked about a topic with which the lesson deals.

Implement/experiment

- *Teacher*. Teach the lesson(s) in question. In respect of the student questions, this exercise, which might perhaps be undertaken in small groups, could be followed by a plenary at which nominated questions can be shared, critiqued (are these the right questions?) and supplemented, and there can be a discussion about how important it is for students, too, to ask questions.

Collect data

- *Teacher or mentor*. Towards the end of the cycle make new lesson video recording, ideally including both the enhanced questioning from the teacher and the discussion during which students talk about their own role as questioners.

Review/refocus

- *Teacher and mentor.* Review progress over the cycle in both teacher and student questioning by reference to repertoire 5 and discuss ways that the questioning repertoires of both the teacher and the students can be further expanded.
- *Final test.* How far does the pattern of questioning meet the six 'bottom line' criteria of dialogic teaching? (Chapter 7, Principles)

* * *

Cycle 6: Extending

The focus in this cycle is on what we do with what students say and with the answers they give to the questions that we or other students pose. Working from the proposition that how the third turn is handled is a critical moment in dialogic teaching, the cycle helps teachers expand their repertoire of moves for probing and extending student contributions.

Signposts

Chapter 7, repertoire 6, extending.
Chapter 6, 'The third turn and the unquestioned answer'.

Review data/plan

- *Teacher.* Select an episode or episodes from the video at the end of cycle 5 that includes students responding to teacher questions and/or making other kinds of oral contribution, both within the three-part exchange and outside it (including how the students' own questions are handled). Seek variety here so as to provide scope for discussing different ways that such contributions can be probed, extended and built upon.
- *Teacher and mentor.* Discuss repertoire 6. Profile the teacher's handling of student contributions. Using a simple number count, which are the most and least common moves? Do some moves seem to be automatic or habitual rather than considered? (We all do it.) Then prepare for teaching during the cycle so as to both enhance questioning as in cycle 5 and try a more varied range of moves to extend students' contributions.

Implement/experiment

- *Teacher.* Teach the lesson(s) in question, concentrating on incorporating some of the extending moves in repertoire 6. As devised by Michaels and O'Connor,[8] these are not random but exert logical leverage on the four priorities for productive talk which preface their list and are turned into the four nominated goals ('share, expand and clarify thinking', 'listen carefully to one another' and so on). So the initial extending moves in a lesson or episode might concentrate on getting students to listen, talk and think, using moves 1–4, while once ideas have been articulated, shared and understood, they can be probed, challenged and extended through moves 5–9.

Collect data

• *Teacher or mentor.* Towards the end of the cycle, make new lesson video recording.

Review/refocus

• *Teacher and mentor.* Review progress over the cycle in the teacher's use of extending moves. Which moves are used most and least? In relation to students' contributions, how appropriate are they? And how effective? Find instances where real 'lift-off' has been achieved in the form of a lively episode of extended student talk. How was this achieved?

• *Final test.* How far does the pattern of questioning meet the six 'bottom line criteria of dialogic teaching', especially that of cumulation? (Chapter 7, Principles) In other words, do the extending moves demonstrably extend not only the exchanges but also the thinking? Consider the implications of this distinction between discursive and cognitive or epistemic extension.

* * *

Cycle 7: Discussing

Here, in its various formats – whole class and small group settings, teacher-led and student-led – we first assess the quality of classroom discussion, then work on ways to improve it. The discussion repertoire calls for skills in organisation, questioning and extending that apply to students no less than to teachers, and for sustained attention to the culture and norms of talk fostered from cycle 1 onwards.

Signposts

Chapter 7, repertoires 7 and 8.
Chapter 7, repertoire 7.
Chapter 3, 'Defining dialogue' and 'Dialogic stance'.
Chapter 4, 'Voice', 'Philosophy for Children' and 'Argumentation'.
Chapter 6, 'Generic explanations' and 'Specific explanations'.

Review data/plan

- *Teacher.* Select two episodes from earlier videos. One should exemplify a whole class or small group discussion led by the teacher. The other will be a small group discussion managed by the students themselves.
- *Teacher and mentor.* Discuss repertoire 7. This is the most synoptic of the eight, for successful discussion requires that we attend to and observe agreed norms such as turn-taking and respect for the voices and opinions of others (repertoire 1) and consider the most appropriate arrangements for student seating and grouping (repertoire 2), as well as revisit the talk forms and moves identified in repertoires 3–6, noting especially the importance but problematic nature of student voice (Chapter 4). On the other hand, if the programme's earlier cycles have progressed as intended, some of the discourse imperatives upon which effective discussion depends should be well on their way to being embedded. So, for example, not only will students be listening to each other and supporting their efforts to articulate their thoughts, but they, as well as the teacher, will also be asking questions (cycle 5) and deploying some of the extending moves that the teacher has modelled (cycle 6).
- *Teacher and mentor.* Review salient video episodes exemplifying teacher-led and student-managed discussion and assess strengths and growth points in light of repertoire 7. In planning for development during this cycle, the teacher-led discussion will be partly a continuation of cycles 5 and 6, in as far as the quality of the teacher's questioning and extending moves will be critical; but the focus will also be on the teacher's ability to shift the locus of interaction, for at least some of the time, from teacher-student to student-student. In such episodes the teacher's role is less one of directing than of chairing. In assessing instances of small group student-led discussion, consider the section 'Conditions for student-led discussion' in repertoire 7. Then plan, within the usual curriculum schedule for this cycle, some lessons during which there will be (a) a heightening of the teacher's attention to good quality whole class discussion and (b) timetabled tasks requiring small group student-led discussion.

Implement/experiment

- *Teacher.* Teach the lesson(s) in question.

Collect data

- *Teacher or mentor.* For the whole class discussion, the usual camera arrangements will apply. For the small group discussions, the students will need to be close-miked so that what they say is audible in the playback, bearing in mind that similar discussions may be taking place in other groups. I suggest placing the audio recorder in the centre of one group and the camera on its tripod further back. The audio recorder should capture the discussion, and the camera will enable you to study its paralinguistics and dynamics and what is going on elsewhere. Repeat the procedure with another group or other groups so that comparisons can be made.

Review/refocus

- *Teacher and mentor*. With reference to repertoire 7, review progress over the cycle in each discussion context. Compare how different groups handled the student-led discussion tasks. Account for what went well and less well. In the latter case, is it a problem of the task you have set, the unique dynamics of the group, both, or something else?
- *Final test*. How far does the pattern of discussion meet the six 'bottom line criteria of dialogic teaching', especially that of cumulation? (Chapter 7, Principles) If by now it is collective, supportive and reciprocal, is it also deliberative, cumulative and purposeful?
- *Teacher and students*. It is important that the students reflect on discussions for which they are responsible. A post-hoc 'How did it go?' will take them only so far, so with the agreement of the students concerned (NB), play them salient clips and invite them to comment and make suggestions for improvement.

* * *

Cycle 8: Arguing

This cycle, like several of the others, is merely an introduction to a repertoire that may take time to refine and establish, for it requires forms of talk with which participants will by now be familiar to be appropriately and incisively applied in furtherance of a particular intellectual discipline, that of making and testing arguments.

Signposts

Chapter 7, repertoires 7 and 8, discussing, deliberating, arguing.
Chapter 7, repertoire 8, arguing.
Chapter 3, 'Defining dialogue', '. . . And argumentation'.
Chapter 4, 'Argumentation'.

Review data/plan

- *Teacher*. Select an episode or episodes from a recent video showing discussion of a deliberative kind and/or students making and defending a proposition or propositions. You may well find an appropriate clip in the data from cycle 7. This is the baseline.

- *Teacher and mentor*. Discuss repertoire 8. All teaching, to express the matter at its simplest, requires attention to both content and process. But to teach argumentation is to foster particular classroom dynamics and modes of discussion at the same time as training students to think and handle ideas in particular ways. If previous cycles have addressed the contexts and forms of talk that are conducive to oral argumentation, they may not have secured this training. So planning for this cycle might consider two types of lesson. The first, analogous to 'talking about talk' in cycle 1, makes explicit to students this cycle's focus on argumentation and explores what argument means and how, building on what has gone before, it can be effectively handled. The second enacts that process in the teaching of the intended curriculum.

- With students of all ages the teacher's modelling of the process is important, and a 'culture of argumentation' can in large measure be established through the patterns of questioning, extension and discussion with which students become familiar through use, without the word 'argumentation' needing to be mentioned. However, with older students (and the age boundary is deliberately left undefined), it is suggested that the nature of argument and the process of argumentation be made the object of a lesson in its own right, with attention given to the stages of argument, its key elements and the vocabulary of position, claim, hypothesis, grounds, evidence, proof and so on. And, as discussed in Chapter 4, this will need to be domain specific, so that students learn to differentiate the generic in argument from the epistemically specific, especially in relation to tests of truth.

- When planning the other lessons – those that enact the argumentation process – aim, if possible, for variety within or across curriculum domains. Think carefully about what will be used to trigger and focus the argument: a text, perhaps, or a practical activity.

Implement/experiment

- *Teacher*. Teach the lesson(s) as described earlier. Explore the viability of Walton's three-stage framework as outlined in repertoire 8 (which Reznitskaya and Wilkinson call 'launch', 'inquiry dialogue' and 'closure')[9] and incorporate their argumentation moves as appropriate.

Collect data

- *Teacher or mentor*. Record at least two lessons, aiming for contrast in the domain or topic which the argument treats.

Review/refocus

- *Teacher and mentor*. View episodes from the three videos so as to (a) track progress between cycles 7 and 8, and (b) reflect differences in the handling of argument within and/or across curriculum domains. Refer to the stages, criteria and practices extrapolated from Reznitskaya and Wilkinson in repertoire 8.

- *Teacher and students.* As with discussion, students take responsibility for the argumentation in which they participate, so allow time for discussion of their part in the featured lessons, ideally – subject to their agreement – using clips from the video recordings.
- In both contexts, evaluation of progress during the cycle will need to reflect on both the process and the content of argumentation. During the cycle, have we exemplified and developed the kinds of talk, and the contingent culture and relationships, in which productive argument can be fostered? Is the process of argumentation better for this intervention? Are we now better at making and substantiating a case, examining a complex question and marshalling and assessing different kinds of evidence?

* * *

Plenary 2: Review and Next Steps

- *Teacher and mentor.* (a) Check: check that video recordings are correctly stored and labelled and that salient episodes are indexed. (b) Record: ensure that planning decisions and review judgements and recommendations from cycles 1–8 have been logged in the programme journal. (c) Flag: identify, in advance of the plenary, one or two examples of interesting practice – either to talk about or to show as a video or audio clip – plus any problems or questions.
- Give extra attention during this review to voice, equity and inclusion. Thus, which students prospered most and least in a dialogic context and why? How did those students fare for whom the language of schooling was not their mother tongue (in England, EAL students) or who had special educational needs and/or disabilities (SEND) or speech, language and communication needs (SLCN)? Did gender or socioeconomic status have a discernible impact on the character and quality of talk?
- *All teachers and mentors.* Come together to share successes (and perhaps clips), review progress and achievements, identify problems and how they can be addressed, and consider how dialogic teaching can be refined and embedded in everyday thinking and classroom practice, and how students themselves can further develop their skill and confidence in using talk to learn, reason and influence events for the better. Refer both to specific repertoires and the more general criteria embodied in the principles and indicators in Chapter 7. Bring together the thoughts and experiences of the various participants on equity and inclusion and consider what steps should be taken to ensure that classroom talk is just and equitable as well as effective.

* * *

Notes

1 The geographical claim is based on sales figures and destinations for *Towards Dialogic Teaching*, citations, email correspondence and direct involvement with fellow-workers outside the UK. Antarctica is obviously a guess, though it is not inconceivable that workers in Antarctic research stations may find their thoughts turning to dialogue during the long winter nights.

2 University of Cambridge, *Personal and Professional Development: mentoring*. www.ppd.admin.cam.ac.uk/professional-development/mentoring-university-cambridge/types-mentoring (accessed September 2019).

3 Cambridge Primary Review Trust/University of York 2015b.

4 Alexander 2001, chapter 16, pp. 427–528.

5 Alexander 2001, 439–440.

6 Cambridge Primary Review Trust/University of York 2015a.

7 Based on Hardman 2015.

8 Michaels and O'Connor 2012.

9 Reznitskaya and Wilkinson 2017, 55–64.

9 Epilogue

This book anticipates a diverse readership. Alongside researchers and research students there will be those who teach or are training to teach in early years, primary, secondary, special or higher education. Some will be teaching the entire curriculum to younger children. Others will be teaching one or two specialist subjects to older students. All will know that the language they use is shaped partly by how they perceive their students' learning needs and capacities, and partly by the character and vocabulary of what they wish their students to understand. These developmental and epistemic conditions combine to create an impressive array of interactive possibilities.

Teachers will be equally responsive to the social and cultural circumstances in which they operate. In the course of developing this book's pedagogical approach, I have visited remote, monolingual and largely monocultural rural schools with a mere 20 or 30 students; bustling multi-cultural, multi-faith and multi-ethnic urban schools where there are more than 1000 students, 30 or more languages are spoken, and student turnover is high; and a wide variety of settings in between. In every school, regardless of size, location or demography, the individual circumstances of students will vary. Alongside those children fortunate to return each day to homes that are stable and economically secure, there are others for whom it is the school rather than the home that provides stability and even basic nourishment.[1] Then there are the students who have specific learning needs and difficulties which have been correctly diagnosed and for whom skilled support has been provided, including perhaps in speech, language and communication; but others whose needs remain unrecognised and who must somehow struggle on against the odds.[2]

Teachers know all this, and my aim is not to state the obvious about the contextual and human diversity that they encounter but to use it to draw attention, one more time, to the imperatives of agency and repertoire that run throughout this book. Having pondered the evidence and arguments in Chapters 1–6, and having studied the dialogic teaching framework and professional development strategy in Chapters 7 and 8, it is the teacher, alive to circumstances and differences such as those exemplified previously, who must decide how the book's ideas and suggestions can most usefully be applied; though it is to be hoped that he or she will do so with close and constant regard to the principles and evidence that we have considered.

There is a further aspect of context that should be mentioned before we close, and it concerns the times in which we live. Researchers have long been exercised by the relationship between language, culture and class, and successive governments have devised (or recycled) various strategies to try to offset the educational consequences of poverty and social disadvantage, usually without attending to their root causes.[3] Yet while the early literature on classroom talk was alive to this challenge, it also managed to convey a sense of optimism, for talk, at its dialogic best, is engaging and inclusive. This certainly shone through the work of the National Oracy Project, whose key text is stirringly upbeat,[4] and it was reflected in a very physical way in the way that, as buildings and communities, schools at that time presented themselves to the world beyond their gates.

Indeed, between the 1960s and 1990s, school gates, whether iron or virtual, were often conspicuously absent. Schools were more readily accessible to their communities than previously ('no parents beyond this line') or subsequently ('press buzzer for entry, stand in front of the camera and clearly state your name and purpose'). During those intervening years, curriculum boundaries and even internal walls came down, and for a while 'open education' captured imaginations on both sides of the Atlantic.[5] By 2010, gates and fences had returned, conventional classrooms had been reinstated, security and safety were imperatives for every school in the land, visitors were vetted and tracked, and those working with children were checked against criminal records.[6] In parallel, the curriculum was closely prescribed, and schools were policed for compliance by a national inspectorate.

The 2006–10 Cambridge Primary Review, which I led, started its enquiries by travelling to far-flung locations in Cornwall, Tyneside, Kent, Lancashire, London, Birmingham, Yorkshire and beyond, and convening 'community soundings' with a wide range of educational stakeholders. During 87 witness sessions, the Review team met groups of children, teachers, teaching assistants, school leaders, governors, parents, administrators, faith leaders and representatives of the police and voluntary agencies, and sought their views on the themes that the Review was tasked with investigating.[7]

Again and again, we encountered a striking contrast between admiration for what goes on inside the school and anxiety about the world outside it. Our resulting report drew attention to:

> the pessimistic and critical tenor of much that we heard. . . . Thus, we were frequently told that children are under intense and perhaps excessive pressure from the policy-driven demands of their schools and the commercially-driven values of the wider society; that family life and community are breaking down; that there is a pervasive loss of respect and empathy both within and between generations; that life outside the school gates is increasingly insecure and dangerous; that the world is

changing, rapidly and in ways which it is not always easy to comprehend, though on balance they give cause for alarm, especially in respect
of climate change and environmental sustainability; that the school curriculum is too narrow and rigid; that the curriculum and children's educational careers are being compromised by the national tests.[8]

But, the report continued:

> Pessimism turned to hope when witnesses felt they had the power to
> act. . . . The children who were most confident that climate change
> need not overwhelm them were those whose schools had decided to
> replace unfocussed fear by factual information and practical strategies
> for energy reduction and sustainability. . . . The teachers who were least
> worried by national requirements were those who responded to them
> with robust and knowledgeable criticism rather than resentful compli-
> ance, and asserted their professional right to go their own way.[9]

Reading these words 13 years later, I am struck by the way they resonate
with two recent events. First, there were those students of Stoneman Douglas
High School in Florida who, in the traumatic wake of the murder of 14 of
their peers and three teachers in February 2018, banded together locally,
regionally and then nationally to demand reform of the US gun laws, notwithstanding attempts to discredit them by the National Rifle Association
and its beneficiaries on Capitol Hill. Then there were the school climate
strikes instigated in Sweden by Greta Thunberg and now, at the time of going
to press, a global movement whose impact can be measured not only by the
millions of students taking part but also by the queue of middle-aged men
eager to patronise or insult them into silence.

Greta Thunberg said she was inspired to strike by the actions of the Stoneman Douglas students, but for our purposes the events are also linked by
the use she and they have made of the spoken word. Both Thunberg and the
Stoneman Douglas students had learned to command language, evidence
and argument and use them to formidable effect. At crowded rallies, the
Florida students demolished the gun lobby's claims and justifications one by
one, citing evidence, exposing special interests and using textbook methods
of refutation;[10] while, disarmingly, Thunberg rehearsed the scientific evidence on climate change and its consequences before insisting, 'But listen to
the science, not to me.' And, like those children in the Cambridge Primary
Review community soundings, all understood that by coming together to
talk, discuss, marshal evidence and argue their case, students may counter
hopelessness, speak truth to power and make a difference.

In a democracy, that should be enough, but democracy is fragile, and
history cautions us against complacency about its prospects; and, as noted
in this book's opening chapter, the gulf between the ways of talking and
reasoning that we try to cultivate inside the school and those that students

encounter outside it appears to be widening. As this book goes to press, Britain is preparing itself for its second general election in two years. The partisan rhetoric on daily display illustrates, as on such occasions it always does, many of the textbook fallacies of argumentation discussed in Chapter 4, with the eristic rampant. This is hardly novel, and in the dialogic classroom it is readily exposed. What is new, however, is the departure from the contest of many Members of Parliament for whom the familiar peppering of political rhetoric with ad hominem/ad feminam argument has become something altogether more dangerous. A record number of women entered the UK Parliament at the 2017 election. Two years later, the list of departing MPs contained a disproportionate number of women, many of them citing abuse and intimidation as their main reasons for stepping down.[11] Their voices, in the formal arena of representative democracy at least, had been silenced. Yet it is on the liberation and protection of voice that democracy, like dialogic teaching, depends.

At the end of his vast and prescient 1990s trilogy *The Information Age*, Manuel Castells concluded that although the enlightenment dream seems forever frustrated by the 'extraordinary gap between our technological overdevelopment and our social underdevelopment', it nevertheless remains within reach; for 'there is no eternal evil in human nature', and 'there is nothing that cannot be changed by conscious, purposive social action'.[12] Dialogue is not a panacea, but it is indeed 'purposive social action' as well as a vital ingredient of effective teaching and a worthy educational end in itself, and hence a manifesto for hope. Dialogue is essential to how we respond to the cultural and existential crises that confront us, but only if we are able to defend those of its ingredients that are currently under attack: voice, argument and truth.[13]

Notes

1 More schools in England are setting up food banks to help feed their pupils' families. BBC News, 3 September 2019. www.bbc.co.uk/news/education-49515117 (accessed October 2019).

2 ICAN 2018 on children with speech, language and communication difficulties; All Party Parliamentary Group for Dyslexia and other Special Learning Difficulties (2019).

3 In England, by way of example, interventions have ranged from the Educational Priority Areas (EPAs) of the 1960s to the Education Action Zones (EAZ) of the 1990s and the Pupil Premium introduced in 2011. For a celebrated analysis of the corrosive impact of inequality and the limitations of such policies, see Wilkinson and Pickett 2009.

4 Norman 1992.

5 See, for example, Silberman 1973 (USA), Pluckrose 1975 (UK).

6 The United States went rather further: there, many schools employ armed security guards, and, following the 2018 Florida school massacre, some armed their teachers too.

7 Alexander 2010b, 532.

8 Alexander and Hargreaves 2007, 1–2.

9 Alexander and Hargreaves 2007, 44.
10 Some of these students were on the AP US Government and Politics programme (AP College Board 2018), and they made a point of acknowledging its impact and praising their teacher's work. Indeed, on the very day of the shootings, the students were investigating political interest groups. NBC News, 14 March 2018. www.nbcnews.com/news/us-news/he-taught-parkland-students-about-nra-then-gunshots-rang-out-n856266 (accessed June 2018).
11 Alarm over number of female MPs stepping down after abuse, *The Guardian*, 31 October 2019. www.theguardian.com/politics/2019/oct/31/alarm-over-number-female-mps-stepping-down-after-abuse (accessed October 2019).
12 Castells 1998, 359–360.
13 It is of course one of this book's key propositions that dialogue is a necessary response to these tendencies and that dialogic teaching can help students acquire the dispositions, understanding and skills to identify and counter them. As this book goes to press there are encouraging signs of a growing synergy here between educational, social and political dialogism. To take just two examples: students in Finland's schools are now taught, as a matter of government policy, to separate evidentially-sustainable information from misinformation and to understand the aims, nature and impact of fake news www.theguardian.com/world/2020/jan/28/fact-from-fiction-finlands-new-lessons-in-combating-fake-news; while, in the UK, the Institute for Strategic Dialogue hopes to develop viable educational responses to 'the rising tide of polarisation, hate and extremism of all forms' www.isdglobal.org.

Appendix 1

Dialogic teaching: the framework in outline

Definitions (page 128)

Dialogue: *the oral exchange and deliberative handling of information, ideas and opinions.*

Dialogic teaching: *a pedagogy of the spoken word that harnesses the power of dialogue to stimulate and extend students' thinking, learning, knowing and understanding, and to enable them to discuss, reason and argue. It unites the oral, cognitive, social, epistemic and cultural, and therefore manifests frames of mind and value as well as ways of speaking and listening.*

Stance (page 128)

- Uniting the cognitive and social
- Towards self-direction and accountability
- Encounters between different ways of knowing and making sense
- Other people, minds, places and times

Justifications (page 130)

- Thinking
- Learning
- Mastery
- Communicating
- Relating
- Acculturating
- Democratically engaging
- Teaching

Principles (pages 131–3)

- Collective
- Supportive
- Reciprocal

- Deliberative
- Cumulative
- Purposeful

Repertoire 1. Interactive Culture (pages 137–9)

- Communicative norms
- Deliberative norms
- Epistemic norms

Repertoire 2. Interactive Settings (pages 139–41)

- Relations   Class – Group (teacher-led and student-led) – Individual (teacher/student and student/student)
- Grouping   Size – Membership – Function
- Space   Rows – Cabaret – Horseshoe
- Time   Lesson length – Talk/text balance – Talk form balance – Pace

Repertoire 3. Learning Talk (pages 142–4)

- Transactional
- Expository
- Interrogatory
- Exploratory
- Deliberative
- Imaginative
- Expressive
- Evaluative

Repertoire 4. Teaching Talk (pages 144–6)

- Rote
- Recitation
- Instruction
- Exposition
- Discussion
- Deliberation
- Argumentation
- Dialogue

Repertoire 5. Questioning (pages 146–50)

- Management   Manage – Bidding and Nomination – Wait time – Rotation and Extension
- Character   Test – Authentic (from Nystrand)

- Purposes   Initiate – Probe – Expand
- Structure   Open/Closed – Leading – Narrow/Discursive

Repertoire 6. Extending (from Michaels and O'Connor) (pages 150–3)

- Share, expand and clarify thinking   Time to think – Say more – Are you saying?
- Listen carefully to one another   Rephrase/Repeat
- Deepen reasoning   Evidence of reasoning – Challenge/Counter example
- Think with others   Agree/Disagree – Add on – What others mean

Repertoire 7. Discussing (pages 153–61) (mainly synoptic: see other repertoires)

- Discourse norms
- Organisational frames
- Learning talk
- Teaching talk
- Questioning
- Extending
- Arguing
- Conditions for teacher-led discussion
- Conditions for student-led discussion

Repertoire 8. Arguing (from Reznitskaya and Wilkinson) (pages 161–4)

- Stages   Opening – Argumentation – Closing
- Foster and explore perspectives   Contestable questions – Share responsibilities – Discuss alternatives
- Clarify language and meaning   Clarify meaning – Connect ideas – Label processes – Track enquiry
- Acceptable reasons and evidence   Evaluate facts – Evaluate values
- Logical connections   Articulate reasons – Evaluate inferences

Indicators

- Respect for the situation, needs and rights of every student, especially those from communities whose voices are not treated equitably or who for social or clinical reasons find it difficult to express themselves in front of others.
- Agreed and respected norms for speaking, listening and discussion.

- A preparedness both to attend to talk for its own sake and to re-think its relationship with reading and writing.
- A broad and flexible repertoire of teaching strategies, modes of interaction and forms of both student and teacher talk.
- Interactions which encourage students to think, and to think in different ways.
- Questions which invite more than simple recall and are posed by students as well as teachers.
- Answers which are justified, followed up and built upon rather than merely received.
- Feedback which takes thinking forward and is offered by students as well as teachers.
- Extending moves which probe and collaboratively expand student contributions.
- Exchanges which chain together into coherent and deepening lines of enquiry.
- Discussion in which ideas are freely shared, heard and explored.
- Argumentation which tests and builds evidence and cases.
- Patterns of organisation which, in the handling of classroom layout, student grouping, time, pace and the balance of whole class, group and individual interactions, are conducive to the previous indicators.
- A classroom culture in which the dynamics of talk are collective, reciprocal and supportive, and its content and trajectory are deliberative, cumulative and purposeful.
- A recognisably dialogic stance on learning, knowledge and human relationships as well as on interaction more narrowly defined.

Appendix 2
Delving deeper

This appendix is primarily for teachers, trainee teachers, teacher educators, school leaders and others who wish to use this book to support professional development, perhaps along the lines suggested in Chapter 8. The appendix contains a small number of publications chosen with further study and discussion in view, together with pointers to video recordings and transcripts. It is followed by a 340-item bibliography that lists all the sources cited in the preceding nine chapters.

Keeping up with the literature in one's field, or trying to do so, is one of any researcher's prime obligations. But some take this to mean that only the most recent publications are worth bothering with, as if date of publication certifies quality. Yet by showering our writing with none but the freshest bibliographic confetti we may deny ourselves access to some of the best thinking available, betray the principle of cumulation which is fundamental to the growth of knowledge, and risk the arrogance of those who are unaware that their ideas are not as original as they think or claim.

So the following list contains both recent and less recent material, and those sharing my suspicion of novelty for novelty's sake will be pleased to discover that while the newest publications in this book's bibliography coincide with its release in 2020, the oldest is dated 1657.

Understanding classroom talk

- Edwards, A.D., Westgate, D.P.G. (1994) *Investigating Classroom Talk*, 2nd edition. London: Falmer Press.

Illustrating the balance of the old and the new, this book by Tony Edwards and David Westgate excludes the most recent research but has scarcely been bettered as a well-structured, expert and accessible account of the workings and problems of classroom talk and the various ways it can be investigated.

Towards dialogue

- Cazden, C.B. (2001) *Classroom Discourse: the language of teaching and learning*, 2nd edition. Portsmouth NH: Heinemann.

- Nystrand, M., with Gamoran, A., Kachur, R. and Prendergast, C. (1997). *Opening Dialogue: understanding the dynamics of language and learning in the English classroom*. New York: Teachers College Press.
- Mercer, N. (2000) *Words and Minds: how we use language to think together*. London: Routledge.

Courtney Cazden's book, whose first edition appeared in 1988, is a classic. It takes us back to the initial charting of the limitations of IRE/recitation with primary/elementary students and ways that teachers can successfully move beyond it. Martin Nystrand and his colleagues, drawing on their research in 8th and 9th grade literature classes (Y9 and 10), make the case for transition to dialogue empirically, epistemically and very persuasively. Mercer's book, also persuasive, popularises the term 'interthinking' and demonstrates the vital role of student-student discussion.

Understanding dialogic pedagogy

- Kim, M-Y. and Wilkinson, I.A.G. (2019) What is dialogic teaching? Constructing, deconstructing and reconstructing a pedagogy of classroom talk. *Language, Learning and Social Interaction*, 21, 70–86.
- Lefstein, A. and Snell, J. (2014) *Better Than Best Practice: developing teaching and learning through dialogue*. London: Routledge.
- Resnick, L.B., Asterhan, C.S.C. and Clarke, S.N. (ed) (2015) *Socializing Intelligence Through Academic Talk and Dialogue*. Washington DC: AERA.
- Mercer, N., Wegerif, R. and Major, L. (ed) (2020) *The Routledge International Handbook of Research on Dialogic Education*. Abingdon: Routledge.

These four are more recent, and because they survey the field as a whole they needed to be. The research review by Kim and Wilkinson seeks to make sense of dialogic teaching by comparing and contrasting some of its major variants, spotlighting an earlier version of the framework in this book's Chapter 7. Lefstein and Snell unpack dialogic teaching, compare models, confront challenges and make good use of case studies, transcripts and, via a link to a companion website, videos. The schools from which their case material is drawn are those with which I worked during the 2003–2006 Barking and Dagenham Teaching Through Dialogue Initiative, and that project's influence remains evident, so again there's a direct link. In different ways, Kim, Wilkinson, Lefstein and Snell provide direct commentaries on some of the ideas explored here.

Ranging more widely, the edited collections of research papers by Resnick *et al.* and Mercer *et al.* capture something of the scale and scope of work now being undertaken in the field of dialogic pedagogy: between them they include over 80 studies from 160 contributors, though there are some surprising omissions. Yet both are valuable points of reference, especially for researchers and research students. Deep pockets will be needed for the Routledge book.

This book's version of dialogic teaching

If I were obliged to reduce to just three those of my preceding publications that best support this one, they would probably be:

- Alexander, R.J. (2001) *Culture and Pedagogy*. Oxford: Blackwell/Wiley.
- Alexander, R.J. (2008b) *Essays on Pedagogy*. London: Routledge.
- Alexander, R.J (2018) Developing dialogue: genesis, process, trial. *Research Papers in Education* 33(5), 561–598.

The 2018 journal article provides a detailed account and discussion of the 2014–17 Education Endowment Foundation (EEF) dialogic teaching project and trial referred to frequently in the foregoing pages. The long section on classroom interaction and discourse with which *Culture and Pedagogy* culminates – a book within a book – analyses and compares, and with transcripts illustrates, patterns of classroom talk in England, France, India, Russia and the United States, uncovering commonalities as well as differences. It also initiates the approach to dialogic teaching whose latest version appears in this book. *Essays on Pedagogy* also deals with talk and yet much more than talk, embedding it in pedagogy, as the title suggests, but also in culture and history, ending with reflections on pedagogical responses to a world in peril. Twelve years later, that discussion has even greater urgency.

There is a full list of my publications on classroom talk and dialogic teaching at www.robinalexander.org.uk/dialogic-teaching/

Dialogic specifics

Questioning

- Dillon, J. (1988). *Questioning and Teaching: a manual of practice*. Eugene, OR: Wipf and Stock.

From the leading authority on this vital, ubiquitous, yet sometimes inadequately exploited ingredient of classroom talk, Dillon turns convention on its head by starting with the questions that students might and ought to ask but mostly don't. Full of provocative and useful ideas.

Extending

- Michaels, S. and O'Connor, C. (2012) *Talk Science Primer*. Cambridge MA: TERC.

A booklet whose value is infinitely greater than its brevity (20 pages) might suggest, because its wisdom and clarity are the distillation of many years of research, thinking and discussion. It, and other works by Sarah Michaels and/or Cathy O'Connor, are my key source for the 'extending' repertoire in Chapter 7. The booklet may be accessed and downloaded at https://inquiry-project.terc.edu/shared/pd/TalkScience_Primer.pdf. The focus is science teaching, but the approach is readily adaptable to other curriculum domains.

Small group discussion

- Barnes, D. and Todd, F. (1995) *Communication and Learning Revisited.* Portsmouth, NH: Heinemann.

Another classic. Douglas Barnes, together with James Britton and Harold Rosen, was among the first to problematise classroom talk in the UK. Here, with Frankie Todd, Barnes sets up and illustrates the influential approach to discussion in general, and small group discussion in particular, on which Mercer and others have since built. Barnes's deep understanding of teaching, from his own direct experience as well as from observation of others, is evident throughout.

Argumentation

- Reznitskaya, A. and Wilkinson, I. (2017) *The Most Reasonable Answer: helping students build better arguments together.* Cambridge, MA: Harvard Education Press.

This deals clearly and systematically with a complex topic and is the acknowledged key source for the argumentation repertoire in Chapter 7. Alina Reznitskaya and Ian Wilkinson also commend and illustrate (pp. 163–170) a process of teacher 'peer coaching' that is similar to the model of video-informed mentoring which forms part of the professional development strategy in Chapter 8.

Lesson video and transcript study materials

As those who follow or adapt the programme in Chapter 8 will rapidly confirm, there is no substitute for making your own video or audio recordings in the settings within which you work. However, some readers may wish to access additional or alternative material. For those working with older students this may not be easy, for while the literature on dialogic pedagogy draws on research undertaken in settings ranging from early years to higher education, most of the video material which has been cleared for use outside the research projects in question comes from primary or lower secondary classrooms. That, I hope, will incentivise those who work with older students to create their own.

Transcripts are useful too, and, as noted in Chapter 8, the act of turning talk into text permits study of a sustained and forensic kind that is possible with video only after many viewings. However, we should remember that while classroom talk may be planned in outline and often follows well-trodden paths – very well-trodden in the case of recitation – it is essentially unscripted, improvisatory and reactive. So to subject it to the same kind of critical scrutiny as, say, the text of a play whose every word has been weighed, drafted and polished is not necessarily appropriate or even fair to the participants. It is as talk that talk should always be judged.

Transcribed lesson extracts

There are abundant examples in the following books, all of them accompanied by analysis:

- Alexander 2001 (UK, France, India, Russia, United States)
- Barnes and Todd 1995 (UK)
- Cazden 2001 (USA)
- Edwards and Westgate 1994 (mainly UK)
- Lefstein and Snell 2014 (UK)
- Mercer 2000 (UK)
- Reznitskaya and Wilkinson 2017 (USA)

The transcripts in Alexander, Lefstein and Snell, Mercer, and Reznitskaya and Wilkinson are from primary/elementary schools. In Barnes and Todd, they are from secondary, in Edwards and Westgate from both and in Cazden from pre-school through primary and secondary.

A selection of transcribed lesson extracts, including some of those used for training purposes on the 2014–17 EEF dialogic teaching project, may be accessed at www.robinalexander.org.uk/dialogic-teaching/

Video-recorded lesson extracts

The use of video recordings acquired as research data is usually governed by ethical codes and data-protection laws that restrict its use to the projects in question. This is as it should be, but it means that in proportion to the amount of video material collected, relatively little becomes more widely available. Here are three useful exceptions:

- Those who use the Lefstein and Snell book are given password-protected access to a website containing the eight video-recorded lesson episodes that the authors and commentators discuss. Faces are pixilated to conceal identity.

  Link: http://dialogicpedagogy.com/the-episodes/

- Strict confidentiality was part of the participation agreement with schools for the 2014–17 EEF dialogic teaching project referred to in this book, so it is not possible to provide access to the excellent video material that emerged. However, a somewhat older (2006) selection from the North Yorkshire project is available. It comprises 24 clips from primary classrooms in a range of subjects with children from Reception to Year 6 (US K1 to 5th grade). The clips were chosen to provoke professional discussion and emphatically not as models of 'best practice'.

Link: www.robinalexander.org.uk/dialogic-teaching/video/

• The *Talk Science Primer* of Michaels and O'Connor referred to earlier is part of the larger Inquiry Project whose website includes a web-based professional development programme. Its resource library contains a wealth of video material, all of it well presented and clearly structured. One series of clips illustrates the various 'extending' moves in this book's Chapter 8, repertoire 6, and overall this extensive collection leans more than the other two towards modelling how dialogue can be fostered – in any setting or subject domain, not just science.

Link: https://inquiryproject.terc.edu/prof_dev/library.cfm.html

Website

I hope to add to these lists from time to time, so for further information about this or my other work, visit www.robinalexander.org.uk.

Bibliography

Adamson, S., Alexander, G.R. and Ettenhuber, K. (eds) (2007) *Renaissance Figures of Speech*. Cambridge: Cambridge University Press.

Alexander, R.J. (1984) *Primary Teaching*. London: Cassell.

Alexander, R.J. (1988) Garden or jungle? Teacher development and informal primary education. In W.A.L. Blyth (ed) *Informal Primary Education Today: Essays and Studies*. London: Falmer Press, 148–188.

Alexander, R.J. (1997) *Policy and Practice in Primary Education: Local Initiative, National Agenda*. London: Routledge.

Alexander, R.J. (1999) Culture in pedagogy, pedagogy across cultures. In R.J. Alexander, P. Broadfoot and D. Phillips (eds) *Learning From Comparing: New Directions in Comparative Educational Research, Volume 1*. Oxford: Symposium Books, 149–180.

Alexander, R.J. (2001) *Culture and Pedagogy: International Comparisons in Primary Education*. Oxford: Blackwell.

Alexander, R.J. (2003) *Talk for Learning: The First Year*. Northallerton: North Yorkshire County Council. www.robinalexander.org.uk/docs/NYorks_EVAL_REP_03.pdf.

Alexander, R.J. (2004) Still no pedagogy? Principle, pragmatism and compliance in primary education. *Cambridge Journal of Education*, 34(1), 7–33.

Alexander, R.J. (2005a) *Talk for Learning: The Second Year*. Northallerton: North Yorkshire County Council. www.robinalexander.org.uk/docs/TLP_Eval_Report_04.pdf.

Alexander, R.J. (2005b) *Teaching Through Dialogue: The First Year*. London: Barking and Dagenham Council. www.robinalexander.org.uk/bardagreport05.pdf.

Alexander, R.J. (2006) *Education as Dialogue: Moral and Pedagogical Choices for a Runaway World*. Hong Kong: Hong Kong Institute of Education with Dialogos.

Alexander, R.J. (2008a) *Education for All, the Quality Imperative and the Problem of Pedagogy* (CREATE Research Monograph 20). Universities of Sussex and London, with the Department for International Development: Consortium for Research on Educational Access, Transitions and Equity.

Alexander, R.J. (2008b) *Essays on Pedagogy*. London: Routledge.

Alexander, R.J. (2009a) Towards a comparative pedagogy. In R. Cowen and A.M. Kazamias (eds) *International Handbook of Comparative Education*. New York: Springer, 922–941.

Alexander, R.J. (2009b). De l'usage de la parole en classe: une comparaison internationale. *Revue Internationale d'Éducation – Sèvres*, 50, 35–48.

Alexander, R.J. (2010a). 'World class schools': Noble aspiration or globalised hokum? *Compare: A Journal of Comparative Education, 40*(6), 801–817.

Alexander, R.J. (ed) (2010b) *Children, Their World, Their Education: Final Report and Recommendations of the Cambridge Primary Review*. London: Routledge.

Alexander, R.J. (2012a). Neither national not a curriculum? *Forum, 54*(3), 369–384.

Alexander, R.J. (2012b). Moral panic, miracle cures and educational policy: What can we really learn from international comparison? *Scottish Educational Review, 44*(1), 4–21.

Alexander, R.J. (2014) Evidence, policy and the reform of primary education: A cautionary tale. *Forum, 56*(3), 349–375.

Alexander, R.J. (2015a) Dialogic pedagogy at scale: Oblique perspectives. In L.B. Resnick, C.S.C. Asterhan and S.N. Clarke (eds) *Socializing Intelligence Through Academic Talk and Dialogue*. Washington, DC: AERA, 429–440.

Alexander, R.J. (2015b) Teaching and learning for all: The quality imperative revisited. *International Journal of Educational Development, 41*(1).

Alexander, R.J. (2015c) True grit. *CPRT Blog*, 30 January. https://cprtrust.org.uk/cprt-blog/true-grit/ (accessed July 2019).

Alexander, R.J. (2015d) True grit – The sequel. *CPRT Blog*, 18 September. https://cprtrust.org.uk/category/robin-alexander/page/2/ (accessed July 2019).

Alexander, R.J. (2016) What's the point? Select committee ponders the meaning of education. *Forum, 58*(2), 155–165.

Alexander, R.J. (2017) *Towards Dialogic Teaching: Rethinking Classroom Talk* (5th edition). York: Dialogos.

Alexander, R.J. (2018) Developing dialogue: Genesis, process, trial. *Research Papers in Education, 33*(5), 561–598.

Alexander, R.J. (2019) Whose discourse? Dialogic pedagogy for a post-truth world. *Dialogic Pedagogy: An International Online Journal, 7*, E1–E20. https://dpj.pitt.edu/ojs/index.php/dpj1/article/view/268/182.

Alexander, R.J., with North Yorkshire County Council. (2006) *Talk for Learning: Teaching and Learning Through Dialogue* (CD/DVD pack with 24 lesson extracts and accompanying texts). Northallerton and York: NYCC and Dialogos.

Alexander, R.J. with J. Willcocks (1995) Task, time and talk. In R.J. Alexander, with J. Willcocks, K. Kinder and N. Nelson (eds) *Versions of Primary Education*. London: Routledge, 103–219.

Alexander, R.J. with J. Willcocks, K. Kinder and N. Nelson (1995) *Versions of Primary Education*. London: Routledge.

Alexander, R.J., Broadfoot, P. and Phillips, D. (eds) (1999) *Learning From Comparing: New Directions in Comparative Educational Research. Volume 1, Contexts, Classrooms and Outcomes*. Oxford: Symposium Books.

Alexander, R.J., Hardman, F. and Hardman, J., with Rajab, T. and Longmore, M. (2017) *Changing Talk, Changing Thinking: Interim Report From the In-house Evaluation of the CPRT/UoY Dialogic Teaching Project*. York: University of York. www.robinalexander.org.uk/wp-content/uploads/2017/07/Alexander-et-al-EEF-in-house-interim-report-final-170714.pdf.

Alexander, R.J. and Hargreaves, L. (2007) *Community Soundings: The Cambridge Primary Review Regional Witness Sessions*. Cambridge: University of Cambridge Faculty of Education.

Alexander, R.J., Rose, J. and Woodhead, C. (1992) *Curriculum Organisation and Classroom Practice in Primary Schools: A Discussion Paper*. London: Department for Education and Science.

Alexander, R.J., Willcocks, J. and Nelson, N. (1996) Discourse, pedagogy and the national curriculum: Change and continuity in primary schools. *Research Papers in Education*, 11(1), 83–122.

All-Party Parliamentary Group for Dyslexia and other Special Learning Difficulties (2019) *Educational Cost of Dyslexia*. London: British Dyslexia Association.

Andal, A.G. (2019) Whose discourse, whose ears? Harmony in dialogic pedagogy amidst the post-truth noise (Commentary on Alexander 2019). *Dialogic Pedagogy: An International Online Journal*, 7, C1–C5. https://dpj.pitt.edu/ojs/index.php/dpj1/article/view/276/184.

AP College Board (2018) *AP US Government and Politics: Course Framework*. Princeton, NJ: AP Services. https://apcentral.collegeboard.org/pdf/ap-us-government-and-politics-course-and-exam-description-effective-fall-2018-0.pdf?course=ap-united-states-government-and-politics (accessed June 2018).

Applebee, A.N., Langer, J.A., Nystrand, M. and Gamoran, A. (2003) Discussion-based approaches to developing understanding: Classroom instruction and student performance in middle and high school English. *American Education Research Association Journal*, 40(3), 685–730.

Arendt, H. (2004) *The Origins of Totalitarianism*. New York: Schocken Books.

Argyris, C. and Schön, D.A. (1974) *Theory in Practice: Increasing Professional Effectiveness*. San Francisco: Jossey-Bass.

Armstrong, M. (2019) The Cambridge Primary Review. In P. Yarker, J. Smith, M.J. Drummond, S. Cox and M. Fielding (eds) *Another Way of Looking: Michael Armstrong's Writing for Forum*. Oxford: Symposium Books, 185–187.

Assessment Reform Group (1999) *Assessment for Learning: Beyond the Black Box*. Cambridge: University of Cambridge Faculty of Education.

Asterhan, C.S.C. (2015) Introducing online dialogues in co-located classrooms: If, why, and how. In L.B. Resnick, C.S.C. Asterhan and S.N. Clarke (eds) *Socializing Intelligence Through Academic Talk and Dialogue*. Washington, DC: AERA, 205–218.

Asterhan, C.S.C., Schwarz, B.B. and Butler, R. (2009) Inhibitors and facilitators of peer interaction that supports conceptual learning: The role achievement goal orientations. In N.A. Taatgen and H. van Rijn (eds) *Proceedings of the 31st Annual Conference of the Cognitive Science Society*. Mahaw, NJ: Erlbaum.

Atkinson, P. and Delamont, M. (1977) Mock-ups and cock-ups: The stage management of guided discovery instruction. In P. Woods and M. Hammersley (eds) *School Experience: Explorations in the Sociology of Education*. London: Croom Helm, 87–108.

Austin, J.L. (1962) *How to Do Things With Words*. Oxford: Oxford University Press.

Bakhtin, M.M., ed M. Holquist (1981) *The Dialogic Imagination*. Austin TX: University of Texas Press.

Bakhtin, M.M., eds C. Emerson and W.C. Booth (1984) *Problems of Dostoevsky's Poetics*. Minneapolis: University of Minnesota Press.

Bakhtin, M.M., eds C. Emerson and M. Holquist (1986) *Speech Genres and Other Late Essays*. Austin, TX: University of Texas.

Bantock, G.H. (1966) *The Implications of Literacy*. Leicester: Leicester University Press.

Barnes, D. (1969) Language in the secondary classroom. In D. Barnes, J. Britton and H. Rosen (eds) *Language, the Learner and the School*. Harmondsworth: Penguin, 9–77.

Barnes, D. (1988) The politics of oracy. In M. MacLure, T. Phillips and A. Wilkinson (eds) *Oracy Matters: The Development of Talking and Listening in Education*. Milton Keynes: Open University Press.

Barnes, D. (2008) Exploratory talk for learning. In N. Mercer and S. Hodgkinson (eds) *Exploring Talk in School*. London: Routledge, 1–15.

Barnes, D. and Sheeran, Y. (1992) Oracy and genre: Speech styles in the classroom. In K. Norman (ed) *Thinking Voices: The Work of the National Oracy Project*. London: Hodder, 90–99.

Barnes, D. and Todd, F. (1977) *Communication and Learning in Small Groups*. London: Routledge and Kegan Paul.

Barnes, D. and Todd, F. (1995) *Communication and Learning Revisited*. Portsmouth, NH: Heinemann.

Bennett, N., Desforges, C., Cockburn, A. and Wilkinson, B. (1984) *The Quality of Pupil Learning Experiences*. London: Lawrence Erlbaum Associates.

Berliner, D.C. (2002) Educational research: The hardest science of all. *Educational Researcher*, 31, 18–20.

Berliner, D.C. (2004) Expert teachers: Their characteristics, development and accomplishments. *Bulletin of Science, Technology and Society*, 24(3), 200–212.

Bernard, E. (2015) Teaching the N-word: A black professor, an all-white class, and the thing nobody will say. *The American Scholar*, 1 September. https://theameri canscholar.org/teaching-the-n-word/#.XVu3JC3My-p (accessed August 2019).

Bernstein, B. (1971) *Theoretical Studies Towards a Sociology of Language* (Class, Codes and Control, Volume 1). London: Routledge and Kegan Paul.

Bernstein, B. (1975) Class and pedagogies: Visible and invisible. *Educational Studies*, 1(1), 23–41.

Bernstein, B. (1990) *The Structuring of Pedagogic Discourse* (Class, Codes and Control, Volume 4). London: Routledge.

Black, P., Harrison, C., Lee, C., Marshall, B. and Wiliam, D. (2003) *Assessment for Learning: Putting It Into Practice*. Maidenhead: Open University Press.

Blakemore, S.J. and Frith, U. (2005) *The Learning Brain: Lessons for Education*. Oxford: Blackwell.

Blatchford, P., Hallam, S., Ireson, J., Kutnick, P. and Creech, A. (2010) Classes, groups and transitions: Structures for teaching and learning. In R.J. Alexander with C. Doddington, J. Gray, L. Hargreaves and R. Kershner (eds) *The Cambridge Primary Review Research Surveys*. London: Routledge, 548–588.

Bloom, B.S., Engelhart, M.D., Furst, E.J., Hill, W.H. and Krathwohl, D.R. (1956) *Taxonomy of Educational Objectives. Handbook 1: Cognitive Domain*. London: Longman.

Board of Education (1931) *Report of the Consultative Committee on the Primary School* (Hadow Report). London: HMSO.

Boyd, M. and Markarian, W.C. (2011) Dialogic teaching: Talk in service of a dialogic stance. *Language and Education*, 25(6), 515–534.

Boyd, M. and Markarian, W.C. (2015) Dialogic teaching and dialogic stance: Moving beyond interactional form. *Research in the Teaching of English*, 49(3), 272–296.

Boyd, M. and Rubin, D. (2006) How contingent questioning promotes extended student talk: A function of display questions. *Journal of Literacy Research*, 38(2), 141–169.

Brown, A. and Palincsar, A.S. (1989) Guided co-operative learning and individual knowledge acquisition. In L.B. Resnick (ed) *Knowing, Learning and Instruction*. Hilsdale, NJ: Erlbaum, 393–490.

Bruner, J.S. (1971) *The Relevance of Education*. London: George Allen and Unwin.

Bruner, J.S. (1978) The role of dialogue in language acquisition. In A. Sinclair, R. Jarvella and W. Levelt (eds) *The Child's Conception of Language*. New York: Springer.

Bruner, J.S. (1983) *Child's Talk: Learning to Use Language*. Oxford: Oxford University Press.

Bruner, J.S. (1996) *The Culture of Education*. Cambridge, MA: Harvard University Press.

Bruner, J.S. (2006) *In Search of Pedagogy*, Volume 1. London: Routledge.

Bruner, J.S. and Haste, H. (1987) Introduction to *Making Sense: The Child's Construction of the World*. London: Routledge, 1–25.

Buber, M. (1937) *I and Thou*. Edinburgh: Clark.

Burbules, N.C. (1993) *Dialogue in Teaching: Theory and Practice*. New York: Teachers College Press.

Cambridge Primary Review Trust/University of York (2015a). *The CPRT/UoY Dialogic Teaching Project, Trial Stage 2015–16: Handbook for Schools*. York: University of York.

Cambridge Primary Review Trust/University of York (2015b). *The CPRT/UoY Dialogic Teaching Project, Trial Stage 2015–16: Planning and Review Forms*. York: University of York.

Carter, R. (1990) *Knowledge About Language and the Curriculum: The LINC Reader*. London: Hodder and Stoughton.

Carter, R. (1997) *Investigating English Discourse: Language, Literacy and Literature*. London: Routledge.

Carter, R. (2004) (Main contributor) *Introducing the Grammar of Talk*. London: QCA.

Castells, M. (1998) *End of Millennium* (The Information Age: Economy, Society and Culture, Volume 3). Oxford: Blackwell.

Cazden, C.B. (2001) *Classroom Discourse: The Language of Teaching and Learning*. Portsmouth, NH: Heinemann.

Cazden, C.B. (2005) *The value of eclecticism in education reform*. Paper presented at the 2005 AERA Annual Meeting.

Central Advisory Council for Education (England) (CACE). (1967) *Children and Their Primary Schools* (Plowden Report). London: HMSO.

Chafe, W.L. (1982) Integration and involvement in speaking, writing and oral literature. In D. Tannen (ed) *Spoken and Written Language: Exploring Orality and Literacy*. Norwood, NJ: Ablex.

Chapin, S., O'Connor, C. and Anderson, N. (2009) *Classroom Discussions: Using Math Talk to Help Students Learn, Grades 1–6*. Sausalito, CA: Math Solutions Publication.

Clarke, S.N. (2015) The right to speak. In L.B. Resnick, C.S.C. Asterhan and S.N. Clarke (eds) *Socializing Intelligence Through Academic Talk and Dialogue*. Washington, DC: AERA, 167–180.

Comenius, J.A. [1657] trans. M.W. Keatinge (1896) *The Great Didactic*. London: A. and C. Black.

Confederation of British Industry (CBI) (2006) *Working on the Three Rs: Employers' Priorities for Functional Skills in Maths and English*. London: DfES.

Cox, B. (1991) *Cox on Cox: An English Curriculum for the 1990s.* London: Hodder and Stoughton.

Crystal, D. (2005) *The Stories of English.* London: Penguin Books.

Daniels, H. (2001) *Vygotsky and Pedagogy.* London: Routledge.

Davie, D. (1982) *These the Companions: Recollections.* Cambridge: Cambridge University Press.

Dawes, L., Mercer, N. and Wegerif, R. (2004) *Thinking Together: A Programme of Activities for Developing Speaking and Listening.* Birmingham: Imaginative Minds.

Delpit, L. (1988) The silenced dialogue: Power and pedagogy in educating other people's children. *Harvard Educational Review, 58*(3), 280–299.

Department for Children, Schools and Families (2008) *A review of services for children and young people (0–19) with speech, language and communication needs* (the Bercow Report). London: DCSF.

Department for Children, Schools and Families (2009a) *Developing Language in the Primary School: Literacy and Primary Languages.* London: DCSF.

Department for Children, Schools and Families (2009b) *The Key Stage 2 Framework for Languages.* London: DCSF.

Department for Children, Schools and Families (2009c) *Independent Review of the Primary Curriculum: Final Report* (the Rose report). London: DCSF.

Department for Education (2011a) *Review of the National Curriculum in England: Summary Report of the Call for Evidence.* London: DfE.

Department for Education (2011b) *The Framework for the National Curriculum: A Report by the Expert Panel for the National Curriculum Review.* London: DfE.

Department for Education (2013a) Freedom of Information response, case reference 2013/0047506. London: DfE.

Department for Education (2013b) *The National Curriculum in England: Framework Document.* London: DfE.

Department for Education and Employment/Qualifications and Curriculum Authority (1999a). *The National Curriculum: Handbook for Primary Teachers in England.* London: DfEE.

Department for Education and Employment/Qualifications and Curriculum Authority (1999b). *The National Curriculum: Handbook for Secondary Teachers in England.* London: DfEE.

Department for Education and Skills (2003) *Excellence and Enjoyment: A Strategy for Primary Schools.* London: DfES.

Department for Education and Skills (2006) *Independent Review of the Teaching of Early Reading: Final Report by Jim Rose.* London: DfES.

Department of Education and Science (1975) *A Language for Life: Report of the Committee of Inquiry Appointed by the Secretary of State for Education and Science under the Chairmanship of Sir Alan Bullock FBA.* London: HMSO.

Department of Education and Science (1979) *Aspects of Secondary Education in England: A Survey by HM Inspectors of Schools.* London: HMSO.

Department of Education and Science (1988) *Report of the Committee of Inquiry Into the Teaching of English Language* (the Kingman Report). London: HMSO.

Department of Education and Science (1989) *Report of the English Working Party 5 to 16* (the Cox Report). London: HMSO.

Department of Education and Science (1993) *The Initial Training of Primary Teachers: Criteria for Courses* (Circular 14/93). London: DES.

Derewianka, B. (2018) Creating dialogic contexts for learning. In P. Jones, A. Simpson and A. Thwaite (eds) *Talking the Talk: Snapshots From Australian Classrooms.* Newtown, NSW: PETAA, 7–18.

Dewey, J. (1916) *Democracy and Education: An Introduction to the Philosophy of Education*. New York: Macmillan.

Dillon, J. (1988) *Questioning and Teaching: A Manual of Practice*. Eugene, OR: Wipf and Stock.

Doyle, W. (1983) Academic work. *Review of Educational Research*, 53, 159–199.

Driver, R. (1983) *The Pupil as Scientist?* Milton Keynes: Open University Press.

Dunkin, M.J. and Biddle, B.J. (1974) *The Study of Teaching*. New York: Holt, Rinehart and Winston.

Dysthe, O. (1996) The multivoiced classroom: Interactions of writing and classroom discourse. *Written Communication*, 13(3), 385–425.

Dysthe, O., Bernhardt, N. and Esbjørn, L. (2013) *Dialogue-Based Teaching: The Art Museum as a Learning Space*. Copenhagen: Skoletjenesten/Fagbokforlaget.

Eagleton, T. (2016) *Culture*. New Haven: Yale University Press.

Education Endowment Foundation (2018) Voice 21: Oracy curriculum, culture and assessment toolkit. *Key Conclusions*. https://educationendowmentfoundation.org.uk/projects-and-evaluation/projects/voice-21-pilot/ (accessed June 2019).

Education Endowment Foundation (2019) Voice 21: Improving Oracy (re-grant). Summary of research results. https://educationendowmentfoundation.org.uk/projects-and-evaluation/projects/voice-21 (accessed June 2019).

Edwards, A.D. (1992) Teacher talk and pupil competence. In K. Norman (ed) *Thinking Voices: The Work of the National Oracy Project*. London: Hodder, 235–242.

Edwards, A.D. (2010) A remarkable sociological imagination. *British Journal of Sociology of Education*, 23(4), 527–535.

Edwards, A.D. and Westgate, D.P.G. (1994) *Investigating Classroom Talk* (2nd edition). London: Falmer Press, 235–242.

Edwards, D. and Mercer, N. (1987) *Common Knowledge: The Development of Understanding in the Classroom*. London: Routledge.

Edwards, J. (1989) *Language and Disadvantage* (2nd edition). London: Cole and Whurr.

Equality and Human Rights Commission (2019) *Tackling Racial Harassment: Universities Challenged*. London: EHRC. https://equalityhumanrights.com/sites/default/files/tackling-racial-harassment-universities-challenged.pdf (accessed October 2019).

Feldman, C.F. (1977) Two functions of language. *Harvard Educational Review*, 47.

Feldman, C.F. (1987) Thought from language: The linguistic construction of cognitive representations. In J.S. Bruner and H. Haste (eds) *Making Sense: The Child's Construction of the World*. London: Routledge, 131–146.

Ferretti, R.P. and Fan, Y. (2015) Argumentative writing. In C. MacArthur, S. Graham and J. Fitzgerald (eds) *Handbook of Writing Research*. New York: Guildford Press, 301–315.

Fisher, R. (2003) *Teaching Thinking: Philosophical Enquiry in the Classroom*. London: Continuum.

Flanders, N.A. (1960) *Interaction Analysis in the Classroom: A Manual for Observers*. Ann Arbor: University of Michigan.

Flood, A. (2019) Professor who quoted James Baldwin's use of N-word cleared by university. *The Guardian*, 19 August. www.theguardian.com/books/2019/aug/19/professor-who-quoted-james-baldwin-n-word-cleared-by-university-laurie-sheck (accessed August 2019).

Freire, P. (1986) *Pedagogy of the Oppressed*. New York: Continuum.

Galton, M. (2008) *Creative Practitioners in Schools and Classrooms*. Cambridge: University of Cambridge Faculty of Education.

Galton, M., Hargreaves, L., Comber, C., Wall, D. and Pell, A. (1999) *Inside the Primary Classroom: 20 Years on*. London: Routledge.

Galton, M. and Simon, B. (eds) (1980) *Progress and Performance in the Primary Classroom*. London: Routledge.

Galton, M., Simon, B. and Croll. P. (1980) *Inside the Primary Classroom*. London: Routledge.

Galton, M. and Williamson, J. (1992) *Group Work in the Primary Classroom*. London: Routledge.

Ginsburg, A. and Smith, M.S. (2016) *Do Randomized Control Trials Meet the 'Gold Standard'?* Washington, DCX: American Enterprise Institute.

Goody, J. (1987) *The Interface Between the Written and the Oral*. Cambridge: Cambridge University Press.

Goswami, U. (2005) The brain in the classroom? The state of the art. *Developmental Science*, 8(6), 467–469.

Goswami, U. and Bryant, P. (2010) Children's cognitive development and learning. In R.J. Alexander, C. Doddington, J.M. Gray, L. Hargreaves and R. Kershner (eds) *The Cambridge Primary Review Research Surveys*. London: Routledge, 141–169.

Graff, H.J. (1991) *The Legacies of Literacy: Continuities and Contradictions in Western Culture and Society*. Bloomington, IN: Indiana University Press.

Graham, S. and Perin, D. (2007) *Writing Next: Effective Strategies to Improve Writing of Adolescents in Middle and High Schools – A Report to Carnegie Corporation of New York*. Washington, DC: Alliance for Excellent Education.

Halliday, M.A.K. (1961) Categories of a theory of grammar. *Word*, 17, 241–292.

Halliday, M.A.K. (1975) *Learning How to Mean*. London: Arnold.

Halliday, M.A.K. (1982) Linguistics in teacher education. In R. Carter (ed) *Linguistics and the Teacher*. London: Routledge, 10–16.

Halliday, M.A.K. (1989) *Spoken and Written Language*. Oxford: Oxford University Press.

Halliday, M.A.K. (1993) Towards a language-based theory of learning. *Linguistics in Education*, 5.

Hamlyn, D.W. (1967) The logical and psychological aspects of learning. In R.S. Peters (ed) *The Concept of Education*. London: Routledge and Kegan Paul, 24–43.

Hardman, F. (2015) The mentoring process. In Cambridge Primary Review Trust/ University of York (ed) *The CPRT/UoY Dialogic Teaching Project, Trial Stage 2015–16: Handbook for Schools*, 19–22.

Hardman, F., Smith, F. and Wall, K. (2003) 'Interactive whole class teaching' in the National Literacy Strategy. *Cambridge Journal of Education*, 33(2), 197–215.

Hardman, J. (2019) Developing and supporting implementation of a dialogic pedagogy in primary schools in England. *Teaching and Teacher Education*, 86. https://doi.org/10.1016/j.tate.2019.102908 (accessed September 2019).

Hardman, J. (2020) Analysing student talk moves in whole class teaching. In N. Mercer, R. Wegerif and L. Major (eds) *The Routledge International Handbook of Research on Dialogic Education*. London: Routledge, 152–166.

Hargreaves, L. and Galton, M., with C. Comber, T. Pell and D. Wall (2002) *Transfer From the Primary Classroom: 20 Years on*. London: Routledge.

Harlen, W. (2014) *Assessment, Standards and Quality of Learning in Primary Education* (CPRT Research Survey New Series 1). York: Cambridge Primary Review Trust. https://cprtrust.org.uk/about_cprt/cprt-publications/ (accessed June 2019).

Haslam, J. (2018) Beware of enormous effect sizes. *Schools Week*, 20 December.

Hattie, J.A.C. (2009) *Visible Learning: A Synthesis of 800 Meta-analyses Relating to Achievement*. London: Routledge.

Heath, S.B. (1983) *Ways With Words: Language, Life and Work in Communities and Classrooms*. Cambridge: Cambridge University Press.

Hinsliff, G. (2019) How Thunberg became a new front in Britain's culture war. *The Guardian*, 17 August. www.theguardian.com/commentisfree/2019/aug/17/greta-thunberg-brexit-culture-war-nigel-farage (accessed August 2019).

Hirst, P. (1967) The logical and psychological aspects of teaching a subject. In R.S. Peters (ed) *The Concept of Education*. London: Routledge and Kegan Paul, 44–60.

H.M. Government (2019) *Official Statistics: Hate crime, England and Wales, 2018–2019*. www.gov.uk/government/statistics/hate-crime-england-and-wales-2018-to-2019 (accessed October 2019).

Holmes, B. and Myles, F. (2019) *White Paper: Primary Languages Policy in England – The Way Forward*. RiPL. www.ripl.uk/policy/ (accessed October 2019).

Holquist, M. (1990) *Dialogism: Bakhtin and his World*. London: Routledge.

House of Commons Digital, Culture, Media and Sport Committee (2018) *Disinformation and 'Fake News': Interim Report*. London: House of Commons.

Howe, C. and Abedin, M. (2013) Classroom dialogue: A systematic review across four decades of research. *Cambridge Journal of Education*, *43*(3), 325–356.

Howe, C., Hennessy, S., Mercer, N., Vrikki, M. and Wheatley, L. (2019) Teacher-student dialogue during classroom teaching: Does it really impact on student outcomes? *Journal of the Learning Sciences*. https://doi.org/10.1080/10508406.2019.1573730.

ICAN and the Royal College of Speech and Language Therapists. (2018) *Bercow Ten Years On: An Independent Review of Provision for Children and Young People with Speech, Language and Communication Needs in England*. London: ICAN/RCSLT.

Jackson, P.W. (1968) *Life in Classrooms*. New York: Holt, Rinehart and Winston.

Janke, R.W. and Cooper, B.S. (2017) *News Literacy: Helping Students and Teachers Decode Fake News*. London: Rowman and Butterfield.

Jay, T., Taylor, R., Moore, N., Burnett, C., Merchant, G., Thomas, P., Willis, B. and Stevens, A. (2017) *Dialogic Teaching: Evaluation Report and Executive Summary*. London: Education Endowment Foundation with Sheffield Hallam University. https://educationendowmentfoundation.org.uk/public/files/Projects/Evaluation_Reports/Dialogic_Teaching_Evaluation_Report.pdf (accessed June 2019).

Johnson, J., Hutton, R. and Yard, L. (1992) Capturing talk: Description and development. In K. Norman (ed) *Thinking Voices: The Work of the National Oracy Project*. London: Hodder, 5–15.

Johnson, M. (2004) *Developmental Cognitive Neuroscience* (2nd edition). Oxford: Blackwell.

Jones, P.E. (2013) Bernstein's 'codes' and the linguistics of 'deficit'. *Language and Education*, *27*(2), 161–179.

Jones, P.E., Simpson, A. and Thwaite, A. (2018) *Talking the Talk: Snapshots From Australian Classrooms*. Newtown, NSW: PETAA.

Juzwik, M., Borsheim-Black, C., Caughlan, S. and Heintz, A. (2013), *Inspiring Dialogue: Talking to Learn in the English Classroom*. New York: Teachers College Press.

Kakutani, M. (2018) *The Death of Truth*. London: William Collins.

Kalantzis, M., Cope, B., Chan, E. and Dalley-Trim, L. (2016) *Literacies*. Cambridge: Cambridge University Press.

Keiner, J. (1992) A brief history of the origins of the National Oracy Project. In K. Norman (ed) *Thinking Voices: The Work of the National Oracy Project*. London: Hodder, 247–255.

Kennedy, G.A. (1999) *Classical Rhetoric and Its Christian and Secular Tradition.* Chapel Hill: University of North Carolina Press.

Kim, M.-Y. and Wilkinson, I.A.G. (2019) What is dialogic teaching? Constructing, deconstructing and reconstructing a pedagogy of classroom talk. *Language, Learning and Social Interaction, 21,* 70–86.

Koedinger, K.R. and Wiese, E.S. (2015) Accounting for socializing intelligence with the knowledge-learning-instruction framework. In L.B. Resnick, C.S.C. Asterhan and S.N. Clarke (eds) *Socializing Intelligence Through Academic Talk and Dialogue.* Washington, DC: AERA, 275–286.

Kotulak, R. (1997) *Inside the Brain: Revolutionary Discoveries of How the Mind Works.* Kansas City: Andrews McMeel.

Krathwohl, D.R., Bloom, B.S. and Nasia, B.B. (1956) *Taxonomy of Educational Objectives. Handbook 2: Affective Domain.* London: Longman.

Kuhn, D., Wang, Y. and Li, H. (2011) Why argue? Developing understanding of the purposes and values of argumentative discourse. *Discourse Processes, 48*(1), 26–49.

Kumar, K. (1991) *Political Agenda of Education: A Study of Colonialist and Nationalist Ideas.* New Delhi: Sage.

Lefstein, A., Pollak, I. and Segal, A. (2018) Compelling student voice: Dialogic practices of public confession. *Discourse: Studies in the Cultural Politics of Education.* https://doi.org/10.1080/01596306.2018.1473341.

Lefstein, A. and Snell, J. (2014) *Better Than Best Practice: Developing Teaching and Learning Through Dialogue.* London: Routledge.

Lefstein, A., Trachtenberg-Maslaton, R. and Pollak, I. (2017) Breaking out of the grip of dichotomous discourse in teacher post-observation debrief conversations. *Teaching and Teacher Education, 67,* 418–428.

Lipman, M. (2003) *Thinking in Education* (2nd edition). New York: Cambridge University Press.

Littleton, K. and Mercer, N. (2013) *Interthinking: Putting Talk to Work.* London: Routledge.

Luxton, R. (2000) *Interactive Whole Class Teaching: A Briefing Note.* London: London Borough of Barking and Dagenham.

MacCabe, C., Yanacek, H. and the Keywords Project (2018) *Keywords for Today: A 21st Century Vocabulary.* Oxford: Oxford University Press.

MacLure, M., Phillips, T. and Wilkinson, A. (eds) (1988) *Oracy Matters: The Development of Talking and Listening in Education.* Milton Keynes: Open University Press.

Major, L. and Warwick, P. (2020) Affordances for dialogue: The role of digital technology in supporting productive classroom talk. In N. Mercer, R. Wegerif and L. Major (eds) *The Routledge International Handbook of Research on Dialogic Education.* London: Routledge, 394–410.

Major, L., Warwick, P., Cook, V., Rasmussen, I. and Ludvigsen, S. (2018) Interactions between classroom dialogue and digital technologies: A scoping review of empirical research analysing opportunities and challenges. *Education and Information Technologies.* https://doi.org/10.1007/s10639-018-9701-y (accessed August 2019).

Matusov, E. (2009) *Journey Into Dialogic Pedagogy.* Hauppauge, NY: Nova Science Publishers.

Mayall, B. (2010) Children's lives outside school and their educational impact. In R.J. Alexander, C. Doddington, J.M. Gray, L. Hargreaves and R. Kershner (eds) *The Cambridge Primary Review Research Surveys.* London: Routledge, 49–82.

Mayer, S.J., O'Connor, C. and Lefstein, A. (2020) Distinctively democratic discourse in classrooms. In N. Mercer, R. Wegerif and L. Major (eds) *The Routledge*

International Handbook of Research on Dialogic Education. London: Routledge, 196–209.

McKeown, M.G. and Beck, I.L. (2015) Effective classroom talk *is* reading comprehension. In L.B. Resnick, C.S.C. Asterhan and S.N. Clarke (eds) *Socializing Intelligence Through Academic Talk and Dialogue*. Washington, DC: AERA, 51–62.

Mead, G.H., ed. C.W. Morris (1962) *Mind, Self and Society*. Chicago, IL: University of Chicago Press.

Mehan, H. (1979) *Learning Lessons: Social Organization in the Classroom*. Cambridge, MA: Harvard University Press.

Mercer, N. (2000) *Words and Minds: How We Use Language to Think Together*. London: Routledge.

Mercer, N. and Dawes, L. (2008) The value of exploratory talk. In N. Mercer and S. Hodgkinson (eds) *Exploring Talk in School*. London: Routledge, 55–72.

Mercer, N., Hennessy, S. and Warwick, P. (2017) Dialogue, thinking together and digital technology in the classroom: Implications of a continuing line of inquiry for developing dialogic teaching practices. Special Section of *International Journal of Educational Research* on the role of teacher practice in promoting academically productive dialogue in the classroom. http://bit.ly/2yPq2Qe (accessed August 2019).

Mercer, N. and Littleton, K. (2007) *Dialogue and the Development of Children's Thinking: A Sociocultural Approach*. London: Routledge.

Mercer, N., Mannion, J. and Warwick, P. (2020) Oracy education: The development of young people's language skills. In N. Mercer, R. Wegerif and L. Major (eds) *The Routledge International Handbook of Research on Dialogic Education*. London: Routledge, 292–305.

Mercer, N., Warwick, P. and Ahmed, A. (2016) An oracy assessment toolkit: Linking research and development in the assessment of students' spoken language skills at age 11–12. *Learning and Instruction*. https://doi.org/10.1016/j.learninstruc.2016.10.005.

Mercer, N., Wegerif, R. and Major, L. (eds) (2020) *The Routledge International Handbook of Research on Dialogic Education*. Abingdon: Routledge.

Michaels, S. and O'Connor, C. (2012) *Talk Science Primer*. Cambridge, MA: TERC.

Michaels, S. and O'Connor, C. (2015) Conceptualizing talk moves as tools: Professional development approaches for academically productive discussions. In L.B. Resnick, C.S.C. Asterhan and S.N. Clarke (eds) *Socializing Intelligence Through Academic Talk and Dialogue*. Washington, DC: AERA, 347–361.

Michaels, S. and O'Connor, C. (2017) From recitation to reasoning: implementing science and engineering practices through talk. In C. Schwarz, C. Passmore and B.J. Reiser (eds) *Bringing Next Generation Science and Engineering Practices Into Our K-12 Classrooms: Moving Beyond 'Knowing' Science to Making Sense of the World*. Arlington, VA: NSTA Press, 309–334.

Michaels, S., O'Connor, C. and Resnick, L.B. (2008) Deliberative discourse idealized and realized: Accountable talk in the classroom and in civic life. *Studies in Philosophy and Education*, 27(4), 283–297.

Mills, K.L. (1996) *Questions, Answers and Feedback in Primary Teaching: International Perspectives*. University of Warwick: Centre for Research in Elementary and Primary Education.

Ministère de l'éducation nationale (2010) *Qu'apprend-on à l'école élémentaire? Les programmes officiels*. Paris: Ministère de l'éducation nationale.

Mortimer, E.F. and Scott, P.H. (2003) *Meaning Making in Science Classrooms*. Maidenhead: Open University Press.

Mortimore, P., Sammons, P., Stoll, L., Lewis, D. and Ecob, R. (1988) *School Matters: The Primary Years*. Wells: Open Books Publishing.

Moyles, J., Hargreaves, L., Merry, R., Paterson, F. and Esarte-Sarries, V. (2003) *Interactive Teaching in the Primary School*. Maidenhead: Open University Press.

Murphy, P.K., Wilkinson, I.A.G., Soter, A.O., Henessey, M.N. and Alexander, J.F. (2009) Examining the effects of classroom discussion on students' high-level comprehension of text: A meta-analysis. *Journal of Educational Psychology*, 101, 740–764.

Myhill, D. (2005) *Teaching and Learning in Whole Class Discourse*. Exeter: University of Exeter School of Education.

Myhill, D. and Newman, R. (2020) Writing talk: Developing metalinguistic understanding through dialogic teaching. In N. Mercer, R. Wegerif and L. Major (eds) *The Routledge International Handbook of Research on Dialogic Education*. London: Routledge, 360–372.

Newell, G.E., Beach, R., Smith, J., VanDerHeide, J., Kuhn, D. and Andriessen, J. (2011) Teaching and learning argumentative reading and writing. *Reading Research Quarterly*, 46(3), 273–304.

Norman, G. (2003) RCT = results confounded and trivial: The perils of grand educational experiments. *Medical Education*, 37, 582–584.

Norman, K. (ed) (1992) *Thinking Voices: The Work of the National Oracy Project*. London: Hodder.

Nystrand, M. (1986) *The Structure of Written Communication: Studies in Reciprocity Between Writers and Readers*. London: Academic Press.

Nystrand, M. (1997) Dialogic instruction: When recitation becomes conversation. In M. Nystrand, with A. Gamoran, R. Kachur and C. Prendergast (eds) *Opening Dialogue: Understanding the Dynamics of Language and Learning in the English Classroom*. New York: Teachers College Press, 1–29.

Nystrand, M. (2019) *Twenty Acres: Events That Transform Us*. London and Paris: KiwaiMedia.

Nystrand, M., with Gamoran, A., Kachur, R. and Prendergast, C. (1997) *Opening Dialogue: Understanding the Dynamics of Language and Learning in the English Classroom*. New York: Teachers College Press.

Nystrand, M. and Gamoran, A. (1997) The big picture: Language and learning in hundreds of English lessons. In M. Nystrand, with A. Gamoran, R. Kachur and C. Prendergast (eds) *Opening Dialogue: Understanding the Dynamics of Language and Learning in the English Classroom*. New York: Teachers College Press, 30–74.

Nystrand, M., Wu, L.L., Gamoran, A., Zeiser, S. and Long, D.A. (2003) Questions in time: Investigating the structure and dynamics of unfolding classroom discourse. *Discourse Processes*, 35(2), 135–198.

O'Connor, C. and Michaels, S. (2018) Supporting teachers in taking up productive talk moves: The long road to professional learning at scale. *International Journal of Education and Research*. https://doi.org/10.1016/j.ijer.2017.11.003.

O'Connor, C., Michaels, S. and Chapin, S. (2015) 'Scaling down' to explore the role of talk in learning: from district intervention to controlled classroom study. In L.B. Resnick, C.S.C. Asterhan and S.N. Clarke (eds) *Socializing Intelligence Through Academic Talk and Dialogue*. Washington, DC: AERA, 111–126.

O'Connor, C., Michaels, S., Chapin, S. and Harbaugh, A.G. (2017) The silent and the vocal: Participation and learning in whole class discussion. *Learning and Instruction*, 48, 5–13.

Ofsted (2005) *English 2000–2005: A Review of Inspection Evidence*. London: Ofsted.

O'Hear, A. (1991) *Education and Democracy: The Posturing of the Left Establishment*. London: Claridge Press.

Oracy All Party Parliamentary Group (2019) *New inquiry: Speak for change*. www.oracyappg.org.uk (accessed June 2019).

Organisation for Economic Co-operation and Development (1995) *Literacy, Economy and Society*. Ontario: OECD.

Organisation for Economic Co-operation and Development (2014) *Education at a Glance 2014: OECD 2014 Indicators*. Paris: OECD.

Orwell, G. (1968) [1946] Politics and the English language. In S. Orwell and I. Angos (eds) *The Collected Essays, Letters and Journalism of George Orwell*. New York: Harcourt, Brace, Javonovich, 127–139.

Osborne, J. (2010) Arguing to learn in science: The role of collaborative, critical discourse. *Science*, 328, 463–468.

Osborne, J. (2015) The challenges of scale. In L.B. Resnick, C.S.C. Asterhan and S.N. Clarke (eds) *Socializing Intelligence Through Academic Talk and Dialogue*. Washington, DC: AERA, 403–414.

Osborne, J., Erduran, S. and Simon, S. (2004) *Ideas, Evidence and Argument in Science Education: A CPD Pack*. London: King's College London.

Palincsar, A.S. and Brown, A.L. (1984) Reciprocal teaching of comprehension-fostering and comprehension-monitoring activities. *Cognition and Instruction*, 1, 117–175.

Park, J., Michaels, S., Affolter, R. and O'Connor, C. (2017) Traditions, research and practice supporting academically productive classroom discourse. *Oxford Research Encyclopedia of Education*, December. Oxford University Press. https://oxfordre.com/education/view/10.1093/acrefore/9780190264093.001.0001/acrefore-9780190264093-e-21 (accessed July 2019).

Pluckrose, H. (1975) *Open School, Open Society*. London: Evans.

Pollard, A. (1985) *The Social World of the Primary School*. London: Cassell.

Popper, K.R. (1963) *Conjectures and Refutations: The Growth of Scientific Knowledge*. London: Routledge and Kegan Paul.

Prideaux, D. (2002) Researching the outcomes of educational interventions: A matter of design. *BMJ*, 324, 126–127.

Pring, R. (2017) Educational philosophy of John Dewey and its relevance to current dilemmas in education. *Education in the North*, 24(1), 3–15.

Qualifications and Curriculum Authority (2005) *Opening up Talk* (DVD). London: QCA.

Resnick, L.B. (2015) Talking to learn: The promise and challenge of dialogic teaching. In L.B. Resnick, C.S.C. Asterhan and S.N. Clarke (eds) *Socializing Intelligence Through Academic Talk and Dialogue*. Washington, DC: AERA, 441–450.

Resnick, L.B., Asterhan, C.S.C. and Clarke, S.N. (eds) (2015) *Socializing Intelligence Through Academic Talk and Dialogue*. Washington, DC: AERA.

Resnick, L.B., Libertus, M.E. and Schantz, F. (2020) The future of dialogic education. In N. Mercer, R. Wegerif and L. Major (eds) *The Routledge International Handbook of Research on Dialogic Education*. London: Routledge, 559–569.

Resnick, L.B., Michaels, S. and O'Connor, C. (2010) How (well structured) talk builds the mind. In R. Sternberg and D. Preiss (eds) *From Genes to Context: New Discoveries About Learning From Educational Research and Their Applications*. New York: Springer.

Reznitskaya, A. (2012) Dialogic teaching: Rethinking language use during literature discussions. *Reading Teacher, 65*(7), 446–456.

Reznitskaya, A., Anderson, R.C., McNurlen, B., Nguyen-Jahiel, K., Archodidou, A. and Kim, S. (2001) Influence of oral discussion on written argument. *Discourse Processes, 32*(2/3), 155–175.

Reznitskaya, A. and Glina, M. (2013) Comparing student experiences with story discussions in dialogic versus traditional settings. *The Journal of Educational Research, 106*(1), 49–63.

Reznitskaya, A., Kuo, L., Glina, M. and Anderson, R.C. (2009) Measuring argumentative reasoning: What's behind the numbers? *Learning and Individual Differences, 19*, 219–224.

Reznitskaya, A. and Wilkinson, I. (2017) *The Most Reasonable Answer: Helping Students Build Better Arguments Together*. Cambridge, MA: Harvard Education Press.

Reznitskaya, A., Wilkinson, I., Oyler, J., Bourdage-Reninger, K. and Sykes, A. (2016) *Using the Argumentation Rating Tool to Support Teacher Facilitation of Inquiry Dialogue in Elementary Language arts Classrooms*. Paper presented at the Annual Meeting of the American Educational Research Association, Washington, DC.

Robinson, C. (2014) *Children, Their Voices and Their Experience of School: What Does the Evidence Tell Us?* CPRT Research Survey 2. York: Cambridge Primary Review Trust.

Rosen, H. (1971) Towards a language policy across the curriculum: A discussion document prepared and introduced by Harold Rosen on behalf of the London Association for the Teaching of English. In D. Barnes, J. Britton and H. Rosen (eds) *Language, the Learner and the School*. London: Penguin, 117–168.

Rosen, H. (1972) *Language and Class: A Critical Look at the Theories of Basil Bernstein*. Bristol: Falling Wall Press.

Rosenthal, R. and Jacobson, L. (1968) *Pygmalion in the Classroom: Teacher Expectations and Pupils' Intellectual Development*. New York: Holt.

Rowe, M.B. (1986) Wait time: Slowing down may be a way of speeding up. *Journal of Teacher Education, 37*(1), 43–50.

Rudduck, J. (1976) *Dissemination of Innovation: The Humanities Curriculum Project*. London: Evans/Methuen.

Rudduck, J. and Flutter, J. (2000) Pupil participation and pupil perspective: Carving a new order of experience. *Cambridge Journal of Education, 30*(1), 75–89.

Rudduck, J. and McIntyre, D. (2007) *Improving Learning Through Consulting Pupils*. London: Routledge.

Scheffler, I. (1971) *The Language of Education*. Springfield, IL: Charles C. Thomas.

Schön, D.A. (1983) *The Reflective Practitioner: How Professionals Think in Action*. London: Temple Smith.

School 21 (2019) *The Oracy Project*. www.school21.org.uk/voice21 (accessed June 2019).

Schopenhauer, A., ed. A.C. Grayling (2004) [1831] *The Art of Always Being Right*. London: Gibson Square Books.

Schwarz, B.B. (2015) Discussing argumentative texts as a traditional Jewish learning practice. In L.B. Resnick, C.S.C. Asterhan and S.N. Clarke (eds) *Socializing*

Intelligence Through Academic Talk and Dialogue. Washington, DC: AERA, 157–166.

Schwarz, B.B. and Baker, M.J. (2017) *Dialogue, Argumentation and Education: History, Theory and Practice*. Cambridge: Cambridge University Press.

Schwarz, B.B. and Glassner, A. (2003) The blind and the paralytic: Fostering argumentation in social and scientific domains. In J. Andriessen, M.J. Baker and D. Suthers (eds) *Arguing to Learn: Confronting Cognitions in Computer-supported Collaborative Learning Environments*. Dordrecht: Kluwer Academic, 227–260.

Sedova, K. (2017) A case study of a transition to dialogic teaching as a process of gradual change. *Teaching and Teacher Education*, 67, 278–290.

Sedova, K., Salamounova, Z. and Svaricek, R. (2014) Troubles with dialogic teaching. *Learning, Culture and Social Interaction*, 3(4), 274–285.

Segal, A. and Lefstein, A. (2015) *Exuberant Voiceless Participation: Dialogic Sensibilities in the Israeli Primary Classroom*. Working Papers in Urban Language and Literacies 156. London: King's College.

Segal, A., Pollak, A. and Lefstein, A. (2016) Democracy, voice and dialogic pedagogy: The struggle to be heard and heeded. *Language and Education*. https://doi.org/10.1080/09500782.2016.1230124.

Shi, Y., Matos, F. and Kuhn, D. (2019) Dialog as a bridge to argumentative writing. *Journal of Writing Research*, 11, 300–321.

Shulman, L.S. (1987) Knowledge and teaching: Foundations of the new reforms. *Harvard Educational Review*, 57(1), 1–22.

Shweder, R.A. (1991) *Thinking Through Cultures*. Cambridge, MA: Harvard University Press.

Silberman, C.E. (1973) *The Open Classroom Reader*. New York: Vintage Books.

Simon, B. (ed) (1957) *Psychology in the Soviet Union*. London: Routledge and Kegan Paul.

Simon, B. (1981) Why no pedagogy in England? In B. Simon and W. Taylor (eds) *Education in the Eighties: The Central Issues*. London: Batsford, 121–145.

Simon, B. and Simon, J. (eds) (1963) *Educational Psychology in the USSR*. London: Routledge and Kegan Paul.

Simon, J. (1966) *Education and Society in Tudor England*. Cambridge: Cambridge University Press.

Simon, J. (1987) Vygotsky and the Vygotskians. *American Journal of Education*, August.

Sinclair, J.M. and Coulthard, M. (1975) *Towards an Analysis of Discourse: The English Used by Teachers and Pupils*. Oxford: Oxford University Press.

Skidmore, D., Perez-Parent, M. and Arnfield, S. (2003) Teacher-pupil dialogue in the guided reading session. *Reading: Literacy and Language*, 37(2), 47–53.

Small, H. (2016) *The Value of the Humanities*. Oxford: Oxford University Press.

Smith, F., Hardman, F., Wall, K. and Mroz, M. (2004) Interactive whole class teaching in the National Literacy and Numeracy Strategies. *British Educational Research Journal*, 30(3), 395–412.

Smith, J. (2010) *Talk, Thinking and Philosophy in the Primary Classroom*. Exeter: Learning Matters.

Sortkaer, B. (2019) Feedback for everybody? Exploring the relationship between students' perceptions of feedback and students' socioeconomic status. *British Educational Research Journal*, 45(4), 717–735.

Stahl, G. (2015) Computer-supported academically productive discourse. In L.B. Resnick, C.S.C. Asterhan and S.N. Clarke (eds) *Socializing Intelligence Through Academic Talk and Dialogue*. Washington, DC: AERA, 219–230.

Standage, T. (2014) *Writing on the Wall: The Intriguing History of Social Media, From Ancient Rome to the Present Day*. London: Bloomsbury.

Stubbs, M. (1989) The state of English in the English State: Reflections on the Cox report. *Language and Education*, 3(4), 235–250.

Sullivan, G.M. (2011) Getting off the 'gold standard': Randomized control trials and educational research. *Journal of Graduate Medical Education*, 3(3), 285–289.

Tannen, D. (ed) (1982) *Spoken and Written Language: Exploring Orality and Literacy*. Norwood, NJ: Ablex.

Taylor, C. (1991) *The Ethics of Authenticity*. Cambridge, MA: Harvard University Press.

Thunberg, G. (2019) *No One Is Too Small to Make a Difference*. London: Penguin Books.

Tobin, J.J., Hsueh, Y. and Karasawa, M. (2009) *Preschool in Three Cultures Revisited: China, Japan and the United States*. Chicago: University of Chicago Press.

Tobin, J.J., Wu, D.Y.H. and Davidson, D.H. (1989) *Preschool in Three Cultures*. New Haven, CT: Yale University Press.

Tough, J. (1979) *Talk for Teaching and Learning*. London: Ward lock Educational.

Toulmin, S. (2003) *The Uses of Argument*. Cambridge: Cambridge University Press.

United Nations (1990) *The United Nations Convention on the Rights of the Child*. New York: UNICEF.

VanDerHeide, J., Juzwik, M. and Dunn, M. (2016) Teaching and learning argumentation in English: A dialogic approach. *Theory Into Practice*, 55, 287–293.

Voice 21 (2019) *The Oracy Benchmarks*. https://voice21.org/wp-content/uploads/2019/10/Benchmarks-report-Digital.pdf (accessed October 2019).

Vrikki, M., Wheatley, L., Howe, C., Hennessy, S. and Mercer, N. (2018) Dialogic practices in primary school classrooms. *Language and Education*. https://doi.org/10.1080/09500782.2018.1509988.

Vygotsky, L.S. (1962) *Thought and Language*. Cambridge, MA: MIT Press.

Vygotsky, L.S. (1963) Learning and mental development at school age. In B. Simon and J. Simon (eds) *Educational Psychology in the USSR*. London: Routledge and Kegan Paul, 21–34.

Vygotsky, L.S. (1978) *Mind in Society: The Development of Higher Psychological Processes*. Cambridge, MA: Harvard University Press.

Vygotsky, L.S. (1981) The genesis of higher mental functions. In J.V. Wertsch (ed) *The Concept of Activity in Soviet Psychology*. London: M.E. Sharpe.

Walton, D. (2013) *Methods of Argumentation*. Cambridge: Cambridge University Press.

Wattenberg, B. (1991) *The First Universal Nation*. New York: The Free Press.

Wegerif, R. (2007) *Dialogic Education and Technology: Expanding the Space of Learning*. New York: Springer.

Wegerif, R. (2013) *Dialogic Education for the Internet Age*. London: Routledge.

Wegerif, R. and Major, L. (2018) Buber, educational technology and the expansion of dialogic space. *AI & Society*. https://doi.org/10.1007/s00146-018-0828-6.

Wegerif, R., Mercer, N. and Major, L. (2020) Introduction. In N. Mercer, R. Wegerif and L. Major (eds) *The Routledge International Handbook of Research on Dialogic Education*. London: Routledge, 1–8.

Welch, K.E. (1990) *The Contemporary Reception of Classical Rhetoric: Appropriations of Ancient Discourse*. Hillsdale, NJ: Lawrence Erlbaum.

Wells, G. (1999) *Dialogic Inquiry: Towards a Sociocultural Practice and Theory of Education*. Cambridge: Cambridge University Press.

Wilkinson, A. (1965) *Spoken English*. Birmingham: Birmingham University Press.

Wilkinson, A., Davies, A. and Berrill, D. (1990) *Spoken English Illuminated*. Milton Keynes: Open University Press.

Wilkinson, I.A.G., Murphy, P.K. and Binici, S. (2015) Dialogue-intensive pedagogies for promoting reading comprehension: What we know, what we need to know. In L.B. Resnick, C.S.C. Asterhan and S.N. Clarke (eds) *Socializing Intelligence Through Academic Talk and Dialogue*. Washington, DC: AERA, 37–50.

Wilkinson, R. and Pickett, K. (2009) *The Spirit Level: Why Equality Is Better for Everyone*. London: Allen Lane.

Williams, R.D. (2008) *Dostoevsky: Language, Faith and Fiction*. London: Continuum.

Williams, R.H. (1998) *Keywords: A Vocabulary of Culture and Society*. London: Fontana Books.

Wood, D., Bruner, J.S. and Ross, G. (1976) The role of tutoring in problem-solving. *Journal of Child Psychology and Child Psychiatry*, 17, 89–100.

World Bank (2019) *Non-cognitive Skills: What Are They and Why Should We Care?* http://blogs.worldbank.org/education/non-cognitive-skills-what-are-they-and-why-should-we-care (accessed July 2019).

Wragg, E.C. (ed) (1991) *Classroom Teaching Skills*. London: Routledge.

Wragg, E.C. (1993) *Primary Teaching Skills*. London: Routledge.

Index